CHILDREN AND YOUTH
Social Problems and Social Policy

CHILDREN AND YOUTH
Social Problems and Social Policy

Advisory Editor

ROBERT H. BREMNER

Editorial Board
Sanford N. Katz
Rachel B. Marks
William M. Schmidt

CHILDREN

IN

CONFINEMENT

Introduction by
Robert M. Mennel

ARNO PRESS
A New York Times Company
New York — 1974

Reprint Edition 1974 by Arno Press Inc.

The Forgotten Adolescent was reprinted
    from a copy in The Newark Public Library

CHILDREN AND YOUTH
Social Problems and ·Social Policy
ISBN for complete set: 0-405-05940-X
See last pages of this volume for titles.

Manufactured in the United States of America

Library of Congress Cataloging in Publication Data
Main entry under title:

Children in confinement.

    (Children and youth: social problems and social
policy)
    Reprint of Westboro State Reform School reminiscences,
by J. A. Allen, first published in 1877; of Juvenile
reformatories of the United States, by T. J. Charlton,
first published in 1900; of The Federal courts and the
delinquent child, by R. Bloodgood, first published in
1922; of The forgotten adolescent, by the New York Law
Society, first published in 1940; and of Correctional
treatment of youth offenders, by L. V. Harrison,
first published in 1944.
    1. Reformatories--United States--History--Addresses,
essays, lectures. 2. Rehabilitation of juvenile
delinquents--United States--History--Addresses, essays,
lectures. I. Series.
HV9104.C44   364.36'0973   74-1675
ISBN 0-405-05954-X

CONTENTS

Introduction

The roots of the juvenile court lay in the inadequacies of the nineteenth century criminal justice system as it applied to children. Youths, often guilty of only vagrancy or petty crimes were sometimes detained in or sentenced to jail. Prison reformers and other citizens believed that the creation of a special probate tribunal emphasizing probation would eliminate this practice. Equally significant in stimulating the origin of the juvenile court was the failure of reform schools. These institutions, which existed in nearly every state outside the South, no longer adequately cared for the children entrusted to them if in fact they ever had. By 1900, however, the reality of institutional life — riots, exploitation in the workshop, cruel punishments — mocked the reform schools' parental ideal to the point where a new alternative disposition was required. In 1891, the social work executive, Homer Folks voiced a common sentiment when he listed "the contaminating influence of association" and "the enduring stigma . . . of having been committed" as reasons to avoid sending children to reform school.

The popularity of probation plans which antedated the court was also related to increasing distrust of children's institutions. In Pennsylvania and New York, voluntary children's aid societies successfully promoted legislation to enable them to supervise children who otherwise would have been committed to reform schools. In Massachusetts, a state probation and parole agency was established in 1869. The first juvenile court, begun in Illinois in 1899, combined the Massachusetts and New York probation systems with two New York laws providing delinquents with special court sessions and separate detention facilities. By developing probation staffs, detention homes, and auxiliary services, juvenile courts relegated reform schools to places of last resort to be used only when the authority of the probation officer was repeatedly disobeyed. In effect, juvenile courts relieved the beleaguered institutions of the parental power of the state *(parens patriae)* by claiming that primarily non-institutional approaches would humanely discipline and care for delinquent children.

The initial response to the juvenile court was enthusiastic. Jane Addams, a promoter of the Chicago Court, believed that the new tribunal effected "almost a change in *mores*" and "absolutely eliminated . . . all notions of punishment." By 1909, a decade after the passage of the Illinois act, ten states and the District of Columbia had authorized localities to establish juvenile courts. Twelve other states followed suit in the next three years, and by 1925, all but two states, Maine and Wyoming, had juvenile court laws. There were, of course, significant differences between courts. In rural areas and small towns, juvenile courts often did not exist or involved little more than a county judge hearing children's cases on Saturday morning. Here children continued to be confined with adults prior to court hearings and probation officers were only intermittantly available to advise the judge or to accept responsibility for supervising children following hearings. Even in urban areas, as Helen Jeter's 1922 study of the Chicago court reveals, judges were not specially chosen for the juvenile court and detention homes and probation staffs were often crowded with cases involving destitution or parental neglect which were more properly the function of domestic relations or family courts. The 1929 U.S. Children's Bureau study by Bernard Flexner, Reuben Oppenheimer and Katharine P. Lenroot discusses the development of these courts and the imprecise legal and bureaucratic borderlands which they shared with juvenile courts.

Often conflicts also tarnished the juvenile court from the outset. Many juvenile court laws, contrary to the parental ideal, allowed judges to remand children to the adult criminal justice system and ultimately to jail. Richard S. Tuthill, first judge of the Chicago juvenile court sent thirty-seven children to the Grand Jury during the court's first year of operation. Because of actions such as this, some judges such as Edward Lindsey and Edward F. Waite questioned the benevolent intent of the court itself. In 1914, Lindsey wrote, "Every child accused of crime should be tried and subjected to neither punishment nor restraint of liberty unless convicted. No child should be restrained simply because he has been accused of crime, whether he is guilty or not." However, Lindsey's opinion and other criticism were forgotten in the general approbation which the court received because it supposedly systematized and destigmatized juvenile justice. A 1905 Pennsylvania decision (Commonwealth v. Fisher) upholding the legality of the juvenile court in that state became the precedent for subsequent cases upholding court authority. The Pennsylvania case concluded, "the legislature may surely provide for the salvation of . . . a child, if its parents or guardians be unable or unwilling to do so, by bringing it into one of the courts of the state without any process at all, for the purpose of subjecting it to the state's guardianship and protection."

This rationale remained viable as long as popular and professional opinion supported the court's benevolent purposes. Beginning in the 1950s, however, this faith began to erode in a direct relationship with the increasingly chaotic conditions attending the urban migration of large numbers of poor white and poor black families and individuals. Scholars such as Francis A. Allen began to question not so much the court's lack of commitment to the rehabilitative ideal but the incapacity of the court to deal effectively with the conditions giving rise to delinquent behavior. Robert Vinter summarized criticism for the President's Commission on Law Enforcement and The Administration of Justice (1967): "The juvenile court typically lacks sufficient resources to handle the level of demands placed upon it, whether these focus on adjudication, on rehabilitation of offenders, or on the provision of social services." Other scholars such as the Columbia sociologists Richard Cloward and Lloyd Ohlin went further to declare on the basis of their case studies that juvenile court systems no longer helped children but instead channeled them into stigmatizing institutions and programs which virtually guaranteed recidivism and eventually adult criminal status. Charges such as these brought into question the court's humanitarian pretensions and hence the parental power of the state itself. Supreme Court decisions began to question whether juvenile court proceedings in fact offered sufficient protection to warrant immunity from providing children with the safeguards of criminal law. Kent v. U.S. (1966) warned juvenile courts against "procedural arbitrariness" while In re Gault (1967) recognized the rights of juveniles in such matters as notification of charges, cross examination of complainants and often witnesses, and warning against self-incrimination. Several of the selections in this anthology discuss the significance of "the Gault revolution" on the juvenile justice system.

Recently, the juvenile court's reputation as a humanitarian agency has been somewhat revived in part because of favorable legal decisions but also because recent delinquency prevention programs have diverted children from the courts and reform schools altogether. In Massachusetts, for example, state reform schools have been closed down in favor of a variety of community programs and surrogate homes located in or near the child's own neighborhood. In California, local youth community programs are subsidized by the state so that at least some children will not have to be incarcerated. Also the increasingly conservative Supreme Court has recently shored up the court's parental power. In 1971, in McKiever v. Pennsylvania, the court divided 6-3 on the necessity for jury trials in juvenile court cases. Justice Harry A. Blackmun, spokesman for the majority, agreed that "trial by jury in the juvenile courts is not a constitutional requirement." Justice William O. Douglas, dissenting, maintained, "the Fourteenth Amendment which makes trial by jury provided in the Sixth Amendment applicable to states speaks of denial of rights to 'any person,' not denial of rights to 'any adult person.'" For the present, we might conclude that while the juvenile court will continue to receive many delinquent children, in the future it may not be the sole or even the principal public agency concerned with definition of juvenile delinquency or the care of juvenile delinquents.

March, 1974
Durham, New Hampshire

Robert M. Mennel
University of New Hampshire

WESTBORO'

STATE REFORM SCHOOL

REMINISCENCES.

BY

JOSEPH A. ALLEN.

BOSTON:
LOCKWOOD, BROOKS & CO.
1877.

WESTBORO' STATE REFORM SCHOOL

REMINISCENCES.

WHILE in charge of the Westboro' Reform School, I was often requested, by persons whose opinion I valued, to write a short history of my connection with the school, with anecdotes and incidents relative to the boys; and especially to give, somewhat minutely, my methods of discipline.

I was too much occupied to undertake it at that time; but the school has attracted so much attention of late, that it has been thought that something of the kind would be useful now. With that hope the following pages have been written.

Late in the autumn of 1860, two letters came to me in Syracuse, N. Y., my residence for the previous eighteen years. Each was from a prominent gentleman of Massachusetts, both now dead, and each inquired if I would accept the position of Superintendent of the Westboro' Reform School if it should be offered me. The letters gave some

information concerning the history of the school,
and of its then recent troubles ; and I was requested
to visit the writers, and consult with friends of
the school who believed in a more humane system
of discipline than ever had been practised there,
and in a religion more liberal and unsectarian.
Nothing could have surprised me more than the
contents of these letters. I knew but little of
the school, and had never been connected with
such an institution. With all questions relating
to education and reform I was indeed somewhat familiar, but not with this in particular. After consulting with my friends in Syracuse, who seemed
to think me adapted to such a position, and considering that my wife's health was precarious, and
that a change of climate might be beneficial, I decided to visit my friends in Massachusetts for con-
sultation ; the result of my visit was that I very
soon received the appointment.

As my brothers and many relatives were well
known as successful teachers in Massachusetts,
and as I had formerly taught in the State and
was acquainted with the leading educators, my
appointment was well received, judging by the
notices in the leading papers ; although there was
little faith in the community that the school would
ever be a success.

We arrived at the institution January 10, 1861,

and were met by several of the trustees, and introduced to the officers and boys congregated in the chapel. My few words to the boys were to the effect that I came to work with and for them; that the institution was established for their benefit and not for mine, and that when I could be of no service to them I should give place to some one who could do more and better.

The condition of the school in 1860, or its previous history, cannot be better shown than by the following extract from the "Christian Examiner," of 1867 : —

"It is also known, that after more than ten years of experiment, the result had been a gloomy and painful disappointment to many of the most hopeful friends of the noble experiment, until, in 1859, the question of abandoning it was seriously raised ! The method of treatment,— which was, in great part, the vulgar and harsh method of convict discipline, enforced by the carrying of bludgeons and loaded weapons by some of the officers,— and the well-meant, though compulsory and unjust, enforcement of a system of religious instruction excited jealousy and alarm, especially among the Catholic families of the boys, which more than neutralized, in many cases, whatever moral influence the school could bring to bear. Friends who visited the school at that period speak of the cowed and 'hang-dog' look prevalent among the inmates. Escapes, or attempts to escape, were constant. The building was repeatedly set on fire, till in the 'fortunate' conflagration of 1859, at least two thirds of the entire structure was destroyed. Wise, merciful, and faithful men, serving on the Board of Trustees, were inured to the evils of a system they could not remedy, or else had come to regard them as hopeless evils, to be borne and made the best of. At length the 'vicious circle' into which the school had settled, in a sort of despair, was violently broken up by the discovery of a case of discipline among the boy-convicts, for some time hidden from the inspectors, so abominably cruel, beyond all limits permitted in a state penitentiary for adults, that a crisis was inevitable. Governor Banks took the responsibility of discharging all the trustees, and appointing a new Board."

It was at this time, through the influence of Dr. S. G. Howe, George B. Emerson, Samuel J. May, and such men, that I was appointed Superintendent, though the opposition on account of my being called a Unitarian was very strong. It is stated, that at several informal ballots only one vote was cast in my favor, no reason being assigned except that of my supposed religious opinions. As Governor Banks favored my appointment, and was impatient at their want of promptness in making a change, and, also, as the governor-elect was John A. Andrew, the Board, at the first formal ballot, elected me unanimously. Had these facts been known to me at that time, I should hardly have considered it prudent to accept the position; but, living in another State, I was not aware of the strength of the opposition. Thus, in January, 1861, with the institution in the disorganized condition above described, — a Board of Trustees almost unanimous in opposition; all the officers, including a resident chaplain, if not unfriendly, at least not in sympathy, — I entered upon my duties. Furthermore, as it soon afterward proved, there were, unknown to the officers, three sets of duplicate keys to the institution in the hands of the boys, stolen from the store-room the day before I arrived.

My first efforts were to gain the confidence and good-will of the boys, banish weapons of all kinds, and every appearance of harshness, and establish pleasant personal relations with each individual, as far as possible. This, as I anticipated, was not a difficult matter; for these boys are more quick to respond to kind treatment, and to appreciate efforts made for their comfort, than those in what are called the upper classes. I was soon acquainted with the general workings of the institution, and the particular duties of each officer. The Trustees were generally ready to acquiesce in such changes as I desired to make; and my personal relations with almost every member were entirely agreeable. In any school, the subject of discipline requires much study, and especially in such a school as this.

DISCIPLINE.

Having, as a boy, taken sides with Horace Mann and his friends upon the question of corporal pun-

ishment, and, later, having taught district and high
schools, private family-schools, and academies,
without the ferule or rod, not to speak of year-
long efforts, as a member of a board of education,
to banish corporal punishment from the schools, I
began in Westboro' with a firm determination to
do away with its use, as far as possible. I felt
sure of my position, but not certain how far my
theories could be put in practice under the circumstances in which I was placed, and with the talent
which could be secured in my assistants. On
consulting Samuel J. May in regard to the advisa-
bility of beginning with the determination, never,
under any circumstances, to inflict corporal punishment, he laughingly replied, after waiting a
moment, "I would let the boys know indirectly
that you can lift nine hundred pounds with your
bare hands. It will have a good moral influence."
However, he advised me to say nothing about punishment to the boys, but to eliminate it as fast as
possible; that my success would depend upon the
character of the officers; but he had no doubt I
would be able to dispense with it almost entirely
in a short time. Securing the best officers I could,
I labored in season and out of season to instil
into their minds correct ideas and principles, and
aided in having these put into practice. Thanks
to their earnest and untiring efforts, in a short

time corporal punishment, although not entirely unknown, was rarely resorted to. Some officers requested of me and the Trustees that they should have more liberty in this respect; and some of the Trustees would advise it, not on account of a lack of good discipline, which was never questioned, but on account of the great labor required of officers to get along without it. Perhaps no member in the Board would restrict an officer as much as I in this respect; for, admitting that a boy might be benefited by a flogging occasionally, the danger that the officer will punish too much and too often will more than balance the possible good.

In a public institution it is very doubtful whether corporal punishment should be permitted at all, it being so easy to keep a knowledge of its abuses from the public, and even from the Trustees themselves. Contrary to what many may think, boys will very rarely report an officer for abusing them. Such boys are generally troublesome, and feel that they deserve some punishment; and they act on the principle that " makes us rather bear the ills we have than fly to others that we know not of."

However, to have something definite to go by, the regulations of the Boston schools, which permit the use of the rattan upon the hand, were

adopted. Daily reports of every case of punishment were required, and every case carefully
investigated. Boys were occasionally put into the
lodge ; but, to guard against its too frequent use,
I ordinarily took the whole charge of it myself.
It is well to hedge punishments about with considerable inconvenience. The lodge was a large,
well-lighted, comfortable room, where boys could
be isolated, and where they could work, if necessary. I have passed three months without putting
a boy into it, and I think a whole year without
having one in over night. Once, having foolishly
threatened to put a small boy into the lodge under
such circumstances as seemed to require me to do
so, I found him at night so nervous and afraid to
remain alone, that I determined to occupy the next
cell myself, to keep him company. This had an
excellent effect upon him and others, showing that
the punishment was not vindictive.

The following answer to the question, " What
punishments are employed ?" a question pro-
pounded by the "Inspectors of Prisons and Reformatories of the United States and Canada," in
a report to the Legislature of New York, 1865,
gives my opinion and practice at that time.

" Deprivation of privileges, simple diet, isola-
tion, and returning from the 'Families' to the
congregate department. Flogging, and such cheap

punishments, so easily inflicted, and so readily resorted to by the passionate and unskilful or inexperienced, we have but little faith in as a means
of reformation. *Fear* may restrain, but *love*
only can reform." The officers found at the institution were persons of intelligence and experience, but more or less in sympathy with the
previous order of things. I was advised to make
an entire change as soon as possible ; but a different course was considered more just, and at a
meeting of the officers it was stated that all might
feel secure in their places if they proved faithful
and efficient, and would aid earnestly in carrying
out such new measures as might be introduced.
My experience, however, was that officers in sympathy with one method of discipline do not heart-
ily work for another; and for new measures we
require new men. Some were outwardly friendly,
who were not so really. Anonymous letters were
written, one to a member of the Governor's Coun-
cil, endeavoring to create sectarian prejudices
against me. Upon an officer who was almost in-
stantly killed by an accident, we found a diary in
which he had kept a note of every unpleasant circumstance that came under his notice, with com-
ments, ready for reference in case it might be
useful. The assistant superintendent, however,
who had been in the institution from its organiza-

tion, was of great service to me, knowing, as he
did, all the minutiæ of the place. He remained
during my whole term of service; and without
his assistance and advice my labors would have
been much more difficult. He is now at the head
of an institution of similar character in a neighboring State.

SCHOOLS.

While the institution was under repairs, after
the great fire, of course not much attention could
be given to the schools, and they were found entirely ungraded and over-crowded — each teacher
having about eighty pupils, many not provided
with desks. The principal teacher had given his
notice, and was to leave in a few days, he having
been attacked by the boys, and somewhat injured,
a short time before. Another teacher left the day
I arrived. He had found a revolver requisite to
protect himself a few weeks previous. It was
necessary immediately to procure substitutes, and
some that I was so fortunate as to secure at that
time remained with me several years, and are now
occupying honorable and responsible positions as
educators. The schools were thoroughly graded
at once, and a course of study prepared. The
number of pupils was reduced, and extra teachers
employed. The teachers' desks were supplied

with the usual reference books, and other suggestive ones, such as "Krumacher's Parables," "Power of Kindness," "Kiss for a Blow," "Æsop's Fables," etc., to take the place of straps and sticks which were previously found there. The following extracts from a late letter in the "Evening Transcript," June, 1877, by one of these teachers, will give a good idea of the schools at this time : —

"I often think over the time I spent there, and how the boys appeared when I entered the room as teacher — the primary department, of eighty boys. The monitor, a boy of nineteen years, handed me a stick or club, saying, 'This is what you will have to lick them with.' I was alone in the room with the boys, but I never felt the least afraid, any more than in other schools I have taught. It was such a pleasure to teach them; they knew nothing of kindness, and were so grateful for all I did. Not one in the room could tell me why we kept the Fourth of July, or Thanksgiving, or Fast, or who George Washington was ; therefore I spent many evenings giving such information. I often sang to them when they were restless. I remember once singing a little song about Benny, how 'the angels came and took him,' etc. After I was through I saw several crying, while others were trying to hide their tears. One little boy said, 'I can't help it ! it makes me think of my little sister that died.' I think the singing had a very good effect. I went into school one morning with the first flower I had seen that spring, and they all seemed so happy to see a flower, and held up their hands, saying, 'Can't I have it, please?' I said, 'I hardly know what to do, when so many good boys want it. You all say that L. B. is the naughtiest boy in the school, and I think I will give it to him — he looks as if it would make him a better boy.' He took it and hugged it to his bosom, crying and laughing, but never letting it out of his hands, till, in parade for supper, with hands behind him, a boy took it from him. He then gave such a scream that the officers all came running to see what was the matter, he all the time crying, 'He's got my flower.'

"I remember a nice little boy from P——, that I tried to teach to knit, but he was so sad and homesick that I pitied him very much. The boys called my attention to his pockets, so crammed. I asked him to let me see what he had. He said, 'I am afraid you will not let me keep them.' I said, 'Let me see.' So he pulled out two dirty stockings, saying, 'I want to keep them; my mother knit them, and I may never see her again.' I told him I would have them washed and mended for him, which I did. Afterwards he was sent home, and his mother wrote me a nice, kind letter. I never struck a blow all the time I was there, or requested any one to do so for me. I remember those days with great satisfaction."

The object aimed at was to give the boys thorough elementary instruction, sufficient to make them good citizens, not great scholars; and to inspire them with a love of learning. Some peculiarities are, perhaps, worth mentioning. In the lowest department, reading was taught by a purely phonetic method. In this way the boys secured a thorough drill in the elementary sounds of the language, and the different brogues were eradicated. Among the pupils were some who would never learn to read our language by ordinary class-teaching. A number had been in school several years, and yet were unable to read a word.

About twenty such boys were put into a room by themselves, and taught by a very enthusiastic and accomplished female teacher, one who entered into the work with her whole heart, and secured surprising results.[1] Her interest was such, that, although many years have passed since she left the school, in telling of her experience there, the tears will sometimes come to her eyes. Much labor was given to teaching all to write a simple letter; special time was set apart for this exercise. Occasionally, each boy would write a specimen letter to me. A spelling-book was compiled of words misspelled in their letter-writing, which we made thorough work with. The proper use of capitals and the period was especially taught. A good deal of time was given to the rapid combination of numbers, in oral exercises. During the war, daily lessons were given from war maps, and the boys were always supplied with a number of the leading daily papers. The army movements of every prominent officer were at once traced out by a boy appointed for that particular purpose, who held himself in readiness to report to the school. In this way all were kept thoroughly informed in

[1] It would be an interesting fact to know how many boys in Massachusetts get a hatred of school, play truant, form bad habits, and are sent to the Reform School, on account of the difficulty of learning to read our language, the spelling of which, according to Max Müller, "is unhistorical, unsystematic, unintelligible, unteachable;" and, according to Gladstone, "without rule, method, or system."

regard to the progress of the war, and all gained
a good knowledge of the geography of the country. This exercise was particularly interesting,
and, we thought, very useful. During the war,
twenty-six boys enlisted directly from the school,
and six hundred and twenty-nine of those who
had been connected with the institution; and
they did good service. Many left their bounty
money in our hands, and sent us their wages for
safe keeping.

A certain time of each week was set apart for
the reading of library books. According to my
experience, young persons first read voluntarily,
for pleasure, afterwards for information, and finally
for profit. Such books were procured for the
library, therefore, as were adapted to these various
conditions. In the lower departments the teachers read aloud to the school, and in this way a
taste for reading was acquired, which I considered
of great importance. The *ability* to read and the
desire to read are quite different things. Special
efforts were made to secure the latter. I gave
much personal attention to the schools, often conducting the class exercises, and with my violin
drilling the boys in singing. Great care was
taken in the selection of officers to find those who
could sing, but particularly so in regard to the
teachers, and we were fortunate in having a large

number of fine singers and musicians during the
whole time I had charge of the school. My wife
and my two little girls often spent a session in the
schools, the girls reciting in the classes. In the
families more attention was given to natural history : large collections of insects were made, and
neatly arranged in cases. Daily journals were
kept by the boys, containing full records of all
garden and farm work in which they were employed : when the different crops were planted, the
quantity and kind of seeds and fertilizers used,
and how the crops were cared for and harvested.
The boys worked six hours a day, and attended
school four ; and their progress, according to the
opinion of all the teachers, was more rapid than
in ordinary schools where the pupils attend six
hours and do no outside work. The teachers
were generally graduates of some normal school
or college, having had experience. I cannot re-
frain from mentioning one of these teachers, whose
early death was a public loss,—Mr. Walter Seaver,
of Northboro', Mass. After being graduated with
honor from the Bridgewater Normal School, he
taught a large and difficult school with great success, and came recommended as one whose influence for good over his pupils was marvellous. To
see him walking about the school-yard, with each
arm around some large, rough boy, and followed

by a crowd of interested listeners while he told some pleasant story, was a sight never to be forgotten.

MUSIC.

As before intimated, the influence of music over the boys, whether listening or taking part themselves, was considered of great importance. I should have been glad to adopt the custom which Pythagoras did, of "having his pupils lulled to sleep every night, and waked every morning, by the soothing appeals of sweet sounds," regarding music as something celestial and divine. Little attention was given to the abstract science of music; its refining and elevating influence was what was desired, and for that I labored in every practicable way, introducing singing daily in the schools and work-rooms, and often in the yard.

The old German proverb, "When music is in, the devil is out," I believe to be true. Special preparation was made for singing in the chapel and at evening devotions. Sunday-school concerts were often given, at which the teachers and the family took a prominent part, my wife always presiding at the organ. It was uncommon to see a boy or officer not joining in the choruses. A great many fine old songs, psalms, and hymns were committed to memory; but none containing

sectarian sentiments were ever taught. I never
thought it practicable to organize a band of musicians in the school, although many of my officers
could play upon different instruments, as I could
myself. Before a boy could have time to learn
to play well, he should be through with the institution. In the excellent school on Thompson's
Island, I have heard very fine playing; but there
the boys are of a different class, and they can remain longer.

Much more female help was introduced than
before, the influence of which was very excellent.
In the three families the teachers were females.
In the chair-shop the teacher of work had always
been a man; a cultivated woman was appointed
in his place. A woman was also employed to assist the baker and aid in the cooking, in the
congregate department; and the female teachers
were always in the dining-room during the meals,
to teach the boys table manners. These things,
like " little drops of water, little grains of sand,"
gradually changed the atmosphere of the whole
place.

WORK.

All the boys, except those engaged in domestic
work, as cooking, washing, sewing, knitting, etc.,
were employed in cane-seating chairs — a very

neat, healthy, and active kind of work, but one
from which not much profit could be realized.
Having been brought up on a farm, and being
always interested in agriculture and horticul-
ture, I was satisfied that farm work was in every
respect the most desirable, when there was an
opportunity to make use of it.[1] Arrangements
were, therefore, made at once to introduce it.
We had a fine, large farm, formerly under the
control of the State Board of Agriculture, who
had laid out the ground, and had done very
much to improve, beautify, and prepare it for
the work I now proposed to undertake. The
State had built several houses on the grounds,
now called "trust houses," for small families of
thirty, which were ready for occupancy. Officers
were selected for them, and the families immediately organized with special reference to the
introduction of agricultural and industrial employment. A particular department was assigned
to each family. The first, made up of large boys,
had the heavy farm labor and the care of the
stock. The second, of smaller boys, raised small
fruits and vegetables. The third, of the smallest
boys in the institution, had the care of the grounds
about the buildings, and they also cultivated flow-

[1] "The principal business of the school will be agriculture."—*Thedore
Lyman, 1846.*

ers and gathered flower-seeds for sale. Besides
these particular employments, each family did a
large amount of miscellaneous work. To see, as
I often have seen, an experienced and skilful
teacher, full of fun, leading, not driving, some
twenty boys into the fields, to join in the labor
himself, and not to act the overseer, is something
pleasant to remember. One of these teachers has
since been assistant professor at Harvard College,
and is now at the head of one of the first schools
in the State. Each boy in the different families
had two rods of ground for his own, to cultivate
in his leisure time, we finding the fertilizers and
he the labor, and sharing profits. These grounds
were always well kept, and the boys realized from
one to three dollars apiece, annually. This was a
very excellent arrangement, and tended to form
industrious habits and to inspire a love of work.
Voluntary labor is quite a different thing from enforced labor, in its influence upon the young.

In the winter and in bad weather, boys were
seating chairs, making paper boxes, and doing any
similar work that could be found for them. This
experiment of introducing farm labor was in every
respect satisfactory; farm labor proved more
healthful, more interesting, more profitable than
mechanical labor, and it better prepared the boys
to go to homes in the country. The year before

I went to the institution (1860) the income from the product of the farm was $7,004.63. The year I left (1866) it was $14,796.63. The valuation of the farm had also increased upwards of $6,000 as appraised. The income from mechanical labor had increased from $2,483.80 in 1861, to $3,595.-96 in 1866. A head farmer had been employed at a salary of $650, and a steward at $500, and support. These officers were no longer necessary, as their particular duties were transferred to me, thereby securing unity of administration, while reducing the expense. The annual amount paid for salaries in 1866 was upwards of $5,000 less than in 1876.

Experiments and improvements had to be made gradually. Several acres of grapes were planted. One year, forty thousand heads of cabbages were raised, and always large quantities of roots and berries. The spring I left, more than fifteen hundred dollars' worth of strawberries were raised. Instead of allowing large quantities of the sewage of the institution to run to waste, as was previously the case, every particle was utilized, and hundreds of loads of peat-muck yearly composted. The number of cattle and hogs was largely increased, and extra fertilizers, to some extent, were purchased. The stock, which was of a miscellaneous character, was gradually changed to pure Ayrshire. Hundreds of cords of stone were sunk, and many acres of poor pasturage made into excellent tillage. The ruins of the great fire were removed, the grounds graded, and many shrubs and ornamental trees planted around the institution. To show how the Trustees regarded the experiment of gardening and farming, the following extract, taken from their report of 1866, is given : —

"The Trustees have long felt the desirableness of turning as much of the labor of the boys as possible to agricultural pursuits, and especially to gardening, and have, therefore, been yearly extending the grounds devoted to this purpose, and raising thereon a large variety of vegetables and small fruits. We have a tract of about forty acres of plain land, easy to cultivate, and admirably adapted to this purpose; and we have now a vegetable and fruit garden of about thirty acres, which, we think, will compare favorably with any garden of its size in the county. The returns of the crops herewith rendered will show how successful we have been in our cultivation the present season. We were particularly favored in our crop of strawberries, which brought us quite a sum of money; while many of the other articles we have produced are largely consumed by the inmates of the school as food. We have also raised a good crop of grapes, and have grown new vines enough the present year to double our number for the coming season. We are convinced by experience that boys placed with farmers in the country are almost certain to do well, and, if not disturbed by their parents, they generally become steady, respectable men ; while those placed in large towns and cities are about equally sure to return to their former evil habits. By employing our boys in gardening, we gradually form in them a love for such labors, and, at the same time, we prepare them to be useful at once to the farmers with whom we so much desire to place them."

The style of our cultivation will be understood, when it is stated that the appraisers one year estimated the entire growth upon one acre of cabbages, roots and tops, at upwards of sixty tons. These boys should do much more than they ever have done towards their own support; and it can be accomplished by a well-arranged system of labor upon the land, adapted to their capacity, in connection with some mechanical labor during the winter and stormy weather. It would be better for the boys and the State.

The earnings of one family of thirty boys at Westboro' during the year 1866 were $4,544.72, at least half their support. Boys in the families can earn much more than in the congregate department, which is contrary to the general impression.

HEALTH.

The health of the boys was remarkably good. The whole number of deaths during my administration was but ten, and three of these from accidents, averaging about one a year from sickness,— a number much less than before or since. In 1861, the physician's salary was reduced from $200 to

$100, and it continued at that sum during the time I was there; when I left, it was increased to $250, at which sum it has remained since. A new hospital was built, and supplied with such books as Florence Nightingale's work on Nursing, and "The Family Physician," by Joel Shew, M. D. The duties of the nurse were so light that she was occupied much of her time in the sewing and knitting room. No boy was taken to the hospital without the case being reported to me immediately, when, if nothing serious was the matter, I gave directions concerning the treatment. Having read the leading works upon Homœopathy and Hydropathy so as to enjoy the visits of my family-physician, who was an Allopath, and once having spent a vacation of some weeks at the celebrated Water Cure at Glen Haven, N. Y., under Dr. Jackson, where the principal medicines were fresh air, pure water, exercise, sunshine, and fasting, I was enabled to prescribe these remedies with remarkable success, and found them sufficient for ordinary troubles among the boys. As our physician was an elderly man, and not expert in extracting teeth, the boys had become much prejudiced against him in this part of his practice. Informing myself as thoroughly as I could, by the aid of an excellent dentist of Westboro', of the art, I therefore did that work myself. This was

an excellent thing, for it gave me the opportunity
of relieving severe pain, and being of personal
service to many boys. By this experience I was
led more fully to see that all things have their
times and seasons, like measles and marbles ; for
I have sometimes extracted twenty-five teeth in a
day, and then not one for as many days. Such
facts the thoughtful disciplinarian turns to account. I remember, one stormy day, asking the
boys in the sewing-room if any one wished a
tooth extracted, when immediately half a dozen
hands were raised. Some people have a prejudice
against this operation, but many of these boys
seemed to consider it an amusement. It is certainly a fact, that they bear pain better than ordinary boys. I have known boys to get permission
to go to the office to have a tooth extracted when
their teeth were not troubling them in the least.
Perhaps what prompted them was to speak to
some one, and be spoken to, individually ; for in
such schools many boys, especially the quiet and
well-behaved, may not be spoken to, individually,
by an officer for many days ; and they are often
very lonely, even when surrounded by their school-
mates. Such things show the evils of a congregate system, which I endeavored to counteract in
every possible way.

The boys were not so large as ordinary farmers'

sons of the same age, owing, doubtless, to their previous unhealthy manner of living, and the almost universal habit of using tobacco. They would give anything they had in exchange for a stub of a cigar, and risk any discipline to obtain it. It would sometimes take many weeks for boys who had lived in cellars, and had eaten when and what they could get, to become accustomed to regular habits and wholesome food. After a while they would gain rapidly; but I think they seldom reached what should have been their normal size, and that their average length of life was shortened.

FOOD.

Most persons can be influenced through the stomach, and especially the young. It was, therefore, made a point to have the food as palatable as possible, and not too expensive. It was as good as that of the officers, though with less variety. They had the same bread, vegetables, and meat; but the latter was more simply cooked. In the families, all ate at the same table with the officers, and of the same food. There was no more difference than is made in ordinary families where there are children. This, I am certain, had great influence upon the boys. For similar reasons I usually had a suit of clothes made from the same cloth as theirs, and wore it about the institution, some one of the boys always making it for me.

CHAPLAIN.

A resident chaplain had been employed in the institution since its organization ; but my judgment, as expressed to the Trustees, was in favor of employing clergymen of the different denominations in the neighboring towns to supply the pulpit on Sunday ; thus securing a variety of talent, making the exercises more interesting to the officers and boys, and saving an annual expense of at least $500. This opinion, formed after careful consideration, was confirmed by experience, and, as I afterwards learned, was generally held by superintendents of such schools ; as was shown by a discussion of the question in a convention of " Managers and Superintendents of Houses of Refuge and Schools of Reform in the United States," held in the city of New York, in 1857. The gentleman occupying the position of Chaplain was physically feeble, and unfortunate in being a cripple, but seemingly well satisfied with the situation. Such misfortunes enlist the sympathies of the wise and good ; but upon thoughtless boys, such as those at Westboro', they are likely to cause a repetition of the rudeness and irreverence manifested

by the forty-and-two children of Bethel towards
the Prophet Elisha.

A great deal depends upon the personal appearance of a man when addressing an audience, especially of boys; and of all subjects, religion
should have every advantage. I am inclined to
the opinion that Moses was right when he men-
tions what should disqualify a man physically for
the office of priest. Our chaplain was a Methu-
selah among the old-school theologians. However,
he took a good deal of interest in the Sunday-school, often making out the questions for
the lessons, and printing them himself upon cards.
His favorite subjects were from the Old Testament, such as the story of Jonah swallowed up
by the whale, and Elisha and the saucy boys. As
he always took the most literal view of these stories, and preached upon the subjects, it was sometimes difficult for me to conduct the recitation in
my Sunday-school class, without conflicting with
his expositions. To illustrate: Once, when the
lesson was concerning Jonah, the boys in the class
inquired immediately, if I believed that story,
saying that they did not believe a word of it. I
told them I thought we all believed it. I then explained to them the situation of Nineveh and
Tarshish. "Now," I said, "when our conscience,
which may be called the voice of God, tells us to

do a certain thing, and we do not obey, we do
just the opposite — we disobey; so Jonah, when
told to go to Nineveh, went the opposite way to
Tarshish. Then when we do what we know is
wrong, we soon feel badly, and worry over it, and
cannot sleep, and toss about in bed, and everything looks dark and troublesome; so it was with
Jonah,— he is said to be in a vessel during a
storm, tossed about and frightened. When we
have done very wrong, we are likely to feel over-
whelmed, and, as it were, swallowed up with re-
morse and grief; and so Jonah is represented as
cast into a sea of trouble, and swallowed up by a
whale. Ignorant and superstitious people are
very likely to think that calamities of all kinds
are sent by God as punishments for somebody's
sin; so the sailors laid the storm to Jonah, and
threw him overboard. After a person is over-
taken in his sin, and trouble comes, he is likely
to see his error, and repent; and so it was with
Jonah,— he came to himself, and prayed for for-
giveness. When a person truly repents and
makes good resolutions, he soon experiences a
kind of happiness, and feels as strong as though he
stood upon a rock; so it was with Jonah, — he is
said to have been thrown upon the solid land.
Then, if a person is sincere in his repentance he
will follow the voice of conscience; so Jonah,

after he was safe upon the land, went immediately
to Nineveh, as he was to do at first." After going
through the story something in this way, which
pleased them very much, they all said the story
was true. For a long time afterwards it was a by-
word in the yard, when a boy was behaving badly,
to say he was on the road to Tarshish. In this
way I tried to get something useful out of any
subject that the chaplain might choose, without
openly differing with him. In his farewell sermon, the chaplain, in alluding to this style of
interpretation, took occasion to condemn such
want of reverence for the Bible, in strong terms.
The Trustees were well aware that he was not
suited to such a position; but out of consideration for his misfortune, I suppose, he was permitted to remain more than a year. When
informed that his services were no longer desired,
he was very much annoyed, and preached a farewell sermon, entitled, "A Plea for the Bible in
the State Reform School," in which he made a
bitter attack upon the evangelical Board of Trustees for appointing a man of my religious opinions
as superintendent. The following is a part of the
text: "For I know this, that after my departure
shall ravenous wolves enter in, not sparing the
flock." The sermon was full of insinuations and
misrepresentations in regard to my religious influ-

ence; so much so, that Governor Andrew said the Trustees should have stopped him during its delivery. When visited after the service by the president of the Board, he manifested such a spirit that I was requested, in writing, to demand his keys, and not allow him to enter the institution again. A large edition of the sermon was published, and copies placed upon the desk of every member of the Legislature, and sent to prominent men in this and other States. We had always been on the most friendly terms; and, to show that it was only the welfare of Zion he had at heart, he took occasion to say, "My personal relations with the Superintendent have been marred by no act, no word or syllable of a word; my intercourse with the household has been marked by mutual courtesy;" and he returned me public thanks. From this time, no resident chaplain was appointed while I was there. The usual daily devotional exercises I conducted, and occasionally I spoke to the boys in the chapel on Sunday.

SUNDAY.

On Sunday, the boys, under the direction of the teachers, prepared their Sunday-school lessons, and assembled at nine o'clock, in the chapel, for recitation. A number of intelligent ladies and

gentlemen of Westboro' took charge of the school,
selecting one of their number for superintendent;
and I have never seen persons better qualified for
such positions. Many of the officers of the institution, including my wife and myself, always
took a class. Besides the regular lessons, many
parables and psalms, and such chapters as Rom.
xii., 1 Cor. xiii., were committed for concert
recitation. The regular services in the afternoon
were always interesting and instructive. Clergymen of different denominations, from the neighboring towns, generally officiated. Of these
preachers, no one was more acceptable to the
boys than the late venerable Dr. Allen, of Northboro',— not so much for what he said, as for what
he was.

"E'en children followed, with endearing wile,
    And plucked his gown, to share the good man's smile."

One summer, many of the clergymen of Wor-
cester spoke to the school, and we had occasionally prominent men from different parts of the
State; so that, upon the whole, we thought we
had better preaching than any society in the
county. But it is not the preaching we hear, so
much as the practice we see, that influences for
good; and therefore I was much more anxious in
regard to the character of my officers, who associated daily with the boys, than for the preaching

that occupied their attention for a few moments each Sunday.

After supper, in pleasant weather, many of the officers, male and female, and any Trustee who might be at the institution, took small classes out to walk in the neighborhood, gathering flowers and specimens of natural history. The chaplain, in his farewell sermon, thus alluded to this custom: "The evangelical idea of the holy Sabbath already waning from these walls and these yards, already trampled upon by company strolls into the surrounding fields and woods, will be lost to these young hearts." At the devotional exercises in the evening, there was more singing than on week-day, and often concert recitations from the Bible, after which the boys retired with the impression that "the Sabbath was made for man, and not man for the Sabbath."

Sometimes, to vary the exercises and make them more interesting, I read from "The Altar at Home," published by the American Unitarian Association; sometimes from "Selections from Scripture, for Families and Schools," for Episcopalians, published by E. P. Dutton & Co.; sometimes from "Stories from the Lips of the Teacher," by O. B. Frothingham; and also from a copy of an old edition of the New Testament, once owned by John Hancock, containing his autograph. The translation was in the ordinary language, and not according to King James' version. One of the Trustees, in his anxiety to guard against heresy, objected to this miscellaneous reading, and I was requested to confine myself to the common version. In speaking to the boys, I often took for my subject the character of some great man; and, as nearly one half of the boys were Catholics, often such as Fénelon, O'Connell, and Father Matthew; and, on St. Patrick's day, the excellent man in whose honor the day is celebrated. Soon after going to Westboro' I observed, one morning, that the officer whose duty it was to look over and distribute the mail threw the "Pilot" into the waste-basket. Upon inquiry I found that this was the usual disposition made of that paper, when sent to the boys. It was always given out, afterwards, with other papers.

A Catholic priest, from a neighboring town, called occasionally, and sometimes spoke to the boys. He left copies of the Catholic catechism to give to such boys as wished them, which were distributed accordingly. It was my intention to treat all sects alike — Jews and Gentiles, Protestants and Catholics; to teach the great principles of religion and morality, and require all my officers to do the same; but, in a State institution, I considered I had no right to teach sectarian dogmas ; and I think all the officers, as many have done, will bear witness that the management was unsectarian, in the highest and best sense. That there was no disposition to favor, unduly, so-called liberal men and preaching, is shown by the fact that two thirds of all the officers, and three fourths of the preaching, were "evangelical," so-called, during the whole time I was in charge of the school.

ELOPERS.[1]

In many institutions boys are punished severely for running away. This is a mistake. It may deter some from making the attempt, but even this is doubtful. Fear, except for immediate consequences, has but little influence. A large number of the boys, after being away a few hours, will come back of themselves, if they are sure of kind treatment when they return — a much larger number than will be kept from running away by fear of punishment. I found it was not always the worst boys that ran away, but often the best. An act is sinful according to the motive that prompts it, and in this case it is not often bad. My first experience in this direction was with two boys who ran away soon after I arrived. They were

[1] Boys who escape from the school and are not returned are reported "Elopers."

caught in a few hours, with their feet badly frozen.
I took charge of them, and did all I could to re-
lieve their sufferings, inflicting no punishment.
These boys never gave me trouble afterwards.
Their feelings toward me were quite different from
what they would have been if I had put them in
the lodge for some weeks, and fed them upon
bread and water. Some of the officers thought the
course I took would increase the trouble, but experience proved the reverse. A great deal of
freedom was granted to the boys, often more than
one hundred being at work in the fields, outside
the main building. If boys never ran away, it
would prove that no freedom was allowed; if a
great many, that the officers were negligent or the
building was insecure. A shrewd officer reads the
intentions of the boys in their countenances and
actions, and counteracts their plans. The inefficient officer, having eyes, sees not the things that
most concern him to know. I could illustrate this
by many anecdotes like the following: Some
twenty boys were in line, one morning, ready to
pass out into the fields, as usual, when something
impressed me that a certain boy had better not go
out that day. I called him to me, and gave him
some other duty. In a few moments it came out
that he had made plans to run away that morning.
No one who has not this faculty of "mind read-

ing," to a considerable degree, should be employed in such a school, or perhaps in any other.
The average yearly number of successful escapes
during this period was between one and two;
previously it had been between two and three;
since that time it has been increased to between
ten and eleven.[1]

Furthermore, there was no attempt to fire the
buildings, and no deliberate combination of the
boys to attack and injure the officers. These
are noteworthy facts, considering the previous
and subsequent history of the institution, and
also that between two and three per cent. of the
boys are incendiaries. Previous to this the institution had been set on fire fourteen times, causing considerable damage, before the great fire
of 1859, which destroyed three fourths of the
entire building.

PLAY.

Having always been fond of play, and fairly skilful in all boys' sports, — running, skating, wrest-
ling, and all gymnastic exercises; and, moreover,
being strongly of the opinion that play is an important influence for good in any educational system for the young, as soon as possible I had a

[1] Before 1861, Average No. Boys, 450; escapes yearly, 3: about ⅔ per cent.
1861 to 1867, " " 300; " " 1½ " ⅜ "
Since 1867, " " 309; " " 10¼ " 3½ "

gymnasium built in the yard, and the boys encouraged in all ways to become expert gymnasts. I joined in the sports myself, and endeavored to have all my officers do the same. Besides the gymnasium, there were posts of different heights for leap-frog, a smooth pole for climbing, barrels to run upon, football, etc.

This helped very much in the discipline of the school : a boy is never very troublesome when in a mood for play. In the winter, we had one of the finest ponds in the State for skating. Members of the Chauncy Hall, the West Newton English and Classical, and the Boston Latin schools, sent us nearly a hundred pairs of skates one winter, so we were well supplied. These skates were sent us through the personal influence and exertions of Mr. J. H. Stevenson, a most useful and efficient Trustee. Often all the boys, good and bad, together with the officers, male and female, would skate for an hour or two. It was a sight worth seeing, and a good thing for us all.

The following extract from an article[1] in the " Commonwealth," written in 1863, and entitled, " Christmas at Westboro'," will illustrate this feature : —

[1] The writer, Mr. F. B. Sanborn, Secretary of the Board of State Charities at that time, is a gentleman as familiar with our charitable institutions as any one in the State, and to whom we were indebted for wholesome criticisms.

"About nine o'clock the battalion of boys from the great Hall marched down to the ice with their skates, marshalled by their teachers, and led by Mr. Allen, the Superintendent. The farm-house boys had gone earlier, and two or three *alumni* of the school, just enlisted in the army and furloughed for the holidays, were cutting about on the pond in their blue overcoats. The Hall boys had perhaps one pair of skates to every five boys, — the rest raced or slid or sledded, or waited their turn at the skates. But presently the scene changed. Mr. Stephenson of Boston, one of the Trustees, came driving up from the village, escorting a huge box of skates which had been sent by the boys of the High and Latin schools to the Westboro' boys.

"The box was dumped on the ice, opened, and received by the boys with loud huzzas, nor was it long before the new skates were gliding over the pond to the infinite delight of the wearers, who did not let a fall, now and then, interfere with their sport.

"But Mr. Stephenson had not only brought the skates, but a detachment of skaters, and among them several young ladies. These were joined by the ladies from the Hall, and about the same time appeared a huge sled with a chair or throne mounted on it. In this was placed in turn each of the ladies, who were drawn about by men and boys in fine style. The scene was now gay enough. Here you might see a young lady skating indiscriminately forward or backward, pursued by a troop of boys, — there the Superintendent, dodging among a dozen boys who were trying to catch him, — farther on a boy of the school, with what surgeons call a 'solution of continuity' in his jacket, skating with a little girl in hat and feather, — in another place a State official skating hand in hand with a small mulatto urchin, who was relating portions of his autobiography, and petitioning for favors, — the whole circumfused with an atmosphere of shouts, songs, and general hubbub. A little before noon the party returned to the Hall for dinner, and in the afternoon resumed their sports, quite untired, and continued them till sunset, when we came away, resolved, if possible, to spend another Christmas with the naughty boys at Westboro'.

"We wish all our readers could look in upon the workings of this beneficent institution, whose Principal believes first in making his pupils happy, and then leading them, by affection rather than affliction, along the path of learning and virtue. They could not better employ their first day of leisure."

In early spring, with the first mud, came the interesting game of marbles. He who invented this game should have a monument, as a public benefactor. No game is so generally popular as this in its season. It gives skill to the eye and hand, and cultivates fair dealing between boys. It teaches, in a practical way, that " the best man wins." **Of** course there is sometimes cheating ; but if we allowed nothing where there is cheating, no one could trade horses. I used sometimes to give each boy ten marbles in the morning, and tell him to gain all he could honestly, by skilful play. At night I have often had boys bring hundreds to me to distribute the next morning. Any dispute about a marble gave the smallest boy standing near a right to it. This put a stop to most of the disputing, and was a popular regulation. Who can understand marble-playing? As suddenly as it comes, so suddenly it goes, not to reappear till the following spring.

For some time after marble-playing, the boys

are generally uneasy, and will run away, if their
attention is not taken up in some other direction.
In summer, all "went in swimming," sometimes
every day of the week. I made it a point to have
all taught to swim; and I have never seen better
swimmers. They were very venturesome and
careless; and two officers in a boat were always
near to aid in case of need, which was not uncommon. After the crops are gathered, in the autumn, when the leaves begin to fall, and the birds
are starting for a southern home — then, of all
times in the year, the boys desire to run away,
good and bad, great and small, all the same. It
will take a good deal of ingenuity to direct their
attention to other subjects. In the ability to anticipate trouble, and in judicious plans to avoid it,
lies the secret of good management. A gentleman at the head of one of our families once came
to me to ask what he should do with his boys, as
they were continually getting green apples from
the trees, and eating them; and he feared he
should be obliged to bring some back to the main
building. I advised him to take his boys to the
currant bushes, and let them eat all they would,
which he did twice. Afterwards he had no trouble
with his apples; thus, by supplying the boys' natural desire for acids in the spring, he saved his
apples, and kept the boys.

MILITARY.

Before going to Westboro' I was satisfied that "military drill" was not favorable to good discipline in any school; and with such boys as were in the Reform School, I was certain it would cause trouble. Their belligerent tendencies are already too active, and they need to have developed in them a reverence for human life and a regard for the rights of property, and to be, rather, under the gentle and refining influences, such as music affords. When the war commenced, and the military spirit was so active, the Trustees and officers were anxious that the "drill" should be introduced. I expressed no opposition, and wooden guns were supplied, and competent instructors procured to form and drill the companies.

I was glad to see the practical workings of this exercise, and entered into the experiment with spirit; but watched carefully, and studied its influence. The boys took great interest in it, and enjoyed it very much; and the companies appeared well. In about six months it had become a common thing, and its effect, I thought, could be seen. I therefore wrote to each of the leading officers, asking his opinion of its influence on the discipline of the school. The answer from each was that

it had been bad, which was in accord with my
judgment, and it was given up. When the war
was ended, and the drill given up in many schools,
and was becoming unpopular, some of the Trustees were anxious to introduce it again. As I
had given my testimony against it, before a committee of the Legislature, and in lectures and discussions, and believed it interfered with the best
interests of the school, I opposed it, and procured
the testimony of the most noted educators and
philanthropists against it: Horace Mann, Captain
Machonochie, the author of the Irish System of
Prison Discipline, and many others. This was
the condition of the question when I left, after
which the drill was reintroduced, and its legiti-
mate influence, I have no doubt, has been felt, if
not understood.

MARKS OF DISTINCTION.

Finding on my arrival that the boys were
dressed so as to indicate that they were Reform
School boys, I banished all such distinctions, and
never allowed the wearing of "badges" in school,
to indicate moral character. Their influence is
likely to be as it was in the family of Jacob,
when he dressed Joseph differently from his
brethren.

The best badge for moral worth is the countenance. A boy may be very troublesome, violating the rules constantly, and yet we know him to be a good boy at heart; while another may obey every regulation, and cause no trouble, and still we may not have the least confidence in him. This cannot be indicated by badges.

VISITORS.

We had a great many visitors from time to time, and it was quite interesting to see how different persons would impress the boys. Sometimes a so-called reformer would go through the institution, looking "wondrous wise," and discourse eloquently about the dangerous classes, without manifesting the least interest in the individual specimens before him. Another would appear to think he was in constant danger of having his pocket picked. Another would keep at a respectful distance from the boys, as though he feared to catch some disease; while the boys, with that instinctive knowledge of character which they possess, would be prompted to play tricks on such a one, just from feelings of antagonism. Such visits are productive only of evil. There are other persons whose visits are remembered as a beautiful dream. Boys run to these spontaneously, as to an old, familiar friend; and are better acquainted with them in five minutes than they could ever be with the other class.

That Christian gentleman and genial man, Samuel J. May, appropriately called the "Personification of the Beatitudes," made us several visits. To see him in the yard with the boys was a sight never to be forgotten. They would crowd around him, and listen to his anecdotes and conversation, all who could, taking hold of his hands and garments. I have seen them reach through the crowd surrounding him, to touch his clothes, prompted, I doubt not, by the same feelings as those of old, in Galilee. Such visits were a blessing to the boys, and an inspiration to the officers.

A. Bronson Alcott once read to the boys from "Pilgrim's Progress," and Julia Ward Howe recited some of her poems to them, and they never had a more attentive audience.

An excellent Quaker gentleman used to visit us occasionally and spend the Sunday. He always addressed the boys in the chapel, and after service gave each a present,— once a copy of the New Testament, at another time a beautiful card, upon which were printed appropriate mottoes and hymns. Going into the yard, after chapel, I found the boys had marked the cards, and nearly all, in groups, were quietly playing euchre; making

use of the cards in a way our Quaker friend had
not anticipated. Some excellent persons might
think this an evidence of great depravity; but if
they would look from the boys' standpoint the
prospect might not be quite so gloomy. There is
no better place to study human nature than in
a reform school; here you can see every faculty
of the mind so active as to be recognized easily.
One boy has inherited a gypsy's desire for wan-
dering, and will run away if he can, as surely as
the young partridge from the farmer's barnyard.
Another, like young Pomeroy, has the not uncommon tendency to cruelty developed into a
monstrosity. Here you will find "the artful
dodger," and the simple-minded "Smike," whose
relatives have taken this way to be rid of his support. If special religious exercises secure extra
privileges, one will be sure to find "Uriah Heap,"
" so 'umble," more to be despised, though not so
troublesome, as master "Quilp," with his almost
supernatural power for evil. No one can fully
understand all these boys : he may study particular
specimens for days and months, as a skilful physician studies a patient in a hospital; but, like him,
may never be able to do more than show his good
intentions. Still, after months and years of labor,
one may find an avenue to the *heart*, as was found
to the *mind* of Laura Bridgman. The Board of

State Charities could not do a better thing for
the State than to have such cases as that of young
Pomeroy investigated by eminent specialists.

DR. HOWE.

Great obligations are hereby expressed to the
late Dr. S. G. Howe for his valuable advice and
cordial sympathy. Notwithstanding his other duties,—having charge of the Blind Asylum, the
School for Idiots, and as chairman of the Board of
State Charities,—he accepted an appointment as
Trustee of the Reform School, in order to give
what aid he could to the efforts we were making
to conduct it upon what he thought right principles. His belief was that the Board should allow
the Superintendent to carry on the institution
without interference, and to hold him responsible
for results. He thought a superintendent of a
reform school, as of an insane asylum, should
be an expert in his business, and a trustee should
interfere in the one case no more than in the
other. And my present experience, as trustee of
the Girls' Industrial School, Lancaster, added to
my experience at Westboro', confirms his opinion.
He was very much in favor of the family system
wherever it was practicable.

SCHOOL SHIP.

During the whole time I was at Westboro', the "School Ship" was in existence, under the charge of Captain Richard Matthews; and as the two Boards of Trustees were on the most friendly terms, boys from the ship, not adapted to a sailor's life, were sent to Westboro', and exchanged for those who desired to go to sea.

We received ninety-five such boys, many of them nearly full grown; and sent an equal number to the ship. These boys never caused us extra trouble; and, according to my experience and that of all my officers of whom I have inquired, large boys of eighteen or nineteen were less troublesome than those of fourteen or fifteen. They could much more readily be made to see that it was for their interest to do well. I cannot recall an instance, reported to me, where corporal punishment was deliberately inflicted upon a large boy. The following extract from a letter written by a prominent teacher, now in the Boston schools, who was for several years one of my most earnest and successful teachers at Westboro', contains the same statement: —

"We had, I think, but comparatively little trouble with the large boys; it was the middle-sized ones that made most disturbance. The large boys could, if rightly approached, generally be made to see the folly of their course. You ask if the large boys were whipped. I think not; I believe I never had an encounter of any kind with any of the larger-sized boys."

Having once spent nearly a week upon the School Ship, I think the boys at that time were under excellent discipline. Such an institution can be conducted so as to be a service to the State, and a benefit to the boys.

CAUSES OF FAILURE.

In the "Report on the Prisons and Reformatories of the United States and Canada," before quoted from, it is stated that a "majority of subordinate officers in penal institutions have but a dim idea of their duties and responsibilities." Is not this the reason why, in such articles as "The Child of the State," in a recent number of the "Atlantic," the officers of the Reform School are described as heartless and cruel? When will it seem natural and probable to describe them as intelligent and humane gentleman?

The prophecy of Goldsmith, in the "Vicar of Wakefield," more than one hundred years ago, uttered in the character of Dr. Primrose, and the spirit he manifested among his fellow-prisoners, will some day be fulfilled in the management of our penal and reformary institutions. This "dim idea of their duties and responsibilities" is the cause of the failure of so many institutions to accomplish the object for which they are established. The most difficult thing a superintendent has to do is to select assistants adapted to the work required of them. Such as have more than a "dim idea of their duties and responsibilities" should be demanded in Massachusetts. If he is successful in this, all his other duties will be comparatively light. One inefficient officer will more than neutralize the labors of an excellent one. I was fortunate in having to aid me, a large portion of the time, four gentleman who are now superintendents of similar institutions; and many prominent teachers, male and female, in Boston and the neighboring cities. To these is due, in a great measure, whatever of success the school attained. The four gentleman alluded to (and also their wives) were with me more than four years, on the average, and several other excellent officers were there an equal length of time. Probably no similar institution in the country, during the war, could show such a degree of permanency in its leading officers.

If the Board of State Charities had the charge of the charitable institutions of the State, as the Board of Education has of the educational, and such men as Dr. S. G. Howe were appointed superintendents, then with a Horace Mann for its secretary, a unity and efficiency of action would be secured, and something more satisfactory accomplished. Until we have such a central board, not much improvement can be expected. The recommendations of the Board of State Charities upon this subject, in their last Report, will doubtless be carefully considered by the able commission lately appointed for that purpose. Notwithstanding our shortcomings, Dr. E. C. Wines, D. D., and Theodore W. Dwight, LL. D., say, in their "Report to the Legislature of New York upon Prisons and Reformatories of the United States and Canada," after visiting all these institutions in 1866 : "If we might venture, among so many excellent institutions, to single out any that seem to us to possess an excellence superior to others, we could not hesitate to name the reform schools of Massachusetts." In speaking of harsh methods of discipline, they say : "Are there superintendents of prisons who say, How shall we govern our men without some, at least, of the sterner means of repression? — to such we would say, Go to Massachusetts and learn." A high compliment to Mr. Gideon Haynes, the Warden of our State Prison at that time.

INFLUENCE OF THE SCHOOL UPON ITS OFFICERS.

It was interesting to notice the influence the institution exerts upon different officers. Some begin with great enthusiasm and confidence, but soon become discouraged, and grow unsympathetic and harsh. Others grow cunning and tricky, like the boys, and use discipline on the principle that "it takes a rogue to catch a rogue;" that "the end sanctifies the means." Such officers soon become unreliable themselves, and teach deception by precept and example. We once had a bright, active office-boy to run of errands, very faithful and prompt. I noticed that he gradually grew sober and uneasy, so I concluded something was wrong. I took occasion to talk with him about his general appearance, and told him he must be doing wrong in some way. He was much troubled, and cried, which I had never seen him do before. He finally told me that one of the officers had been giving him tobacco, to keep order in the sleeping hall, for an hour after the boys retired, instead of doing it himself, as was his duty. The boy never fairly recovered his self-respect. After he left the school he used tobacco to great excess, and became a drunkard. How much this result was due to that officer, no one can tell. Women sometimes get too much interested in the work. One of the most self-sacrificing and excellent women was so much interested in the welfare of the boys, that her sympathy for them, in general, passed beyond a philanthropic, into a particular interest, more than Platonic, and I found it necessary to limit the practical workings of so excellent a sentiment as "Love the unlovely and care for the uncared-for." Speaking with Dr. Howe on this subject, I learned that some of the best women ever employed in the Blind Asylum he was obliged to discharge for similar reasons.

Many persons seem to act as though the law of progress or developement, defined by the term "survival of the fittest," sanctioned their doing as little as possible for their inferiors, not comprehending that the best evidence of a fitness to survive is shown by a desire to help the unfit; that the higher faculties (as benevolence) are developed by exercise; that our noble State became the fittest to survive by doing the most for its feeble and unfortunate children; that to be the greatest of all we must be the servants of all. Perhaps all the idiots at the school in South Boston could never be made equal to one ordinary citizen; but every citizen is made better by the existence of the school.

ANECDOTES.

The following, among many anecdotes of similar character which might be given, will indicate something of my dealings with the boys, and our mutual relations. The peculiar circumstances connected with each cannot be written, but must be imagined, to give life and reality to the incidents.

CHRISTMAS EVE.

The night before Christmas the boys always hung up their stockings, expecting Santa Claus to remember them. Many of their friends sent presents at this time, which we gave in this way. Into the stockings of those who had nothing, I used to put some candy or nuts. Once, after all were supposed to be asleep, I put on my felt slippers and went into the sleeping hall to fill the stockings. After I was through, thinking some boy might be awake, and get up to "fish" the stockings, I went quietly back and listened; soon I heard a boy at them; I let him work, but when he returned to his berth I was there, and he walked into my arms. Without a word, I led him with a firm grasp into a lighted room. The boy had been in the institution but a few days, and was

terribly frightened, though not a word had been
spoken by either of us. I sat a few moments,
thinking what to say; then began by telling him
how many boys there were who had no parents or
friends to send them a Christmas present; that I
wanted all to feel that some one thought of them,
so I had been putting a little candy into their
stockings, and now I had found him, a stranger-
boy, creeping around and stealing it away. What
will the boys say when they hear of it, and how
will they treat you in the yard? He now began
to cry, and spoke for the first time, begging me
not to tell them, promising always to be a good
boy, if I would not. He meant what he said, I
have no doubt, and I promised not to tell of it
as long as he was a good boy. He then went
back to bed. Some weeks afterwards, I mentioned the circumstance at evening devotion, but
gave no name; and no officer or boy ever found
out who it was. I inquired if they thought I did
right to take his word, under the circumstances;
and all thought I did. That boy came with a
very bad name, but he always did well afterwards, and has turned out well.

THE STOLEN KEYS.

When keys were lost, I was to be informed immediately, and no one else. One day an officer came and informed me that her keys had been taken from her pocket, but she had no idea by whom. It was just before recess, and the boys all passed into the yard — over two hundred — to play. Standing where I could overlook the yard, I watched their movements, and soon came to the conclusion that a certain boy had the keys. Then sending for an officer (whom I considered very skilful), I informed him of the loss, and my impressions, and asked him to go into the yard and examine for himself. In a few moments he brought me the keys, having found them in the shoe of the boy I mentioned. How shall such a case be dealt with? Here is a cunning, active boy, good-hearted, and popular with his mates. If he is severely punished, he may be more careful in the future ; but he will be sure to do something to "get square," and will have the sympathy of his friends. I consider such a trick as a favorable circumstance to aid in bringing a boy under my influence ; for he knows that he deserves some punishment, and this gives one an opportunity which can usually be turned to good account. I

kept this boy with me for some time, got much
better acquainted with him than I otherwise
should, and showed him by this example that he
could not do mischief and appear innocent. It
resulted in our becoming excellent friends, and he
was ever after a trustworthy boy. He is now a good
citizen, of more than ordinary intelligence. One
can afford to give a good deal of time to get a few
leading boys under one's influence. Succeeding
in this, you can control the whole. The following
will illustrate this : —

LEADING BOYS.

For some reason, one morning, the boys in the
chair-shop were very disorderly, and the officer
was troubled to know what to do. He sent a note
requesting me to come into the shop. When I
went in, all was perfectly quiet and orderly; but
when I returned to the office, it was worse than before, and the officer, fearing some serious trouble,
wrote me again. Instead of going back, I sent
for one of the leading boys and put him quietly
in the lodge, and then for a second and disposed
of him in the same way, explaining to neither
why I did it. After these leading spirits were
out, the boys in the shop were perfectly orderly
the rest of the morning. None of the boys or

officers knew what I had done : the less notoriety
the better in such cases.   At noon, I went to see
the boys in the lodge ; they wanted to know why
I had put them in there, saying they had done
nothing : " That may be, but I can show you that
I have done right." Then I told them that when
I heard that the boys in the chair-shop were disorderly, I made up my mind that if one or two of
the leading boys (who, probably, only encouraged
the others by their looks) were taken out, all
would be quiet; for boys are like sheep, — all
follow the leaders. The difficulty was to know for
certain who the leaders were. I sent for you, and
the question now is, Did I get the right boys?
They were amused at the course I had taken, and
both said I had the right boys, and they guessed
it was orderly after they left, as was the case.
They were surprised that I understood them so
well, and felt that I had done right; for by so
doing, perhaps, several boys were kept out of
trouble. After calling their attention to the influence they had for good or evil, I sent them
back, and this ended the trouble.

THE RUNAWAYS.

One day a small boy in a family wrote me a
note saying that he wished to see me very much;

so I sent for him to come to the office. He seemed to be in great trouble about something, and, when we were alone, said that, about a week before, he and another boy got up in the night and ran away; that he had felt badly ever since, and wanted to tell me that they were very sorry. Thinking that the man they lived with had sent them to me, I inquired what he thought about it. "He knows nothing about it. We went over as far as North-boro', and lay down on some hay in the field, and we thought we would come back; so we did, and got in at the window, and went to bed again. Shall you take us out of the family, now that we came back alone, and we both wanted to tell you all about it?" "Oh no!" I said, "as long as you correct mistakes as soon as you see them, you will grow wiser and better every day." He went back as though relieved of a great trouble; and nothing further was said about it to any one.

A DORMANT CONSCIENCE.

I once put a bright American boy with a shoe-maker, to learn the trade. He did well until his master moved into a large place, and opened a saloon in connection with his shoe-shop. After this there was continual trouble. Finally the boy determined to poison the family, making two attempts, the last nearly fatal to his master. He was suspected, confessed, and was arrested, but, by the advice of the authorities, he was returned to the school; otherwise he would have been put into the State Prison. He was now a large, handsome boy of eighteen, without the least appreciation of his crime. I put him in the lodge, waiting for the action of the Trustees. In the mean time, I spent many hours with him, endeavoring to make him realize what he had done. For a long time he seemed to feel as one might who had attempted to kill a cat. After a while he saw the action in its true light, and realized his condition. Finally the Superintendent of the School Ship secured a place for him on a long voyage. When he returned he visited me, and appeared to be a fine young man.

BREACH OF CONFIDENCE.

I often allowed a certain boy (when he had finished his work) to go outside and walk about the pond for an hour. From something in his appearance when he came in, one day, and brought me some lilies, I was almost sure he had been in mischief, and told him so. He seemed quite troubled, and then I was sure my suspicions were correct. I kept the matter in mind, and a few

days later he came and told me that he had run to
the village and stolen some candy. I persuaded
(not required) him to go to the store, tell the man,
and pay him, lending him the money until he
could earn it by extra work. After such an
experience a boy rarely causes me any further
trouble.

THE PEANUT BOY.

I once put a boy with a man to learn the shoe-
maker's trade, where he remained for a year, when
his master gave up business, and, as the boy had
done well, he was allowed to go to his brother-in-
law, in Boston. Soon his sister died, and her
husband took to drinking, and ran away, leaving
two little boys, nine and eleven, with no one to
care for them but this boy-uncle, sixteen years of
age. He hired an unfurnished room in South
Boston, where they all slept, the neighbors giving him some old blankets to lie upon. He let
himself to a man who roasted peanuts, where he
earned four dollars a week. With this he paid
for his room, clothed and fed himself and his
nephews, with the aid of the neighbors, all
through one winter. Where he worked there
was a bakery, and he occasionally had a chance to
work extra, part of the night, sleeping betimes on
the bags of peanuts. In this way he could earn

WESTBORO' STATE REFORM SCHOOL.

an extra loaf of bread to take home. The little
boys ran about the streets during the day, picking up what they could while keeping out of sight
of the truant and police officers. They were in
no condition to attend school if they had wished,
their clothing barely covering them. Of course
these little fellows soon began to pilfer, as they
were left entirely to themselves during the day and
most of the evening, and the boy-uncle was troubled to know what to do with them, as he feared
they would be arrested and sent to Deer Island.
This was the condition of things when I received
a letter from him requesting me to call and see
him. As the request was not urgent, I thought
I would call the next time I went to the city; but
in a few days I received another letter, asking me
to call very soon. The next day I called at the
place he named, but no one knew of such a boy,
and I was on the point of leaving when some one
said, "There is a boy here we call Jack; perhaps
he is the one you want." By inquiry I found
it must be he, but no one knew his name; he was
only "Jack," who drove the cart delivering the
peanuts after they were roasted. The proprietor
then related the above account of the boy's doings throughout the winter, giving him a good
name; and he seemed much pleased that I had
called to see him. In a few moments "Jack" re-

turned, driving his team. He then told me of his two little nephews; that he did not know what to do with them, as they had begun to be dishonest and he could not help it; so he had sent for me, to ask if I could take them. I told him I would see what could be done, and went immediately to consult Isaac Ames, Judge of Probate, who asked me to bring "Jack" up to his office. I went back and found him just driving out. He said he would ride directly there with me. The idea of riding a mile up Washington Street, in the middle of the day, with "Jack," in a peanut cart, was at first a little distasteful. But when I remembered that here was a boy who had been hungry six months that his little nephews might have something to eat; that he had worked nights, and slept upon bags, to earn an extra loaf for them; that he had been ragged and cold that they might be covered, while I had never done anything so unselfish in my life, — I jumped into the cart, thinking, If he is not ashamed of me, I need not complain. He told his simple story to the judge, who manifested great interest in it, and said, "'That story will do for the Sunday-school next week. It reminds me of the man who cured a dog of a broken leg, and the dog afterwards brought several other dogs for him to cure." The result of this conversation was that the little boys were sent to Westboro'.

THE LOST BILL.

An officer, while dressing a boy to go to a new home, lost from his vest pocket a dollar bill, which he was to give him. He was almost certain that it was swept out into the yard, and probably picked up by a large boy who was about there at the time. He, however, denied it, and the circumstances were told to me. I kept the subject in mind, watched the boy's actions, and soon concluded that he found the bill. I judged that he would not keep it himself (which is rarely done under such circumstances), but pass it to his friend George, the leading boy in the school. This I soon made up my mind he had done. The next Saturday, George asked permission to go to Northboro', to visit a former teacher, about two miles distant. I gave him leave, thinking that he wanted an opportunity to change the bill, and if so I should detect him. But he went to no place where he could do so; still I was sure he had the money. Finally I decided to call him up and have a talk with him. So, after all had retired at night, I went and called him; choosing this time that no one should know of it,—for boys are always more frank if they think the conversation is confidential, and un-

known to others. There we were in the night,
with a strong light so placed as to shine full in
his face, while I was directly opposite, where I
could see every expresssion.

"George," I said, "I have been wishing to speak
to you, for some time, when no one should know
it. Can you think what I wish to speak about ?"
He was silent a moment, and nervous, his eyes
not able to meet mine. He seemed to struggle
with himself, then answered, "I suppose it must
be about some money I have." "That is it," I
said, "now tell me all about it." And the story
was exactly as I supposed, even his object in asking to go to Northboro'. He wished to go immediately and bring the money to me, but I said,
"We can make the money worth more than a dollar, if you will help me : your friend II. has told
falsehoods about this bill; but he is generally a
good boy, and this affair must be used to make
him better, not worse. Without letting him know
that I have said a word to you about it, can you
persuade him that it is his duty to bring the bill
to me and acknowledge his fault? Now, if you
think it is the proper thing to do, and can bring it
about, I should like to have you." He seemed
very much interested in the plan, and said he would
try to do it. The next day the boy II. wished
to see me alone, when he frankly confessed what

he had done, and returned me the bill. I said what I thought proper, and never alluded to the subject again while he was in school. I never had any further trouble with this boy, and he is now a respectable man.

THE UNGOVERNABLE TEMPER.

When I went to Westboro', I found a boy, sent for stabbing a schoolmate, — a quick-tempered, high-spirited boy, but well behaved. He was much more refined in manners than the others, having been well brought up. He talked but little, and rarely engaged in play. I succeeded in gaining his confidence, and soon put him in one of the families, which made him appear like a different boy. One day, while at work with some of the boys, he was hit with a fork, which made him very angry, especially as the boys laughed about it. In a moment the same boy, through heedlessness, hit him again, when he flew into a terrible passion, and struck the boy over the head with a shovel, cutting a frightful gash in his scalp, but not dangerously injuring him. He was brought immediately to me, as a dangerous boy, one not safe to work with others. This otherwise excellent boy was likely to make an utter failure in life, on account of his ungovernable temper. I thought over his case a long time before speaking to him. He seemed utterly broken down and discouraged, — not in the least defiant. We both felt badly. After a while I tried to show him his great danger and real condition, — an excellent boy in all respects, but with a temper which would surely ruin him if it could not be controlled. We had several long talks together, and I succeeded finally in making him realize his danger, and to feel afraid of himself. He was ready to do anything I wished, and expected to return to the congregate department. After consulting with the head of the family, and speaking with some of the boys, who pitied him very much, he was sent back, feeling as thankful as a boy could, and determined to get the control of his temper. He was an excellent boy ever afterwards, enlisted in the army, and was doing well in business when last heard from.

THE PICKPOCKET.

There was a fine little fellow from Boston in the school, sent for picking pockets. One of the Trustees often said he was the finest-appearing boy he ever saw. As there was no opportunity to practise his profession at Westboro', his behavior was in all respects satisfactory. In about a year, his uncle, who had the care of him, wished to try him again; and as his behavior had been good, the Trustees allowed him to leave on probation. In a little more than a year, his uncle brought him back to the school, as entirely beyond control. The boy was now about sixteen, tall, and very polite. He had become a professional gambler and pickpocket, and was dressed in the flashy style common to such persons.

When he came to the office, he met me with all the ease of a gentleman, gave me an account of his doings, manifesting great sorrow for his conduct, and made many excellent promises for the future; so that his uncle was quite affected, and promised to take him again in a short time, if the Trustees were willing. When I went with him to change his clothes, he asked, as a particular favor, to be allowed to keep his boots on. This he said he should consider as a mark of my confidence in him. After he had changed everything but his boots, which I noticed he was very careful to keep, I told him I thought best to keep them for him until he should go away again. I could not be persuaded to let him retain them, and when he pulled them off I found a large quantity of tobacco secreted in them. I remember well the look of shame and utter wretchedness he had at that time. Before a word was spoken, he burst into tears, and cried like a child. I endeavored to have this experience teach him that "the painted hypocrites are known through the disguise they wear." He was always gentlemanly and trustworthy afterwards. What became of him I do not know.

A JOURNEY WEST.

The following will show the restless energy of some of the boys : —

We once had a boy from Boston, about fifteen years of age, very active and uneasy, and always in some trouble ; at the same time quite generous and good-hearted. As he was anxious to be a sailor, he was transferred to the School Ship, where he remained about a year. He then ran away while with a boat crew at the wharf in Boston. Without going to his mother, who lived in the city, he went directly to the Providence depot, and took the first train out, not caring where it went. He had no money, and was put off as soon as the conductor descried him ; but he got on the next train, was put off again, and so on, till in this way he smuggled himself by the next day to New York city, where he was an utter stranger. He started up from the boat upon which he had secreted himself, and told his story to the first boot-black he met. From him he obtained the loan of twenty-five cents, to get some-

thing to eat, and the privilege of blacking boots
for an hour, to earn enough to set up for himself;
and he became self-supporting at once. These
boys will aid one of the same profession, as one
merchant aids another. For several weeks he
blacked boots, slept at the boys' lodging-house,
went to the theatre, and enjoyed himself finely.

Seeing a notice that a number of boys were to
be taken out West, by a benevolent society, and
homes procured for them, he applied for a chance
to go, was provided with an outfit, and went to
Illinois, where he was placed with a farmer. It
took but a short time for him to be satisfied with
that style of living; he left, and made his way,
through Cleveland, back to Buffalo. Here he
found a company of soldiers starting for New
York city by the cars. He crawled under the
seats, and with the help of the soldiers he kept
out of sight, and finally reached the city, sick
with a bad cold. He then went directly to a
hospital, where he was cared for until he was
well, when the authorities, at his request, provided him with a pass home. He arrived in
Boston just three months from the time he left,
having had, he said, a nice time.

After spending the night with his mother, fearing the police, he went twenty miles out into the
country, and let himself to a shoemaker. Here

he remained six months, and it was on his way to
visit his mother that I overtook him; while riding
with me several miles, he gave the above account
of himself. There are but few officers capable
of managing such a boy.

WHY SUSPECT HIM?

One morning the master of one of the families
came to the office and informed me that some one
of his boys had stolen seven dollars from the teacher's purse, which she had left upon her desk. He
had questioned the boys, but all denied taking it,
and he did not know what course to take to find it.
As money in the hands of the boys was almost
sure to cause trouble, he wished my advice about
it. After hearing all the particulars, I requested
him to send a certain boy to the office upon
some errand, that he might not suspect it was connected with the money. When he came, seeming
a little uneasy and nervous, I felt sure he was the
right boy. He was seated near me, where I could
notice him while engaged in other duties. I never
knew a boy so situated to appear natural, if he
was guilty. When we were alone I commenced
talking with him upon general subjects. It seemed
to trouble him to be looked at, and he could not
appear natural. After a while I said, "Do you

know why I sent for you to come to the office? Think a moment, and do not be afraid to tell me the truth." Soon he said, "I think it is about some money I took this morning."

He then told me all about it, and brought the money to me. I gave it to the teacher, but she never knew how I came by it. The boy and I had several conversations upon the question, Why I suspected him, — one boy among thirty, — and what would be necessary for him to do, in order that I should not suspect him again under similar circumstances. "There is no den in the wide world to hide a rogue."

OFFICERS OUTWITTED.

As I was watching the boys play, one day, from my office window, I saw a boy go to the pump, wash his hands and face, and smack his lips, in such a manner that I thought he must have been eating something uncommonly good. One does not make the same motions with his mouth when eating sugar as he does when eating bread. After leaving the pump, he was met by several other boys, all of whom seemed to have been eating, and were in fine spirits. I was curious to ascertain what it was, for I was certain it was something better than the usual dinner. This boy

was one of the shrewdest fellows we had, not
" ugly," but full of fun and mischief. After waiting long enough not to have my intentions suspected, I sent for him to come to the office.
After some pleasant talk on general subjects, I
said, " Supposing something should happen in the
yard, and I should ask you about it, and you
should tell me the truth; and then send for
another boy, and he should tell me the truth ; and
so on, with several, each ignorant of what the
other told, — how would their stories agree?"
"They would be all alike," he said, "no matter
how many were asked, if all told the truth."
" But suppose you and all the rest told lies, but
neither knew what the other told, how would their
stories agree?" "They would not agree at all,"
he said. "How many stories could be true, and
how many false?" I asked. "Only one could be
true ; but there would be as many false as there
were boys," he replied.

"Suppose we try an experiment, to see if this
will prove true : you may tell me why you were
washing your hands and smacking your lips, to-
day, at the pump. There can be but one true
story, you say, about anything ; and now suppose
you tell it." This was the story : He had noticed,
by looking through the window into the cellar, some
molasses-sugar in a pail, and, watching his oppor-

tunity, had sawed the wire grating, so that, by
pulling it to one side, he could get down. Some
of the boys got one officer off into a corner to tell
them stories, and the other was kept busy in the
gymnasium. Then several stood before the cellar
window, while this boy went down and filled his
cap; and I had seen him washing after he had
eaten. He paid for mending the grating, and
that settled it. It was considered a good joke
upon the officers in the yard. Boys enjoy such a
trick very much. It is best to take some trouble
to induce boys to tell the truth, and save the
trouble that would come if they told a lie.

THREE SETS OF KEYS.

The keys in the hands of the boys, referred to
when speaking of the time I entered upon my duties, caused us a good deal of trouble. Several
articles were stolen, from time to time, very mys-
teriously. Finally, in March, three months after
they were stolen, five boys were missing, one
morning. As all the doors and windows were
found secure, it was a mystery how they had escaped. At last, foot-prints were discovered leading from a cellar door, which proved that some
one inside or outside had keys. All the officers
were now busily engaged in trying to find the

keys; but for several days nothing was accomplished — no clue could be obtained. In the mean time I was studying the appearance and actions of the boys, and finally decided that certain ones were in the secret. At night, when all were in bed, I took one of them to the office — one that had the least force of character and was most impressible — and ascertained from him that another boy had the keys. Before morning, I had the three sets of keys, nine in all, and knew all the circumstances. It appeared that the boys who escaped used the keys, and passed them back through a window for others to use. No officer ever knew how I obtained the keys; and no boy knew that any one but himself gave me information. All but one of the runaways were caught in a short time.

The three sets of keys were kept in three different places : one under ground, known only to one boy, and he a "trust boy."

A QUARRELSOME BOY.

One day a quick-tempered but generally pleasant little fellow was brought to the office for fighting with a colored boy. As he had been reported several times before for quarrelling, I was in doubt what course to take, and told him so, asking him to tell me what he thought would be the best way to stop him from fighting. After thinking a moment, he concluded that a good whipping would be the surest thing ; supposing, perhaps, that I would not be likely to punish him in that way.

I said I did not think a whipping would do him much good, for he had just been whipped by the colored boy, without being benefited, so far as I could see ; still, if he really thought it the best thing, I would send for the same boy to whip him again.

He probably could not determine whether I was in earnest or not, but was evidently surprised and amused at the suggestion. He concluded, however, that he would like to try once more, before having me send for the colored boy to cure him ; and he was allowed to go on probation. He reported the conversation to the boys in the yard, which appeared to cause them much amusement. Afterwards, when this boy was angry, some one would propose to send for the colored boy to calm him down. He never was sent to the office again for fighting.

UNFAIR JUDGMENT OF CRIMINALS.

Most people are unjust in their judgment of such boys, or of any so-called criminals. If a boy steals, we consider and treat him as though he were a thief all the time. If a man commits a highway robbery once, we think he is a highwayman all the time; when it may be that neither ever committed a crime before or since, and then only under great temptation, which might have been too strong for us to resist. How should we stand in a community, if we were judged by our worst act? As well judge a man's general health by his sickest day!

I once heard a prominent clergyman of Boston, who visited a condemned pirate some weeks before his execution and became acquainted with his history and temptations, say that he felt that he might have been a worse man under similar circumstances. And I have often thought, when a boy told me his history, that in all probability I should have been worse if similarly situated. I heard the Hon. Gerrit Smith once say, that between us and cannibalism there was only about forty-eight hours.

The faculty we call acquisitiveness is common to us all. How far it may be gratified without trespassing upon the rights of others, is not easily seen by the young and inexperienced. "A thief is one ignorant of the principles of political economy," was the remark of a great and good man. His reasoning faculties, which enable him to appreciate the claims of others, are not so well

developed as his selfish propensities. No matter
how excellent the child, the mother puts the
sugar-bowl out of his reach. I once said to a
gentleman, "There is no one but can remember
stealing something." He was amused, and called
the attention of a highly intelligent company at a
social gathering, and repeated the remark, saying
he wished to test its truth; and called upon each
to give his experience, when every one in that
company recollected taking something when he
knew it was wrong. One lady, a clergyman's
daughter, recollected taking a pumpkin from a
neighbor's garden, when a little girl, and hiding
it. These revelations caused much amusement;
and, perhaps, kept some from repeating the Phar-
isee's prayer.

More than one hundred boys were permitted to
leave the institution yearly; and, as the Visiting
Agency was not then established, it was my duty
to visit them at their homes, so far as practicable.
By these visits I became acquainted with the parents and guardians of these boys, and was thus
able to judge of their surroundings. How many
of them are doing well, I have no means of knowing. I often meet them, and I judge that a large
number are respectable citizens. One, indentured
to a farmer until he was eighteen, has since been
graduated from one of the colleges of this State,

and was a member of the winning crew in a college regatta.

SUGGESTIONS TO THE OFFICERS.

A blank-book was kept in the public parlor, in which suggestions were made from time to time for the consideration of the officers and to cause discussion. The following items taken from it will indicate their general character and probable influence : —

"It is not an uncommon practice among disciplinarians, when a boy is supposed to know the author of some mischief, to force him, by threats and violence, to give information. Is not this on the former principle of law courts, now discarded, of extracting testimony by means of the rack and thumb-screw? and is not testimony valuable in proportion as it is voluntary?"

"It should be remembered that the standard of right and wrong among our boys is in many cases necessarily low ; and, while we endeavor by precept and example to bring it up to ours, in dealing with their delinquencies we should judge them by their own."

"While children should be taught to tell the truth because it is the truth, they should be treated in such a manner that they will not be tempted to tell a lie. A child should never have cause to regret having told the truth. If the father of Washington had *punished* him for injuring his trees, instead of *commending* him for telling the truth, he would not only have lost his pear-tree, but we the the story of the hatchet."

"While it is expected that the officers will treat the boys at all times with kindness, it is especially desirable that particular attention be shown them when they first arrive. 'First impressions are lasting.' Let the impression we make on the boys be such as to convince them they are among friends."

"A very common error among officers is to tell publicly the troubles they have with the boys, and talk of their faults. When nothing good can be said, it is far better to say nothing."

Occasionally I found an officer using a boy as a spy or detective. This I would never allow; for the officer will soon become neglectful of his duties, and the boy a hypocrite.

Tattling among the boys I always discountenanced. It is generally the selfish and mean boys that tattle. The high-minded boy rarely reports a schoolmate even when he should. Tattling, I used to say, was telling something to benefit one's self or injure another, while reporting was to benefit others, which should be done, even at the risk of injuring one's self. I found these boys had the same idea of what was honorable, as those in college.

Some teachers feel that boys should be required to beg their pardon, or make public acknowledgment of their faults, before they can be passed over and forgiven. I have no sympathy with such requirements. If a boy can be made to see his fault and feel contrition, I am satisfied. Punishment should always be for the reformation of the individual, and not for an example to others. What I wanted was the individual reformed. Sentences for a crime, it seems to me, should not be for a certain *time*, but for the accomplishment of a certain *result* — the reformation of the criminal.

If superintendents were selected for our penal institutions as they are for our asylums and hospitals, because of their peculiar fitness for the position, unwise discharging of inmates in one case would not oftener occur than in the others. The hospital is a place for the treatment of physical trouble, an insane asylum of mental, and the prison of moral. No one will deny that the last is of as great importance as the others, and requires in its management as great and as peculiar skill ; and yet scarce a thought, it would seem, is given to find the man fitted by nature and education for so difficult a position. What should we think, if men were put in charge of our insane asylums for political reasons ? And yet this is often done in our penal institutions and reformatories.

COMMENDATIONS OF THE INSTITUTION.

A large number of committees, from this and other States, visited the institution,—legislative, philanthropic and educational committees. The following extracts from a few of their letters and reports will indicate their general spirit. I wish, however, to disclaim any desire to monopolize these commendations, for with such men on the Board of Trustees as the late Dr. S. G. Howe and Mr. George C. Davis, and John Ayres and others now living, I could justly claim but a small share.

FROM THE GRAND JURY OF SUFFOLK COUNTY.

"We find everything in admirable order, and we have no improvements to suggest. All those connected with the institution seem to be the right men in the right place ; and every one, from the Superintendent down, seems to take a personal interest in the welfare of every boy committed to his or her care. We think the institution is as near perfect as it can be, for the purpose the State authorities intended it should be."

In a letter accompanying the report, the foreman says : —

"I am only one of that body, but we all have decided that you have set a pattern for all the institutions."

The chairman of a committee from a distant State, who visited the school in order to obtain information that might assist in establishing a similar institution in that State, writes as follows, in 1864 : —

" During our brief stay with you, so full of interest, I do not remember anything I thought wrong. It seems to me scarcely possible, that those bright, intelligent, and happy boys were but a few months ago on the high road to ruin. There were various incidents of our visit to Westboro' which live with me, and will still live: the unrestrained play of the children at the Peter's House; the simple neatness and beauty of their supper table, adorned by themselves with flowers, showing the 'mother's' influence ; the precision with which one little fellow laid the knives and forks, a lesson to him for life, of wide extent ; the earnestness of the teachers in the different schools; the close attention and prompt reply of the boys to long arithmetic questions ; the knowledge shown in contemporaneous history; the exercises in the chapel-room ; and their orderly retirement for the night, were among these. I honor Massachusetts for her noble example in comprehensive charity."

This committee selected for a superintendent, to organize their State institution, a gentleman we recommended, — one who had been our dependence in the supply of our pulpit for several years, — a man well acquainted with the management of the school.

The following extract is from a late article in the " Sunday Herald," June, 1877 : —

"Being in the Legislature, and a member of the Committee on Charitable Institutions, I visited the school several times under a different management, and I cannot express my own, and the unanimous feeling of the Committee at that time, better than by quoting from a report of a large and influential committee of eminent citizens that visited the school about the same time, by invitation of the Trustees.

"The extract will be particularly interesting at this time, as it was written by the late Isaac Ames, Judge of Probate, Boston, and signed by Hon. A. H. Rice, John D. Philbrick, D. B. Hagar, William E. Sheldon, D. Waldo Lincoln, Hon. Samuel E. Sewall and others:—

"'It is not easy to compress within convenient limits what we should be glad to put on record as to the impressions made upon us by what our eyes have seen and our ears have heard. We select only the salient points.

"'In the schools it was delightful to behold the great mental activity everywhere manifest; each boy was wide awake, the voice decided and distinct, and the answers prompt and correct. Their attention to the business in hand was most remarkable, and such as is rarely witnessed in the very best schools.

"'We can say that the deportment was unexceptionable; and this remark applies not only to the pupils in the schoolroom, but to them also in all the various relations in which we saw them.

"'We remember no instance where interference was required to preserve order. No parent who has a son here need have a moment's anxious thought lest the physical, mental, and moral culture of his child should be neglected.

"'To watch the countenances of these boys, one would hardly think they were prisoners, and some of them snatched from the lowest depths of degradation. They seem rather to be children gathered in what is really a happy home. They have a cheerful air; their faces have the ruddy glow of high health ; they move to their various duties with a quick and willing step; they are neatly dressed, and appear generally as do the sons of a well-regulated family. These results evidently spring not from any slavish fear. Nothing of the kind can be detected. They dread not the haughty frown or the cruel lash. While corporal punishment is not positively interdicted, its practice is almost unknown. It is clear as noonday that there is a mightier influence at work here than fear can exert, and that the hand which guides the various movements of this complicated organism is a "gentle hand." If under such auspices the rough natures that find refuge here cannot be softened, smoothed, and improved, we may well despair of reformation of them anywhere.

" 'If any citizen has a doubt as to the great and good work it is accomplishing, let him do as we have done, and his doubts will vanish as does darkness before the light of day.' "

The following is from a letter by the late George C. Davis, Treasurer and Resident Trustee of the institution during the whole time I was in charge; and in all, thirteen years : —

"You already have the approbation of so many committees, who visited the institution during your superintendency, composed of gentlemen eminently qualified to express opinions on the matters, that any words of mine seem like supererogation. I shall not, however, hesitate to say, your work during the six years you were in charge, though conducting the institution under many annoying circumstances, was an eminent success. You took the school when it had sunk to the lowest condition, and had become a common football for State politicians to kick at, and raised it to the condition spoken of in the reports and the communications alluded to. Of one thing I am certain : you have, and will continue to have, the blessings of hundred of boys, growing up to be men, who ascribe their success in life to your kind and discreet management."

Mr. Davis is now dead. The following is extracted from a tribute given at his funeral, which will show that he himself is entitled to a very large share of the commendation he so generously gave me : —

"As Superintendent of the Westboro' Reform School, I had occasion to consult with and ask advice of him almost daily ; and I wish to bear my testimony, at this time, to his devotion to the duties devolving upon him. Although a man that had many calls upon his time, at home and in business relations, I never went to him, early or late, when he was not ready, and more than ready, to give his first attention to the welfare of the unfortunate lads the State had placed under his supervision. He was a man by nature eminently qualified for this work ; and he spared no pains in making himself acquainted with the most advanced ideas and methods of reform. A personal friend of Governor Andrew, he was in full sympathy with all his noble inspirations, and had his entire confidence and co-operation in all measures taken for the lads in that school.

"I can see him now, as it were, riding up to yonder institution to make his usual call, with a smiling face of welcome in every window; for he was a universal favorite, because a universal friend. How many of those boys, after leaving the school, have walked long and weary miles to see him and ask his advice; and they always carried away more than they came for.

"The notice of his death has been seen in every paper; and hundreds of lads, children of poverty and crime, scattered all over this and other States, will drop the silent tear as the news of his death reaches them; for they all know he was their friend."

CONCLUSION.

Governor Andrew's influence upon the school was very great. He meant the Board of Trustees should be above sectarian influence, and his appointments were made to secure that result.[1] Notwithstanding his arduous labors as the "Great War Governor," he found time to visit the school at other times than officially. He once spent Thanksgiving-day with us, addressing the boys in the chapel, and mingling with them in their exercises during the day. In the afternoon every boy was upon the common and joined in a game of football, not *one* absent from sickness or any other cause, which pleased him very much. He was fond of reciting poetry to the school, giving at one time "Songs of Seven," by Jean Ingelow. He was more than governor; he was a *man*, and the boys forgot his official in his personal character.

[1] The Governor was censured for throwing the balance of power into liberal or unsectarian hands. "I had thought of that," he replied promptly; "and the next time I propose to appoint a Roman Catholic," whereat the remonstrance ceased.

After his death two vacancies soon occurred in the Board of Trustees, which were filled immediately by the appointment of gentlemen not supposed to be in sympathy with its management. One of my friends purposely dropped from the board at this time, was a gentleman who had spared, from a very engrossing business, time to visit as a friend *every* family, in Boston and its vicinity, of the boys of the Westboro' school; and who for four years took not a day's vacation from the cares of business, except what he spent as a visitor at the school,— an example of fidelity in unpaid official duty, to which it would be hard to find a parallel. As this gentleman was reappointed soon after I left, the object of dropping him would seem to be apparent. Seeing such changes in the Board, I thought best to leave the school while it was in good condition, and not remain until I might be held responsible for a different state of things. I therefore gave the following letter of resignation :

To the Trustees of the State Reform School: —

GENTLEMEN : When I took charge of this institution, in January, 1861, a little more than a year after the great fire, the buildings were in a dilapidated condition, and surrounded by ruins. The discipline of the school was necessarily low after such a catastrophe, and the country was just entering upon the late war, which so much disorganized all kinds of business.

It has been my aim to conduct its affairs with economy, to train the boys to habits of industry, to give them a good common-school education, and to instil into their minds and hearts the principles of the Christian religion, carefully avoiding all sectarian or doctrinal teaching.

That the institution has gained the support and confidence of the public is shown by the commendations it has received from the many committees, both public and private, that have visited it, and by the uniform approval of the parents of the boys under my charge.

In carrying out my plans, especially in the matter of religious teaching, I have been obliged to meet the earnest and untiring opposition of your present chairman for nearly five years; and as your Board is now constituted, I cannot expect its sympathy and co-operation.

Under these circumstances, I resign my position as Superintendent.

Yours respectfully,
JOS. A. ALLEN.

WESTBORO', *April* 26, 1867.

The constant and petty-official annoyances to which I was subjected during the last few months are of no consequence to the public, and I pass them over. The last few days of my stay at the institution, after the boys were informed of my resignation, were very interesting to me. An article taken from the "Evening Transcript" of that date, written by the officiating clergyman the last Sunday, will indicate the state of feeling among the boys.

VISIT TO THE STATE REFORM SCHOOL AT WESTBORO'.

To the Editor of the " Transcript:"—

MR. EDITOR : I recently passed a day at this institution, under circumstances of peculiar interest. It was the last Sunday of the administration of the late Superintendent, Mr. Joseph A. Allen, and I was glad of the opportunity of noting the appearance of the boys on such an occasion. As public attention has been somewhat drawn of late to the present condition of the school, I think a short account of my visit will be interesting to your readers.

The institution contains at present about 320 boys, a larger number than usual having been placed in homes this spring. On Saturday evening they all gathered in the chapel for their evening service. This consisted in the singing of two beautiful hymns, and the repeating in concert, by the boys, of the Twenty-third Psalm and the thirteenth chapter of First Corinthians. The repeating from memory of passages from the Bible has always formed a prominent feature of their worship, and I was much impressed by the admirable manner in which it was done. At the close of this simple service, one of the boys, a lad of about sixteen, advanced to the platform, and in a very neat address thanked the Superintendent, in the name of his companions, for his loving and fatherly care of them, expressed their deep sorrow at his departure, and presented, as a gift of their affection, three large volumes of " Wood's Illustrated Natural History." The speech was delivered with a manliness and self-possession which I have never seen surpassed on any similar occasion ; and the whole scene was indescribably touching and beautiful. When I considered who these boys are,—homeless, friendless vagabonds, many of

them the *gamins* of our city streets, — and that every cent
of the money at their command is earned by extra labor
after their day's work is done, I felt that I had never
known anything of the kind more remarkable than this
eager contribution of their little all. Some gave in one
cent, some five, — each what he had, — and some only
tears of sorrow that they had nothing else to give.

The next morning, at the Sunday-school, I dealt as I
could with a class of these intense, sharp-witted youth,
and felt, as never before, what a rare and valuable gift
was that which fitted a man to deal successfully with such
characters. Brim-full of life, instant and positive in their
opinions, keen in judgment, fearless and uncompromising,
one must have infinite tact and readiness, patience and
shrewdness to meet their needs. That the late Superintendent possessed those qualities in no slight degree, no
one will question after five minutes' talk with any of the
boys. They were perfectly prepared with their lesson, —
some verses from the fourteenth chapter of John, — and
I was struck with the readiness and accuracy of their
general information. It was not easy to draw them from
the subject they were so full of, — their love for Mr. Allen,
and their grief at his leaving them. "He doesn't care for
rich boys," they said, "he only cares for such as we." And
there was no dry eye among them when they spoke of
how much good he had done them. When the Sabbath-
school superintendent asked me to speak to the school,
"Oh yes," cried they, "tell us how much more blessed it
is to give than to receive." And I felt, as I spoke, that I
had seldom had more responsive hearers. Their hearts
were full of what they had been so glad to give.

Sunday afternoon it was my privilege to speak the last
words for the Superintendent. I had spent a part of the
day in reading letters to him from the boys. Written or
printed or dictated, according to the capacity of the boy,
they all were alike in the outpouring of their gratitude
and love. There were letters from nearly every boy of

the school. My heart was full, and whatever else may have been wanting, there surely was no lack of inspiration in the occasion. There was a congregation of 300 boys, of just the class that you instinctively avoid in the streets, — reckless, light-fingered, foul-mouthed, — giving themselves up to the emotions that mastered them, and crying and sobbing aloud in all parts of the chapel ; and all because they were to lose a friend, — one who to many of them was the only father they had. The worst class of boys seemed to feel the worst. "He has been so kind to us," they said. And yet no man more firm, decided, and unyielding in matter of discipline or duty.

Altogether it was a most interesting and memorable occasion. I came away feeling more strongly than ever before what a blessed institution this is, and what reason we all have to feel proud of it, as one of our noblest charities. We may hope that under whatever administration it may hereafter be, the Superintendent may be a man combining to an equal degree the rare and essential qualities possessed by him whose services the State has recently lost.

How nearly I conducted the institution in the spirit, and according to the intentions, of its founder, the Hon. Theodore Lyman, those familiar with his letters and communications to the State upon the subject can judge.

But how poor the results at best ! if we consider the hopes and anticipations of its early friends, as set forth in the closing paragraph of the address at the dedication of the school in 1848, by the late Hon. Emory Washburn : —

"In the name, then, of a wise humanity, we bid this institution God-speed! Let it be like a Bethesda's pool, in which the lame and diseased were washed and healed, because an angel had come down and moved its waters. Let it stand, to other times and to coming ages a monument of the munificence of an unknown benefactor of his race, if he will; and of the faithfulness with which the noblest of all charities — a free government — has been hitherto administered by this, our beloved, our 'Model Commonwealth.'"

JUVENILE REFORMATORIES
OF THE UNITED STATES

T. J. Charlton

JUVENILE REFORMATORIES OF THE UNITED STATES.

By T. J. CHARLTON,
Superintendent Reform School, Plainfield, Ind.

The rapid growth of the juvenile reformatories of the United States is marvelous when we consider that it has all taken place in the last fifty years. True, the house of refuge on Randall's Island, New York, was established in 1824, and that at Philadelphia four years later; but their growth was slow, as they were regarded with more or less distrust. Now there are 65 reformatories for juveniles, with an average attendance of 19,410. Since they have been established 209,600 boys and girls have received the benefit of their discipline and teaching. A complete list of these, giving the exact name of each, date of its establishment, name of its superintendent, attendance on the date on which the report was made, and the entire number who have ever been in the school, is made a part of this paper. All institutions which partake of the nature of orphanages have been excluded. These are based on one of

TWO SYSTEMS.

The earlier reformatories, then known as "houses of refuge," were built in large cities and all their inmates were placed in one building, where an official could have charge of a large number. These institutions were said to be managed on the "congregate" plan. Later on, when the States began the establishment of State reformatories for juvenile offenders, most of them adopted the "cottage" system, which was deemed superior because of the better gradation of the inmates in the cottages. The more criminal youths were kept separate from the younger and less hardened ones. The early advocates of the "cottage system" saw nothing good in the "congregate plan," and believed no evils possibly could exist under the "cottage plan." For many years these two systems were the subject of many heated and even acrimonious discussions. Of late years all seem to be ready to say with Pope—

> For forms of government let fools contest;
> Whate'er is best administer'd is best.

There are excellent reformatories managed under each of these systems. The prevailing sentiment is in favor of the cottage system, connected with a large farm. As before mentioned, "house of refuge" was the name given to all of these institutions in their earlier years. A glance at the list reveals quite a variety of names, so that we must conclude that the name is one of the unessential features. There seems to be unanimity in the conclusion that institutions of this kind should not be located in a city. There is a tendency to remove those already established in cities to the country. A notable instance was when the male department of the Philadelphia House of Refuge was removed to Glen Mills, where a typical reformatory on the cottage system was established. This was done largely by the liberality of wealthy philanthropists of that city, many of whom were members of the board of control. Another instance was the removal of the Minnesota Training School from St. Paul to Red Wing. As I stated, these juvenile reformatories were looked upon with distrust for the first two or three decades, yet it was finally conceded that if there were any defects in them it was not because of the system, but because of neglect in the administration. The idea of making them juvenile prisons, organized to make as much money as possible for the State, was abandoned. The gradual decadence in the apprentice system gave rise to the importance of some industrial system which should take its place. Appropriations, in some cases very liberal, were made for the establishment of industrial departments; not particularly in all cases to teach trades in their entirety, but to teach what would lead to the trades. It was recognized that the labor of such juveniles in such institutions should be "instructive," and not "productive;" that the great consideration to keep in mind was not the manufactured article made, but the boy or the girl who made it. They were the output which was to be made ready, so that when restored to society they would be a positive increase to the national wealth. Soon the statistics showed the wisdom of the change. In a few cases, opposition arose because the delinquent children of the State were receiving greater advantages than other children, and, like the elder brother of the prodigal son, certain classes were disposed to block the wheels of progress; but the good sense of the people asserted that no class needed to be made bread earners so much as the very class which had failed. So there were no steps taken backward. It was found that when delinquent children were given an industrial education they were more easily reformed. The best estimate of the success of juvenile reformatories gave the per cent of those who were actually reformed as from 80 to 90 per cent.

If juveniles could be so rescued, the people began to clamor for reformatories for adults. The State Reformatory at Elmira, N. Y., for adults between 16 and 30 years of age, was established, and, fortunately for the experiment, Mr. Z. R. Brockway was made its superintendent. The experiment with adults was a very great success. Other States established reformatories on the Elmira plan which have been successful.

The differences between the juvenile and adult reformatories are those which result from the difference of age. Trade schools are made prominent in both kinds, and education is given due attention. There is necessarily more restriction imposed in a reformatory for adults than in those for juveniles. The juvenile reformatories have play grounds, freer conversation, and more intercourse than in the other class.

As the years have sped the character of the inmates is changing. At first in all the States nearly every juvenile reformatory admitted orphans who were in danger of leading a bad life, but that is not allowed except in a few cases now.

Several States have provided State schools for such. It will be observed that juvenile reformatories are not only those managed by a city or a State, but there are some established by churches. Indeed, the largest juvenile reformatory in the land is the Catholic Protectory of New York, the boys under the Christian Brothers and the girls under the Sisters. The inmates of this protectory are not strictly confined as delinquents. But in the following list this great institution is not included, because a greater part of the children are sent there because they are homeless. If the distinction could be well made it would probably add 1,000 to the list of the daily attendance. There are other church enterprises of this class of less size, such as St. Mary's Industrial School of Baltimore. Most of these church schools for delinquents receive some State aid.

INDUSTRIAL EDUCATION.

The earlier work of juvenile reformatories was patterned entirely too much after the prisons of that day. The school work was made subservient to the contract workshop. Indeed, the labor of inmates seemed to be managed in the interest of contractors. The welfare of the boy was lost sight of. So the inmates of these early reformatories, in many cases, were sent out into the world to make their own living almost wholly unprepared. The great object of the first institutions was to make as much money as possible for the city or for the State. But a change came over the sentiments of the people. They realized that if such reformatories were to be made efficient they must be made, as far as possible, trade schools. The labor was made "instructive" and not "productive." The great consideration now is the boy or the girl. This was the dawning of a brighter era in the American juvenile reformatories. From that time until the present the great object is the welfare of the inmate. He is the "output" that must be prepared with the greatest care. As a result, the best industrial schools of the United States are the juvenile reformatories. Not only is industrial education given its due prominence in these, but the elementary and academic education is given equal prominence. As a rule the boys sent to juvenile reformatories have been habitual "absentees" or "truants" from day schools.

LITERARY EDUCATION.

Their education has been neglected. This want has been promptly met by these juvenile reformatories. All inmates who are deficient in education are placed in well-graded schools and kept there until they make up for past neglect. The schools of the institutions have done their work well, and the consequence is the American boy or girl of a juvenile reformatory is receiving a good elementary education. The best teachers are employed and the results of these schools are among the best in the land.

MORAL INSTRUCTION.

Realizing that the delinquent classes, more than any others, need the strengthening power of moral and religious training, all juvenile reformatory schools provide for the religious and moral instruction which is needed, be they Catholic, Protestant, or Jew. The juvenile reformatories of the United States have been freed from their earlier incumbrances and are now vigorously doing the work for which they were designed. The results are most satisfactory, about 80 per cent of their "output" becoming useful, patriotic citizens. This is no fanciful dream, but the actual fact.

The ultimate aim of all schools is to bring pupils to as high a development as possible, so that our girls and boys of the future may be the good citizens. When Theseus was 16 years of age his mother took him to the huge stone beneath which lay his father's sword and sandals, without which he could never enter Athens. The young hero's training had been such that he lifted the great stone away and entered upon his career of glory. The perfect developed citizen is not the work of a day. They do not spring, Minerva-like, fully armed and equipped from the brain of Jupiter; they are developed by long years of training. The managers of reformatories fully realize this. Boys are not reformed in a day. The average time of detention in the juvenile reformatories of this country is about two years, and we can not overestimate the importance of so preparing them that their hands and hearts may be made stronger in all those higher virtues that ennoble and adorn human character.

Appended to this report is a complete list of the juvenile reformatories of the United States, giving the date of their establishment, the average attendance, and the number who have been admitted up to the present:

Juvenile institutions.

State.	Name of institution.	Established.	Superintendent.	Location of school.	Attendance.	Last consecutive number.
California	Whittier State School	1891	T. B. Van Alstyne	Whittier	304	1,203
	Preston School of Industry	1894	D. S. Hirshberg	Waterman	143	362
Colorado	State Industrial School	1881	Barnard L. Olds	Golden	116	1,384
	State Industrial School for Girls	1895	Elizabeth D. Benthall	Montclair	31	137
Connecticut	Connecticut School for Boys	1853	Charles M. Williams	Meriden	436	6,147
	Industrial School for Girls	1870	W. G. Fairbanks	Middletown	259	1,371
Delaware	Ferris Industrial School	1893	Mrs. Laura E. Brown	Wilmington	26	40
District of Columbia	Reform School, District o Columbia	1886	H. E. Haines	Marshallton	68	279
Indiana	Indiana Reform School for Boys	1870	George A. Shallenberger	Plainfield	245	2,272
	Indiana Reform School for Girls and Women's Prison	1868	Mrs. Sarah Keeley	Indianapolis	549	4,584
Illinois	School of Agriculture and Manual Training for Boys	1873	Oscar L. Dudley	Chicago, 113 Adams street	205	1,163
	State Reformatory	1887	George Torrence	Pontiac	1,397	2,400
	State Home for Juvenile Female Offenders	1893	Ophelia M. Amigh	Geneva	137	3,515
Iowa	Industrial School for Boys	1894	B. J. Miles	Eldora	492	361
	Industrial School for Girls	1808	A. H. Leonard	Mitchellville	172	533
Kentucky	Louisville Industrial School of Reform	1869	P. Caldwell	Louisville	420	738
Kansas	State Reform School for Boys	1865	J. M. Hart	North Topeka	228	4,157
	Industrial School for Girls	1880	Mrs. P. J. Bare	Beloit	108	1,709
Louisiana	Boys' House of Refuge	1889	M. T. Mohler	New Orleans	120	324
Maine	State Reform School	1845	Edwin P. Wentworth	Portland	136	376
	Industrial School for Girls	1853	Helen M. Staples	Hallowell	119	250
Maryland	House of Refuge	1875	R. J. Kirkwood	Baltimore	215	4,380
	Female House of Refuge	1855	Miss M. D. Stuart	do.	92	727
	Industrial Home for Colored Girls	1867	Mrs. H. F. Whittemore	Melvale	114	722
	House of Reformation for Colored Boys	1883	Nathan Thompson	Cheltenham	265	2,174
	St. Mary's Industrial School for Boys	1872	Brother Dominic	Baltimore	511	4,647
Massachusetts	Lyman School for Boys	1866	Theodore F. Chapin	Westboro	295	7,194
	State Industrial School for Girls	1848	Mrs. L. L. Brackett	Lancaster	162	362
	Plummer Farm School	1856	Charles A. Johnson	Salem	26	188
Michigan	Industrial School for Boys	1870	J. E. St. John	Lansing	581	7,032
	State Industrial Home for Girls	1850	Mrs. Lucy M. Sickles	Adrian	317	1,355
Minnesota	State Training School	1881	J. W. Brown	Red Wing	308	2,117
Missouri	Missouri Reform School for Boys	1808	L. D. Drake	Boonville	411	1,127
	State Industrial Home for Girls	1889	Mrs. Anna Clark	Chillicothe	96	118
	House of Refuge	1889	William C. Nolte	St. Louis	338	7,898
Montana	State Reform School for Boys	1854	Benton C. White	Miles City	71	144
Nebraska	State Industrial School for Boys	1894	Charles W. Hoxie	Kearney	150	1,194
	Girls' Industrial School	1881	B. K. B. Weber	Geneva	73	76
New Hampshire	State Reform School	1891	Thomas W. Robinson	Manchester	135	1,831
New Jersey	State Industrial School for Boys	1858	Ira Olterson	Janesburg	363	3,160
	State Reform School	1867	Mrs. Myrtle B. Kyler	Trenton	123	520
	Newark City Home	1871	C. M. Harrison	Verona	272	1,064

Juvenile institutions—Continued.

State.	Name of institution.	Established.	Superintendent.	Location of school.	Attendance.	Last consecutive number.
New York	State Industrial School	1849	Franklin H. Briggs	Rochester	809	10,348
	House of Refuge	1824	E. M. Carpenter	Randalls Island	690	27,231
	Juvenile Asylum	1850	C. K. Bruce, M.D	New York, 176th street and Armstrong avenue.	1,042	33,420
Ohio	Berkshire Industrial Farm	1887	W. W. Mayo	Canaan Four Corners	25	317
	Boys' Industrial School	1858	D. M. Barrett	Lancaster	775	8,911
	Girls' Industrial Home	1869	A. W. Stiles	Rathbone	349	1,942
	Cincinnati House of Refuge	1850	James Allison	Cincinnati	452	8,707
Oregon	State Reform School	1891	E. M. Croisan	Turner	101	345
Pennsylvania	House of Refuge	1828	F. H. Nibecker	Glenn Mills	822	1,592
	Pennsylvania Reform School	1854	J. A. Quay	Morganza	590	7,549
	House of Refuge, Girls' Department	1828	M. A. Campbell	Philadelphia	165	5,411
Rhode Island	Sockanosset School for Boys	1850	James H. Eastman	Howard	373	4,822
	Oaklawn School for Girls	1850	...do	...do	56	361
South Dakota	State Reform School	1848	C. W. Ainsworth	Plankington	116	317
Tennessee	Tennessee Industrial School	1886	W. C. Kilvington	Nashville	763	1,971
Utah	Utah Industrial School	1889	E. M. Allison	Ogden	24	220
Vermont	Industrial School	1866	S. A. Andrews	Vergennes	133	1,284
Virginia	Laurel Industrial School	1879	John W. Cringan	School Post-office	123	420
Washington	State Reform School for Boys and Girls	1891	Thomas P. Westendorf	Chehalis	149	553
West Virginia	Reform School	1890	D. W. Shaw	Pruntytown	200	500
Wisconsin	Industrial School for Boys	1860	Charles O. Merica	Waukesha	300	4,411
	Industrial School for Girls	1875	Mrs. Emma Bland	Milwaukee	260	1,604

Sixty-five reformatories are reported.
Totals: 19,410; 209,600.

U. S. DEPARTMENT OF LABOR
JAMES J. DAVIS, Secretary

CHILDREN'S BUREAU
GRACE ABBOTT, Chief

THE FEDERAL COURTS
AND
THE DELINQUENT CHILD

A STUDY OF THE METHODS OF DEALING WITH CHILDREN WHO HAVE VIOLATED FEDERAL LAWS

By
RUTH BLOODGOOD

❦

Bureau Publication No. 103

WASHINGTON
GOVERNMENT PRINTING OFFICE
1922

CONTENTS.

LETTER OF TRANSMITTAL.

UNITED STATES DEPARTMENT OF LABOR,
CHILDREN'S BUREAU,
Washington, November 19, 1921.

SIR: I transmit herewith a report entitled "The Federal Courts and the Delinquent Child: A Study of the Methods of Dealing with Children Who Have Violated Federal Laws." The report was prepared by Ruth Bloodgood, of the Social Service Division of the Childen's Bureau, with the assistance and under the direction of Katharine F. Lenroot, who has written the last chapter.

The Post Office Department and the Department of Justice have assisted the bureau by making their records available for the purpose of the study, and in many other ways in securing and interpreting the facts on which the report is based.

It will doubtless surprise many who have been interested in the development of the juvenile-court system to find that our Federal laws, like the old common criminal law, makes no distinction between adults and children. In consequence little children are still proceeded against in the United States courts by the ordinary method of arrest, detention in jail with adults pending arraignment for bail, indictment by the grand jury, and final discharge or sentence of fine or imprisonment.

All students of this subject will appreciate, as do most of the judges and officers of the Department of Justice and the Post Office Department, the injustice to the individual child, and more important still, the community loss in this unscientific method of handling juvenile offenders.

Respectfully submitted.

GRACE ABBOTT, *Chief.*

Hon. JAMES J. DAVIS,
Secretary of Labor.

THE FEDERAL COURTS AND THE DELINQUENT CHILD.

CHAPTER I. JUVENILE OFFENDERS AGAINST FEDERAL LAWS.

PURPOSE AND METHOD OF STUDY.

A phase of the problem of juvenile delinquency not heretofore given special consideration is that of the children who violate Federal laws and are taken before United States district courts. Attention has centered on the number of children coming before State courts and on the progress these courts have made in affording special treatment of children's cases. That there are considerable numbers of juveniles arrested and tried on Federal charges is shown in the reports of the Attorney General for the last two years,[1] which give a total of 1,038 persons under 20 years of age committed to institutions for violations of Federal laws by United States district courts; figures are not available for the total number under 20 years of age before these courts.

The attention of the United States Children's Bureau had been called to the problem of children violating Federal laws by several persons in different parts of the country. In one instance a member of a grand jury to which several children's cases had been presented felt very keenly that young children should not be subjected to the formal procedure and limited facilities for treatment in the Federal courts. It seemed particularly appropriate that the Children's Bureau, a Federal agency concerned in raising the standards of child protection and child care, should interest itself in the methods employed by the Federal Government in dealing with children violating the laws of the United States. For these reasons an inquiry was undertaken covering, so far as the information was available, the numbers of children violating Federal laws in 1918 and 1919, their ages, the types of offenses committed, the methods of procedure, the dispositions made, and to a limited extent the home conditions and social histories of the children.

The Department of Justice and the Post Office Department were most helpful in making available the data upon which the inquiry is based.

---

[1] Annual Reports of the Attorney General of the United States : 1919, Exhibit No. 23, opp. p. 534 ; 1920, Exhibit No. 19, opp. p. 606.

Records of the chief inspector of the Post Office Department relating to offenders against postal laws were the first sources of information. Data were obtained on all such offenders under 18 years of age arrested throughout the United States during the calendar years 1918 and 1919.

As the National Training School for Boys in the District of Columbia is the institution to which the largest number of boys under 18 years of age are committed for all types of Federal offenses, the records of this institution were consulted, information being obtained in regard to all children sent to this institution for offenses against Federal laws committed during the years selected. Besides this Federal institution, two State institutions were included in the study—the New York State Reformatory at Elmira and the Iowa State Reformatory at Anamosa. These institutions, located in different parts of the country, are among those with which the Government contracts to receive Federal commitments.

The information from the National Training School for Boys and the Post Office Department furnished the basis for selection of the eight United States courts chosen for special study, namely, the Supreme Court of the District of Columbia [2] and seven United States district courts (Illinois, northern district; Indiana; Maryland; Massachusetts; New York, eastern and southern districts; and Pennsylvania, eastern district). Juvenile and other State courts in these districts were visited for the purpose of obtaining information with regard to any Federal cases which were referred to them.

In each district the seat of the court, which happened in each case to be the largest city of the district, was visited, as were also some of the smaller localities near by. All cases of juvenile postal offenders for which information had already been obtained at the Post Office Department and cases of children committed to the institutions studied were followed through the records of courts, jails, and social agencies knowing the offenders, in order to secure as complete histories as possible.

From the different sources schedules were taken for each case, the following information being obtained: Type of court hearing case, method of handling case in court, age, offense, detention, disposition, length of time between apprehension and disposition, and any social facts available.

In the districts studied, because of the absence of age reports on the court records, it was impossible to obtain an accurate count of all cases of children committing Federal offenses other than postal. Accurate knowledge of the number of Federal offenders referred to juvenile courts could not be obtained as the records of the juvenile

---

[2] The Supreme Court of the District of Columbia is clothed with the powers and authority of a United States district court.

courts seldom noted the case as involving a Federal charge, giving merely the charge preferred in the juvenile court.

The United States judges, attorneys, postal authorities, and representatives of social agencies familiar with the local situations were most cooperative in assisting the Children's Bureau in this study. In addition to the studies of selected localities, interviews were had with the United States attorneys and other officials in Buffalo, Cleveland, Denver, Los Angeles, Minneapolis, New Orleans, St. Louis, San Francisco, and Seattle. Although schedules were not taken in these places, information as to the extent of the problem and the practice in handling juvenile cases was obtained.

LEGAL PROVISIONS AND PRESENT PRACTICE.

Jurisdiction of Federal and State courts in juvenile cases.

The United States district courts have exclusive jurisdiction " of all crimes and offenses cognizable under the authority of the United States." [3] Such offenses are cognizable in these courts only when made so by acts of Congress.[4] No separate provisions exist under Federal law for jurisdiction over juvenile cases; and so the children who violate such acts as the postal, interstate-commerce, internal-revenue, and drug laws, or those who are arrested for larceny of United States property, trespassing on United States property, forgery, and embezzlement of Government property, are under the jurisdiction of the United States district courts.

Although there is no law for the removal to the State courts of cases cognizable in the district or circuit courts of the United States,[5] among many Federal authorities a practice has developed of referring to the State courts juvenile cases which may be brought under the jurisdiction of the State authorities by lessening the charge. For instance, in many cases of larceny of mail the charge preferred is simply that of larceny or "taking the property of another." In some cases the offense may involve both a State and a Federal charge, as in larceny from a post office located in a general store, merchandise also being stolen. In such cases the State charge is often preferred and the Federal charge dropped, the Federal authorities considering the State prosecution sufficient.

Organization and procedure of Federal courts in juvenile cases.

The types of offenses committed against the United States are in many instances not more serious than those bringing children to the juvenile courts, yet in the Federal courts the method of procedure and the attitude of the court toward the offender differ materially

---

[3] The Judicial Code of the United States, Ch. XI. sec. 256 ; 36 Stat. 1161.
[4] U. S. v. Shepherd, 1 Hughes 520 ; 27 Fed. Cas., No. 16274 ; U. S. v. Lewis, 36 Fed. 449.
[5] McCollom v. Pefe, 7 Kans. 189, 1871.

from juvenile-court practice, which considers the delinquent a child to be protected and saved. Procedure in Federal courts, when unmodified by the expedients adopted in some instances, is based on the theory that the child has committed a crime for which he must be punished.

The organization and procedure of the Federal courts do not readily lend themselves to the handling of juvenile cases according to generally recognized standards of dealing with delinquent children. In the first place, prompt action is difficult to obtain because the jurisdiction of each United States district court includes considerable territory, in many instances an entire State. Sessions of the court are held at various places within each district at stated intervals; a child committing an offense against the United States may have to wait for trial until the term of court which meets in his place of residence, or if he does not live in a meeting place of the court he must be taken to the one nearest his home.

The first step in bringing a case before a Federal court is a presentation of the facts to the United States attorney; following this a preliminary hearing is held before the United States commissioner, who fixes the amount of bond. The case is next presented to the court on information filed, or to the grand jury, the former procedure being permissible in cases of misdemeanors. If the case is presented to the grand jury and an indictment returned, or if it is presented direct to court on information, the case is then tried, often by jury. These trials are open to the public and are formally conducted. Because of the organization of the Federal courts, the length of time between apprehension and final court action is sometimes considerable, and cases are often carried from one term of court until the next because of a crowded calendar. Moreover, in the Federal courts there is no provision for social investigation, special detention of juveniles, or probation.

In contrast to the methods of the Federal courts are the following features of juvenile-court organization and procedure: Prompt action, because of easy access to the court and frequency of sessions; informal court procedure, with separate hearings as nearly private as possible; proper facilities for juvenile detention; means for obtaining adequate information concerning the child's physical and mental condition, personality and habits, family history, and home conditions; and probation service, by which children on probation may be kept under close and helpful supervision. The preliminary hearings by attorneys and commissioners and the presentment to the grand jury are eliminated in the juvenile-court procedure. Under this procedure no bond is required, and children are released upon their own recognizance if they can safely remain at home pending the hearing.

Prior to December, 1916, the Federal judges had always used their own discretion in placing offenders on probation, and their right to do so had never been questioned. At that time the Supreme Court of the United States handed down a decision[6] by which it was held that Federal judges had no legal power to place offenders on probation from United States district courts, but could do so from the Supreme Court of the District of Columbia, where a system of probation is legally provided. This decision made the rule against probation absolute.

Immediately following this decision a bill providing for probation was passed in February, 1917, by both the House and the Senate, but did not receive the President's signature. Another bill[7] was introduced in the House of Representatives on January 24, 1920, and was referred to the House Committee on the Judiciary, which held hearings on the subjects of probation in the Federal courts and parole.[8] This bill was not enacted into law, and in April, 1921, a third bill was introduced in the House of Representatives and referred to the Committee on the Judiciary.[9]

In contrast to the lack of probation in the Federal courts is the fact that probation has been provided for by law in every State of the Union. The instances already cited[10] of reference of juvenile Federal offenders to State courts on preferred charges show that many United States attorneys and judges realize their handicap in this matter. Several United States attorneys reported that in cases which they did not consider sufficiently grave to warrant prosecution they often placed boys on probation to themselves, informally, requiring the boys to report from time to time, and later dismissing the cases. This informal probation consisted only of reporting in person or by mail to the office of the attorney. No further supervision was afforded, such as would be exercised by a probation officer through home visits, cooperation with school authorities, employers and recreational agencies, and by other means.

The problem of the detention of juveniles coming before the Federal courts is the more serious because of the long periods that frequently elapse between apprehension and disposition, and because bond is required for release after preliminary hearing. Doubtless detention could often be avoided if the juvenile-court practice were

[6] Kilits case, 242 U. S. 27.
[7] A bill for the establishment of a probation system in the United States courts, except in the District of Columbia. H. R. 12036, 66th Cong., 2d sess.
[8] Hearings before the Committee on the Judiciary, House of Representatives, 66th Cong., 2d sess., Serial No. 20. p. 5. Washington, 1920.
[9] An act to amend an act entitled "An act to parole United States prisoners, and for other purposes," approved June 25, 1910, as amended by an act approved January 23, 1913, and for the establishment of a probation system in the United States courts, except in the District of Columbia. H. R. 4126, 67th Cong., 1st sess.
[10] See p. 3.

followed of releasing children to the custody of their parents without bond. But, for children as well as for adults, jail detention is the common practice, there being no prohibition under Federal law against detaining juveniles in jail and no provision for other forms of detention. Through informal arrangements local detention homes are used in a few instances, but this is by no means a general practice. In New York City, where local ordinances prohibit jail detention of juveniles under 15 years of age, the shelter of the Society for the Prevention of Cruelty to Children is used for all Federal offenders under that age. In Knoxville, Tenn., the law creating the juvenile detention home specifies that Federal offenders may be detained therein. This provision in the law was requested by the Federal judge of that district, who had had several cases of children detained in jail for months.

In Federal cases referred to juvenile courts, when detention is required, the children are detained in special detention homes or other places provided for the detention of juvenile delinquents under the jurisdiction of those courts. In few of these cases were children reported as being detained in jails. The juvenile-court laws in many States prohibit the detention of juveniles under specified ages in jails and frequently require the establishment of special places of detention for them.

Expedients used in juvenile cases.

Certain expedients have been adopted by some of the United States attorneys and judges in the handling of children's cases, by which they are enabled to deal with them more nearly from the standpoint of the children's welfare and potentialities.

The first of these expedients is that mentioned above—the referring of cases of children violating Federal laws to the State courts, charges being preferred which will bring them under the jurisdiction of those courts. The extent to which this policy is followed depends upon the attitude of both attorneys and judges. The cases which are referred are usually reviewed first by the United States district attorneys, though in a few districts the post-office inspectors, knowing the policy of the judges and attorneys, take the children directly to the juvenile courts.

In 7 of the 17 districts in which the United States attorneys were interviewed, a large number of the children reported as violating Federal laws were referred to the State courts—usually to the juvenile courts where they were available, or to the courts having jurisdiction to hear juvenile cases in places not having specially organized juvenile courts. In two of these seven districts special arrangements had been made informally with the juvenile courts to handle all cases of children under 17 years of age who violated Federal laws.

Extracts from letters of the post-office inspectors in five localities other than the seven districts referred to in the preceding paragraph are here cited for the purpose of showing the attitude of attorneys and judges in those places toward referring juvenile cases:

(1) At an interview a few weeks ago the United States attorney informed me that when the State would assume the prosecution and charge of delinquent boys accused of violations of the postal laws he much preferred such action to prosecutions in Federal court, as the State courts can sentence them to reform schools and place them under charge of probation officers, with better results than can be secured by confining them in county jails or sending them to Federal prisons.

(2) One of the United States attorneys advised that in view of the fact that there was a good case against the boy in the State court, and as he was too young for prosecution in the United States court on account of lack of suitable place for his confinement, and also for the reason that, because of the war, the expenses of the United States courts had been increased, and he did not like to burden these courts with a case of this nature when the defendant could be punished in the juvenile court; therefore he advised that the matter be taken up with the probate judge of the county, looking to the confinement of the boy in the reform school of the State.

(3) The facts in this case were reported to the United States attorney. In his reply he stated that a number of cases of similar nature have been submitted to him, and that he has found that the better course is for a charge to be made against the youthful offender (who is 16 years of age) in the juvenile courts (State); that the judge of the court or the probation officer constantly has the boy under surveillance, and that the best results can be eventually worked out. He stated, further, that a charge of forgery under the State law may be made and the boy apprehended and released on such conditions as the court may require.

(4) The matter was submitted to the United States attorney, who, under date of January 18, 1919, replied in part as follows: " I know the attitude toward prosecutions of boys of his age for crimes of this nature, and I am sure that more good could be accomplished by having the boy brought before some local or municipal judge and reprimanded than by his indictment and prosecution."

(5) I have submitted several reports of cases involving violations of the postal laws by persons under 18 years of age to the United States attorney, and in each of these cases he has recommended that the matter be submitted to the county authorities of the county in which the offense was committed, stating that the judge in this district does not care to handle cases of persons who are subject to commitment to the State industrial school.

Great variance was found in the method of prosecuting interstate commerce violations. In the case of juveniles, these usually consist of breaking into and larceny from freight cars in interstate shipment. In some communities all these cases are taken before juvenile or other State courts on larceny charges. In other localities all go before the Federal courts, and in still others some are taken to each type of court. The policy of one eastern railroad is to prosecute all cases in State courts whenever possible.

In two districts the United States attorney ruled that the Federal authorities would not prosecute cases of theft from interstate shipment where the value of the goods stolen was small (in Maryland less than $100). Children seldom commit larceny to a large amount from interstate shipments, and in these two localities few children were taken before Federal courts on this charge. Of the 74 boys committed for such offenses by United States district courts to the National Training School for Boys, 2 were sent from one of these two districts and none from the other.

Informal treatment by United States attorneys is frequent, consisting of an informal conference in the attorney's office and dismissal of the case or arrangement for informal probation either to the attorney himself or to some probation officer of a local court. An example of this method is found in the eastern district of Pennsylvania.[11]

In one district the post-office inspector handled informally postal cases involving children, reporting each case, with his decision, to the district attorney, who usually concurred in the recommendation of the inspector and did not see the child. Cases which were brought formally to this district attorney's office usually went to the grand jury.

In some cases reaching the grand jury, because of the youth of the offender, a finding of "no bill" was returned. This amounts to a dismissal of the case, since no further court action is taken. In many cases the attorney did not wish to prosecute, even though a bill of indictment was returned, and he entered a petition to nolle prosequi—also a form of dismissal without trial.

In disposing of children's cases which are brought for trial and in which the offense does not warrant commitment to an institution, the judges in three of the districts studied frequently imposed a sentence of one day in the custody of the United States marshal, thus satisfying the legal requirement that a sentence shall be passed upon a defendant who is found guilty. The child thus sentenced was required to sit in the marshal's office from the time of pronouncement of sentence by the judge until the office closed for the day. In three other districts short sentences of from one week to sixty days in local jails were reported. In one large city, in preference to committing the boys to the county jail located in the city, they were committed to small county jails outside the city.

Fines are sometimes imposed. As a substitute for probation, judges often continue a case or defer sentence from one term of court until the next, pending the child's good behavior. No close supervision, such as a probation system would provide, is available in these continued cases, the only effort to keep in touch with the child's conduct being the requirement that he shall report to the court on the dates set in the continuance order. Such procedure was

[11] See p. 50.

reported in four of the districts studied. After such cases have been continued for from six months to a year, many are nol-prossed, while in other cases fines are imposed or the children receive sentences of one day in the marshal's custody or short terms in jail.

Two war-time measures [12] included sections on the unlawful wearing of the United States uniform, the procuring of liquor for soldiers and sailors, and vice regulations. Before the courts or in the institutions studied were 50 boys arrested for wearing uniforms illegally or procuring liquor for men in uniform—cases typical only of the war period. Girls arrested during the war in violation of the vice section of this act were usually taken to the juvenile courts through the efforts of the protective agencies and were not recorded separately by these courts as Federal cases. No reports of the number of such cases were available in the courts studied. It was found that 21 girls had been committed on such charges by United States district courts—6 to the Iowa State Reformatory and 15 to the National Training School for Girls, District of Columbia—but they were not included in this study.

Few juveniles are held on charges of the violation of the Mann Act.[13] Several courts reported that in rare instances girls under 18 years of age are held as witnesses in Mann Act cases. If detention is necessary, it is usually in private institutions, though occasionally in jails. In this study no records of such cases were discovered.

Institutions receiving juveniles on Federal commitments.

The National Training School for Boys and the National Training School for Girls, both in the District of Columbia, are the two Federal institutions to which only juvenile delinquents are committed. Under the law these institutions receive boys and girls from the juvenile court and the Supreme Court of the District of Columbia and from United States district courts. A large number of boys are committed to the National Training School for Boys by the district courts throughout the United States; the National Training School for Girls, however, seldom receives girls from such courts.

Legal provision is made for commitment of juvenile offenders against Federal laws to certain State and other local institutions. By statute [14] the Attorney General may contract with local houses of refuge for the confinement of juvenile offenders against the laws of the United States. He must notify the district courts of the places of confinement thus provided, and offenders are sentenced

---

[12] 39 Stat. 166 (national defense act, June 3, 1916) ; 40 Stat. 76 (an act to authorize the President to increase temporarily the Military Establishment of the United States, May 18, 1917).

[13] 36 Stat. 825 (act of June 25, 1910).

[14] U. S. Comp. Stat. 1916. secs. 10550 (R. S. 5549), 10551 (R. S. 5550), 10560 (act 3 Mar., 1891, ch. 529, sec. 9).

to the designated house of refuge nearest the place of conviction. The Federal Government pays for the maintenance of its prisoners committed to such local institutions. The reports of the Attorney General for the years 1919 and 1920[15] show that persons under 20 years of age were confined in the following local institutions, exclusive of jails: State industrial schools of Colorado and Idaho, girls' industrial schools of South Carolina and West Virginia; Tennessee State Training and Agricultural School for Boys, St. Mary's Industrial School[16] and the House of Reformation (for colored boys),[17] Maryland, and the Missouri State Industrial Home; State reformatories in Connecticut, Illinois, Iowa, Minnesota, Missouri, and New York; State reformatories for women in Iowa and Massachusetts, and the Woman's Reformatory of Kansas City, Mo.; State penitentiaries of Colorado, Maryland, Missouri, Oklahoma, and West Virginia; the penitentiaries of Essex County and Hudson County, N. J., and Oahu Prison, Honolulu; the houses of correction of Chicago and Peoria, Ill., of Detroit, Mich., and of Milwaukee County, Wis. State laws in both Pennsylvania and Minnesota[18] provided for the confinement in State institutions of juvenile delinquents convicted in the Federal courts of the State, the State to be reimbursed for their maintenance by the United States.

The majority of the local institutions with which arrangements are made to receive juveniles receive also adult offenders, the ages of prisoners at the State reformatories ranging from 16 to 30 years. Federal prisoners have the same treatment at these institutions as do other prisoners, and no provision is made for separation into groups according to age.

During the two-year period from July 1, 1918, to June 30, 1920, in addition to those committed to the institutions already mentioned, 389 persons under 20 years of age were committed to Federal penitentiaries—204 to Atlanta, Ga.; 158 to Leavenworth, Kans.; and 27 to McNeil Island, Wash. That the majority of these 389 were probably 18 years of age and over is indicated by the fact that only 12 cases of commitment to such institutions were reported in this study of juvenile offenders. All were sent to Atlanta penitentiary, and all but one had violated postal laws.

---

[15] Annual Reports of the Attorney General of the United States : 1919, Exhibit No. 23, opp. p. 534; 1920, Exhibit No. 19, opp. p. 606.

[16] A private institution in Maryland.

[17] A private institution, subsidized by both city and State.

[18] Pa. 1899 P. L. 15, sec. 1 (act of Mar. 22) ; Minn. G. S. 1913, sec. 14064.

CHAPTER II. CHILDREN VIOLATING POSTAL LAWS.

SOURCES OF INFORMATION.

Postal laws and regulations were found to be the Federal laws most frequently violated by juveniles. The information with reference to the postal cases was obtained from the records of the chief inspector of the Post Office Department. The United States is divided into 15 divisions, with an inspector in charge of each, and a varying number of inspectors in each division to handle the cases of postal violations arising therein. The inspectors are vested with the power of arrest but not of search, and they make investigations of all postal cases before referring them to the United States attorneys. If local police officials make the arrest they are required to notify the post-office inspectors at once. The inspectors present the cases, with a report of their investigations, to the United States attorneys. Each case is reported to the office of the chief inspector in Washington, information being given as to the offense, age of defendant, type of court handling the case, preliminary hearing, indictment, and final disposition made. In some cases supplementary information is given with regard to detention, employment, school attendance, and social history.

These records were available for the entire United States, Alaska, and Porto Rico, and are fairly inclusive of the number of juveniles violating Federal postal laws during the period, though a few cases may have been handled informally of which no record was sent in. In a small number of instances the age was not given. The information from the Post Office Department was checked and supplemented by court, jail, and institutional records in those cases reported also from the districts or by the institutions included in other parts of this study.

NUMBER OF CASES REPORTED.

Records from the Post Office Department were obtained for 1,108 cases of juveniles under 18 years of age arrested in 1918 and 1919. The number reported for 1919 was considerably larger than that for 1918, 617 as compared with 491. There were 37 cases of postal-law violation reported in the localities and by the institutions studied for which no record could be found in the Post Office Department. The 1,108 for which records were found in the Post Office Department form the basis for this chapter.

During the two-year period 1,054 boys were arrested for postal offenses, and only 54 girls. Of the boys, 869 were white, 163 were

Negroes, 11 belonged to other races, and in 11 cases race was no reported. Thirty of the girls were white, 23 were Negroes, and in case race was not reported.

Cases of violations of postal laws by juveniles were reported fror each State [1] for the two-year period, 1918–1919, as follows:

Total	1,108	Nebraska	1
		New Hampshire	
Alabama	21	New Jersey	1
Arizona	7	New Mexico	
Arkansas	24	New York	9
California	53	North Carolina	2
Colorado	18	North Dakota	
Connecticut	11	Ohio	3
Delaware	2	Oklahoma	3
District of Columbia	27	Oregon	
Florida	22	Pennsylvania	5
Georgia	38	Rhode Island	
Illinois	119	South Carolina	2
Indiana	19	South Dakota	
Iowa	8	Tennessee	2
Kansas	17	Texas	2
Kentucky	21	Utah	
Louisiana	19	Vermont	
Maine	8	Virginia	3
Maryland	24	Washington	1
Massachusetts	56	West Virginia	4
Michigan	18	Wisconsin	1
Minnesota	34	Wyoming	
Mississippi	34	Alaska	
Missouri	39	Porto Rico	
Montana	6		

TYPES OF POSTAL OFFENSES.

The largest number of cases reported were for larceny of mail—496 cases—and post-office breaking and entering and larceny—24 cases. Fifty or more cases each were reported for forgery, larcen of postal funds or property, "stubbing" special-delivery letters and wrongful use of the mails. A list of the various offenses and th number of children committing each offense follows:

	Number.	Per cent di tribution
Total	1,108	100.
Larceny	555	50.
Of mail	496	
Of postal funds or property	50	
Of money left in rural boxes	3	
Other	6	

[1] No cases reported from Idaho or Nevada.

[2] When a special-delivery messenger fails to attempt to deliver letters given him fo delivery and makes a false return on the return slip. collecting the 8 cents allowed fo delivery of each letter, he is guilty of " stubbing."

	Number.	Per cent distribution.
Breaking and entering and larceny, post office	246	22.2
" Stubbing "	58	5.2
Forgery	56	5.1
Wrongful use of mails	50	4.5
Breaking and entering, post office	41	3.7
Larceny of mail and forgery	31	2.8
Destruction of post-office property	28	2.5
Embezzlement	21	1.9
Having stolen post-office property in possession	8	.7
Attempted robbery	3	.3
Other	11	1.0

Postal offenses committed by the 54 girls reported were confined chiefly to three types: (1) Forgery of mail or of checks contained in stolen mail—15 cases; (2) larceny of mail—15 cases; (3) wrongful use of the mails—10 cases—including 8 cases of sending obscene letters and 2 involving schemes to defraud.

AGES OF OFFENDERS.

Slightly more than half (566) of the children committing postal offenses were reported to be under 16 years of age at the time of apprehension. The 54 girls reported were proportionately older than the boys, as nearly two-thirds of the girls, but less than half the boys, were 16 and 17 years of age. The age distribution of the boys and girls is shown in the following list:

	Boys.	Girls.
Total	1,054	54
Under 10 years	38	--
10 to 11 years	69	1
12 to 13 years	145	5
14 to 15 years	295	13
16 to 17 years	498	34
Age not reported	9	1

Except for post-office breaking and entering and larceny and the " stubbing " of special-delivery letters there seems to be no close relation between the age and type of offense. Of the 244 boys arrested for breaking, entering, and larceny from post offices, 108 were 16 years of age or over. In 55 of the 58 cases of " stubbing " reported the boy was of this age group; this was the largest proportion 16 years of age or over reported for any one offense, and is accounted for by the policy of not employing as special-delivery messengers boys who are under the age of 16.

TYPES OF COURTS.

As stated in Chapter I, United States district courts have original jurisdiction of the violations of postal laws, but the policy of referring cases involving children to juvenile and other State courts is followed in many districts, though no legal provision has been made for such action.[3] Table 1 shows for each State the children before specified types of courts.

TABLE 1.—*Type of court, according to State; children arrested in 1918 and 1919 for violating postal laws.*

State.[1]	Total.	Before specified type of court.			No court action taken.	Court action not reported.
		U. S. district.	Juvenile.	Other State.		
Total	1,108	676	202	136	79	15
Alabama	21	17		1	3	
Arizona	7	1		2	3	1
Arkansas	24	18		4	2	
California	53	[2]11	38		4	
Colorado	18	1	10	6	1	
Connecticut	11	3	2	6		
Delaware	2	1			1	
District of Columbia	27	10	15		2	
Florida	22	20		1	1	
Georgia	38	34		3	1	
Illinois	119	98	9	6	6	
Indiana	19	13		6		
Iowa	8	5		1	1	1
Kansas	17	12	1	3		1
Kentucky	21	16		5		
Louisiana	19	13		2	4	
Maine	8	5		3		
Maryland	24	[3]16	1		7	
Massachusetts	56	5	35	13	3	
Michigan	18	[3]11	5	2		
Minnesota	34	13	15	6		
Mississippi	34	30		1	3	
Missouri	39	30	3	3	3	
Montana	6	2	2	2		
Nebraska	11	1	5		3	2
New Hampshire	7	6	1			
New Jersey	13	12		1		
New Mexico	7	7				
New York	94	41	32	17	4	
North Carolina	21	18				3
North Dakota	2	2				
Ohio	33	21	7	3	1	1
Oklahoma	37	[4]30	3	2		2
Oregon	7	5		2		
Pennsylvania	53	26	9	9	6	3
Rhode Island	3			3		
South Carolina	21	18			2	1
South Dakota	2		2			
Tennessee	20	17		2	1	
Texas	23	21		2		
Utah	1				1	
Vermont	2	1			1	
Virginia	34	26		3	5	
Washington	14	4	5	5		
West Virginia	40	26		5	9	
Wisconsin	10	2	2	6		
Wyoming	1	1				
Alaska	3	3				
Porto Rico	4	3			1	

[1] No cases in Idaho or Nevada.
[2] Includes 5 children before a United States district court, whose cases were later transferred to juvenile courts.
[3] Includes 1 child before a United States district court, whose case was later transferred to a juvenile court.
[4] Includes 1 child before a United States district court, whose case was later transferred to a State court other than juvenile.

In 15 cases court action was not reported; in 79 cases—7.1 per cent—no court action was taken, it being decided by the United States attorney or by the postal authorities not to prosecute. Of the remaining 1,014 cases, 202—19.9 per cent—were before juvenile

[3] See p. 3.

courts, and 136—13.4 per cent—were taken before other State courts—county, district, circuit, or city courts. Some of the last group of courts, though not reported as juvenile courts on the post-office records, probably belonged in the juvenile-court group as having juvenile jurisdiction and organization for dealing with children's cases. The majority of cases—668, or 60.3 per cent—were heard before the United States district courts, and 8 others were first heard by these courts and then transferred to juvenile or other State courts. Cases presented to the United States commissioner for preliminary hearing or to the grand jury for indictment, whether or not a bill was returned, were considered to have had court action.

Half, or more than half, the children's cases reported were referred to juvenile or other State courts in California, Colorado, Connecticut, District of Columbia, Massachusetts, Minnesota, Montana, New York, Rhode Island, South Dakota, Washington, and Wisconsin.

The policy of referring juvenile cases to State courts is much more prevalent in cases involving young children than in cases involving older boys and girls. The majority of postal cases involving children under the age of 12 and exactly one-half of those involving children 12 and 13 years of age were handled by juvenile and other State courts. Of the cases involving children 14 years of age and over, the largest number were before Federal courts. The comparatively small proportion of children 16 years of age and over referred to juvenile courts may be accounted for in part by the fact that their jurisdiction extends in some States only over children under 16 years of age and in others only over children under 17. Furthermore, it may not be considered necessary to refer the older children to the juvenile or other State courts for the more informal procedure available there. Table 2 gives further detail of the ages of children before the different courts.

TABLE 2.—*Age at apprehension and type of court; children arrested in 1918 and 1919 for violating postal laws.*

	Children violating postal laws.					
Age at apprehension.	Total.	Before specified type of court.			No court action taken.	Court action not reported.
		United States district.	Juvenile.	Other State.		
Total................................	1,108	676	202	136	79	15
Under 10 years.........................	38	8	11	4	15	....
10 to 11 years..........................	70	19	33	10	7	1
12 to 13 years..........................	150	60	45	30	11	4
14 to 15 years..........................	308	[1]177	73	33	19	6
16 to 17 years.........................	532	[2]408	38	57	25	4
Not reported...........................	10	4	2	2	2	....

[1] Includes 2 children before a United States district court whose cases were later transferred to a juvenile court.
[2] Includes 5 children before a United States district court whose cases were later transferred to a juvenile court, and 1 whose case was transferred to a State court other than juvenile.

Comparison of the type of offense with the type of court handling the case does not indicate that any definite policy was followed in referring certain types of cases to State courts. In only four groups of offenses was no instance of reference to juvenile or other State courts reported: (1) Larceny of mail from rural mail boxes, involving forgery of checks contained in the letters; (2) larceny of money for stamps left in rural boxes; (3) use of mails in a scheme to defraud; and (4) sending threatening letters. These offenses are not more serious than others reported.

The largest numbers of cases referred involved larceny of mail and post-office breaking and entering and larceny, which were the offenses most frequently committed. Of the 496 cases of larceny of mail, 36.3 per cent were referred to State courts, and 55.6 per cent were brought before United States district courts; of the 246 cases of post-office breaking and entering and larceny only 29.3 per cent were taken to local courts as compared with 63.4 per cent before the Federal courts. A considerable number of the cases of larceny from post offices involved State in addition to Federal offenses, as the post office was often located in a store from which merchandise was stolen at the same time. In a number of instances of larceny of mail from hall letter boxes the Federal authorities ruled that the responsibility of the Post Office Department ended with the delivery of the mail. Table 3 shows the types of offenses involved in cases before the different courts.

TABLE 3.—*Offense and type of court; children arrested in 1918 and 1919 for violating postal laws.*

Offense.	Children violating postal laws.					
	Total.	Before specified type of court.			No court action taken.	Court action not reported.
		United States district.	Juvenile.	Other State.		
Total...............................	1,108	[1] 676	202	136	79	15
Larceny................................	555	311	139	59	41	5
Of mail...........................	496	277	129	51	34	5
Of postal funds or property...........	50	28	10	6	6	....
Of money left in rural boxes..........	3	3	....	....	....	....
Other.............................	6	3	....	2	1	....
Breaking and entering and larceny, post office.........................	246	156	25	47	11	7
"Stubbing".............................	58	57	1	....	....	....
Forgery.............................	56	43	7	3	3	....
Wrongful use of mail..................	50	36	5	1	5	3
Breaking and entering post office..........	41	17	2	16	6	....
Larceny of mail and forgery..............	31	10	11	5	5	....
Destruction of post-office property..........	28	15	6	3	4	....
Embezzlement........................	21	20	1	....	....	....
Having stolen property in possession......	8	5	2	....	1	....
Attempted robbery.....................	3	2	....	1	....	....
Other.............................	11	4	3	1	3	....

[1] Includes 8 children before United States district courts whose cases were later transferred to juvenile or other State courts.

PLACE OF RESIDENCE.

The organization of the United States district courts, each district covering considerable territory, with specified places of holding court at stated intervals, often necessitates taking the child some distance from his home and holding him for some time awaiting trial. The child's place of residence was other than the place of holding court in 310, or 56.2 per cent, of the 552 cases before United States courts in which place of residence was reported. On the other hand, the child lived in the city in which the court was located in 72.3 per cent of the 188 cases reported heard by juvenile courts in which place of residence was reported, and in 52.9 per cent of the 87 cases before other State courts. The place of residence in relation to the place of holding court, for the 881 cases in which the place of residence was reported, is shown in table 4.

TABLE 4.—*Place of residence in relation to place of holding court and type of court; children arrested in 1918 and 1819 for violating postal laws.*

Place of residence.	Children violating postal laws whose residence was reported.										Court action not reported.
	Total.		Before specified type of court.						No court action taken.		
			United States district.		Juvenile.		Other State.				
	Number.	Per cent distribution.	Number.	Per cent distribution.	Number.	Per cent distribution.	Number.	Per cent distribution.	Number.	Per cent distribution.	Number.
Total......................	881	100.0	[1] 552	100.0	188	100.0	87	100.0	45	100.0	9
Same as place of holding court....	448	50.9	242	43.8	136	72.3	46	52.9	20	44.4	4
Other than place of holding court.	433	49.1	310	56.2	52	27.7	41	47.1	25	55.6	5

[1] Includes 7 children before United States district courts, whose cases were later transferred to juvenile courts.

The largest number of the 1,108 children were reported as residing in communities of less than 10,000 population—385, or 34.7 per cent. The next largest group—240, or 21.7 per cent—resided in cities of 500,000 population and over. The size of place of residence and the type of court are shown in Table 5.

TABLE 5.—*Size of place of residence and type of court; children arrested in 1918 and 1919 for violating postal laws.*

Size of place of residence.[1]	Total.	Before specified type of court.						No court action taken.		Court action not reported.	
		United States district.		Juvenile.		Other State.					
		Number.	Per cent.[2]	Number.	Per cent.[2]	Number.	Per cent.[2]	Number.	Per cent.[2]	Number.	Per cent.[2]
						Children violating postal laws.					
Total............	1,108	676	61.0	202	18.2	136	12.3	79	7.1	15	1.4
Under 10,000..........	385	235	61.0	57	14.8	58	15.1	28	7.3	7	1.8
10,000, under 25,000....	47	34	......	3	......	10	......	......	......	......	......
25,000, under 100,000...	90	58	......	19	......	7	......	5	......	1	......
100,000, under 500,000..	109	63	57.8	36	33.0	5	4.6	2	1.8	3	2.8
500,000 and over.......	240	151	62.9	71	29.6	8	3.3	10	4.2	......	......
Not reported..........	237	135	57.0	16	6.8	48	20.3	34	14.3	4	1.0

[1] Derived from Fourteenth Census of the United States, 1920, Vol. I, Popu lation, p. 320 ff
[2] Not shown where base was less than 100.

The percentage of cases referred to juvenile or other State courts was almost as high in towns of less than 10,000 population as in large cities—29.9 in the former as contrasted with 37.6 and 32.9 in cities of 100,000 to 500,000 and of 500,000 and over, respectively. However, in cities of over 100,000 population, less than 5 per cent were referred to State courts other than juvenile, while in communities under 10,000 the percentage was 15.1. This difference is doubtless accounted for by the fact that large cities are much more likely than smaller communities to have organized juvenile courts.

DISPOSITIONS OF CASES.

Types of dispositions.

Because of the absence of probation and power to suspend sentence in the Federal courts, commitments to institutions constitute the most frequent form of disposition in the 1,014 postal cases for which definite court action was reported. The National Training. School for Boys, State reformatories, and jails received the largest number of commitments from the United States district courts, while the State industrial schools received the largest number from juvenile and other State courts. Probation, suspended sentence, or both probation and suspended sentence were used in the majority of cases dealt with by juvenile courts. Both State and Federal courts dismissed cases, Federal courts usually upon preliminary hearing before the United States commissioner. Summarizing the dispositions made by courts of all types in the 1,014 cases, it is found that the Federal grand jury made a return of " no bill " in 79, the cases against 31 children were nol-prossed by the United States district attorney, 68 cases were dismissed, 137 children were placed on probation, 24 were given suspended sentences, 15 others were given suspended sentences and placed on probation, 14 were placed in the custody of the United States marshal for one day, 77 were fined, 417 were committed to institutions and jails, other dispositions were made in the case of 11 children, and dispositions were not reported for 141.

Of the 553 cases before United States district courts, the disposition of which was reported, the children were committed to institutions in 52.3 per cent; in 24.4 per cent other disposition was made, in 9 per cent the case was dismissed, and in 14.3 per cent no bill was returned by the grand jury. In the 289 cases in which commitments were made the children were committed as follows:

Total	289
National Training School for Boys [4]	124
State reformatories [5]	37
State industrial schools	16
Private institutions	1
Jails [6]	94
Other institutions [6]	17

It is significant to note that the commitments to jails formed the second largest group.

The following list shows other dispositions made by the United States district courts:

Total	135
Cases nol-prossed	31
Fined	76
Custody of the United States marshal	14
Informal probation	12
Suspended sentence and probation [7]	1
Other disposition	1

---

[4] Four also fined.
[5] One also fined.
[6] Ten were also fined, and one was ordered to pay costs.
[7] Case was before the Supreme Court of the District of Columbia, where probation is provided for.

Of the cases referred to the juvenile and other State courts, 5.6 per cent were dismissed, commitments were made in 40 per cent, and 54.4 per cent were disposed of otherwise. The following list shows the institutions to which the 128 children committed by juvenile and other State courts were sent:

```
    Total _____  128
                                                                     ———
National Training School for Boys*_____    2
State reformatories_____   18
State industrial schools_____   68
Private institutions_____    8
Jails*_____    5
Other institutions_____   27
```

Of the 174 cases in which disposition other than commitment was made by juvenile and other State courts, the child was placed on probation in 125 cases,[10] in 24 cases sentence was suspended, in 14 sentence was suspended and the child was placed on probation, in 10 some other disposition was made, and 1 child was fined.

Disposition was not reported in 123 cases before the Federal courts, in a considerable number of cases the final disposition not having been made at the time of this study. Of the juvenile-court cases, the disposition was not reported for 18.

Dispositions and types of offenses.

In a majority of the cases of larceny of mail, of post-office larceny, and of "stubbing" tried by the Federal courts, the children were committed to institutions; about one-third of the cases of larceny of mail referred to juvenile and other State courts resulted in commitments. No special relation seemed to exist between type of offense and disposition made in the Federal courts, each court following its own policy. In the juvenile courts disposition was based usually upon the child's need rather than upon the type of offense.

Ages and types of dispositions.

Of the children before Federal courts for whom disposition was reported, a larger proportion of those under 14 years of age than of those 14 to 17 years were committed to institutions—60.6 per cent as compared with 51 per cent. In only 1 of the 5 cases involving children under 10 years of age was the child committed to an institution; of the 66 children 10 to 13 years of age, 42 were sent to institutions; and of the 478 children 14 to 17 years of age, 244 were committed. Other dispositions and expedients used by the Federal

---

* Committed by the Juvenile Court of the District of Columbia, the National Training School being the institution receiving commitments of delinquent boys from that court.
* Two also fined.
[10] One also fined.

courts were reported for 28 children under 14 years of age, and for 234 of those in the group from 14 to 17 years.

The largest number of children before juvenile and other State courts were 14 and 15 years of age, and the next largest number were between the ages of 16 and 17 years, inclusive. In each of these groups more children were committed than were placed on probation, of the former group 40 being committed and 37 placed on probation while of the latter 47 were committed and 34 were placed on probation. In the group under 14 years of age before juvenile or other State courts more children were placed on probation than were committed to institutions.

Length of commitment.

Commitments made by the United States district courts were in the majority of cases for definite terms, only 13 of the 289 commitments being for indeterminate periods or during minority. In contrast, 66 of the 128 commitments by juvenile and other State courts were for indeterminate periods and 25 during minority—a total of 91. The largest number of commitments by the Federal courts were for two years but less than three, 54 not being reported. Further details as to the length of commitment in the cases before the two types of courts are shown in Table 6.

TABLE 6.—*Term of commitment and type of court; children arrested in 1918 and 1919 for violating postal laws, and committed to institutions.*

Term of commitment.	Children violating postal laws who were committed to institutions.				
	Total.	By United States district courts.		By Juvenile and other State courts.	
		Number.	Per cent distribution.	Number.	Per cent distribution.
Total...............................	[1] 404	[2] 284	100.0	[3] 120	100.0
Indeterminate...........................	68	2	.7	66	55.0
During minority.........................	36	11	3.9	25	20.8
Definite terms less than minority....................	300	271	95.4	29	24.2
Less than 1 month...........................	36	33	....	3	....
1 month, less than 3...........................	53	47	....	6	....
3 months, less than 6...........................	15	13	....	2	....
6 months, less than 12...........................	23	19	....	4	....
1 year, less than 2...........................	51	45	....	6	....
2 years, less than 3...........................	55	54	....	1	....
3 years, less than 4...........................	40	34	....	6	....
4 years, less than 5....................	12	12	....	....	....
5 years and over...........................	15	14	....	1	....

[1] Excluding 13 for whom length of commitment was not reported.
[2] Excluding 5 for whom length of commitment was not reported.
[3] Excluding 8 for whom length of commitment was not reported.

Indictment.

Of the 1,108 cases of postal violations 658 were reported as presented to United States grand juries. The remaining 450 cases included those in which no court action was taken, those disposed of in preliminary hearings before United States commissioners, those presented to United States district courts by filing information (as is permissible in cases of misdemeanors), and cases heard by State courts. In 84.2 per cent of the 575 cases in which the finding of the grand jury was reported, a bill of indictment was returned, and in only 15.8 per cent of the cases was "no bill" returned. Of the 38 cases of children under 10 years of age, only 8 were presented to United States grand juries; 5 resulted in indictment, 2 in no indictment, and in 1 case the finding was not reported. The facts regarding indictment and age at apprehension are given in Table 7.

TABLE 7.—*Age at apprehension and grand jury finding; children arrested in 1918 and 1919 for violating postal laws.*

Age at apprehension.	Total.	Children violating postal laws.								Cases not presented to United States grand jury.[1]
		Cases presented to United States grand jury.								
		Total.	Finding reported.						Finding not reported.	
			Total.	No bill of indictment returned.		Bill of indictment returned.				
				Number.	Per cent.	Number.	Per cent.			
Total....................	1,108	658	575	91	15.8	484	84.2	83		450
Under 10 years..............	38	8	7	2	....	5	....	1		30
10 to 11 years.................	70	20	15	......	....	15	....	5		50
12 to 13 years.................	150	56	51	8	....	43	....	5		94
14 to 15 years.................	308	175	155	28	18.1	127	81.9	20		133
16 to 17 years.................	532	395	345	53	15.4	292	84.6	50		137
Not reported, but under 18 years......................	10	4	2	......	....	2	....	2		6

[1] These cases include those in which no court action was taken, those presented to the U. S. district courts on information filed, and cases before State courts.

TIME BETWEEN APPREHENSION AND DISPOSITION.

The length of time between arrest and final disposition is usually much longer in Federal court cases than in cases before juvenile and other State courts. The cases heard in the Federal courts must frequently wait a month or possibly longer until the court meets near the residence of the child; or, when there is a crowded calendar, the more serious cases are given preference, and the juvenile cases are postponed until the next term of court; or the necessity of presenting the case to the grand jury lengthens the period.

The tendency in juvenile courts has been to hear cases as soon as possible after arrest, the period of time between arrest and hearing rarely exceeding one week, though cases may be continued for a somewhat longer period for final disposition.

The time between apprehension and disposition in 544 cases before United States district courts is shown below:

	Number.	Per cent distribution.
Total [1]	544	100.0
Less than 2 weeks	90	16.5
2 weeks, less than 1 month	66	12.1
1 month, less than 2	107	19.7
2 to 3 months	131	24.1
4 to 5 months	55	10.1
6 to 7 months	40	7.4
8 to 9 months	17	3.1
10 to 11 months	11	2.0
1 year or over	27	5.0

Of the 315 cases referred to juvenile and other State courts in which time between apprehension and disposition was known, only 2 cases were reported in which the intervening period was over 6 months, being from 10 to 11 months in 1 case and 1 year or over in the other. The majority of these cases (235) were heard within two weeks from date of arrest. The following list gives the details of this information for the 315 cases:

	Number.	Per cent distribution.
Total	315	100.0
Less than 2 weeks	235	74.6
2 weeks, less than 1 month	36	11.4
1 month, less than 2	11	3.5
2 to 3 months	25	7.9
4 to 5 months	6	1.9
10 to 11 months	1	0.3
1 year or over	1	0.3

In some of the Federal court cases the long interval is due to the policy of continuing cases from time to time as a substitute for probation or as a means of handling the case without commitment. Continuance was reported in 117, or 17.3 per cent, of the 676 cases, the larger number of such cases occurring among those in which intervals of more than six months between apprehension and disposition were reported.

In 25 of the 117 continued cases it was reported that continuance was pending the child's good behavior or to allow for probation informally arranged; 25 were continued for other reasons; and in

---

[1] Excluding 132 cases in which time between apprehension and disposition was not reported.

67 cases the reason was not reported. The length of time between arrest and disposition in the 117 Federal court cases continued is given below:

Total	117
2 weeks, less than 1 month	1
1 month, less than 2	2
2 to 3 months	4
6 to 7 months	9
8 to 9 months	10
10 to 11 months	4
1 year and over	15
Interval not reported	72

Only 3.8 per cent of the cases heard by juvenile and other State courts were reported continued—two on informal probation, six for other reasons, and five for reasons not stated.

DETENTION.

Number detained.

The types of detention used by United States district courts and by juvenile and other State courts before trial or pending admission to institutions were reported in 348 cases—260 heard by United States district courts and 88 by juvenile and other State courts. In 88 cases it was reported that there was no detention; 66 of these were in United States district courts and 22 in juvenile and other State courts. Of the 79 children in whose cases there was no court action 20 were known to have been detained, 17 of them in jail. No information as to detention was available for 578 cases in which court action was taken; in 123 cases children were remanded in default of bond, but it was not reported whether they were actually detained. The number reported detained is probably very much lower than the actual number held. Most of the information concerning detention was obtained from institution and jail records, the former in most cases showing only the boys' statements, since the court papers sent to the institutions seldom reported on the matter.

Type of detention.

Of the 326 children tried before United States district courts for whom information was obtained as to detention, 260—79.8 per cent— were detained. Jail detention was practically the only method used and was reported for 91.2 per cent of the 260 cases. Of the 27 children detained by State courts other than juvenile 24 were reported detained in jail. In contrast, only 16 of the 61 children detained by juvenile courts were held in jail. Table 8 shows the types of detention used by Federal courts and by juvenile and other State courts, together with the ages of the children.

TABLE 8.—*Type of detention used by Federal, juvenile, and other State courts, according to age at apprehension; children arrested in 1918 and 1919 for violating postal laws.*

Type of court and age at apprehension.	Children violating postal laws who were reported as to detention.						
	Total.[1]	Not detained.	Detained.				
			Total.	In jail.	In juvenile detention home or S. P. C. C. shelter.	In other place of detention.	Place of detention not reported.
Total......................	436	88	348	277	51	18	2
Children before United States district courts..................	326	66	260	[2]237	9	12	2
Under 10 years............	2	....	2	2	....	....	....
10 to 11 years..............	9	2	7	5	....	1	1
12 to 13 years..............	34	5	29	25	1	3	....
14 to 15 years..............	84	16	68	[3]57	5	6	....
16 to 17 years..............	196	43	153	[4]147	3	2	1
Age not reported...........	1	....	1	1	....	....	....
Children before juvenile and other State courts.............	110	22	88	40	42	6	....
Under 10 years..............	4	2	2	1	1	....	....
10 to 11 years...............	16	6	10	3	7	....	....
12 to 13 years	23	5	18	6	9	3	....
14 to 15 years................	36	7	29	8	19	2	....
16 to 17 years................	31	2	29	22	6	1	....

[1] Not including 79 children involved in cases in which there was no court action, 15 in which court action was not reported, and 578 not reported as to detention. Twenty of the 79 children for whom there was no court action were known to have been detained, 17 of them in jail.
[2] Includes 6 children detained in jail part of the time, and in juvenile detention home or Society for the Prevention of Cruelty to Children shelter the remainder of the time.
[3] Includes 4 children mentioned in note 2.
[4] Includes 2 children mentioned in note 2.

Because of aversion to placing juveniles in jail or because State laws prohibited such detention, 21—8.1 per cent—of the 260 children whose cases were heard by Federal courts for whom the facts with reference to detention were reported, were by informal arrangement detained in juvenile detention homes, industrial schools, county detention homes (not reported as juvenile detention homes), and family boarding homes. Of the 9 children under 12 years of age, 7 were detained in jail; of those 16 and 17 years of age 96.1 per cent were reported detained in jail.

Of the 79 children with regard to whom no court action was taken 20 were reported detained between arrest and conference with the United States attorney or final decision as to method of handling the case—17 in jail, 2 in a juvenile detention home or a shelter maintained by the Society for the Prevention of Cruelty to Children, and for 1 the place of detention was not reported. In a few instances it was decided to take no action because the child had been detained in jail, and this was considered a sufficient punishment. The ages of the 17 children detained in jail were as follows:

Total _____ 17

Under 10 years of age	7
10 to 11 years	2
12 to 13 years	1
14 to 15 years	4
16 to 17 years	3

The 7 children under 10 years of age detained in jail comprised all the children in this age group in whose cases no court action was taken. The 3 children for whom detention other than jail was reported were 14 years of age or over.

Length of detention.

The longer period between apprehension and disposition in the Federal court cases necessitated longer periods of detention than were required in cases before juvenile and other State courts. Sixteen children were reported detained for four months or over. Detention was sometimes longer than the time between apprehension and disposition, since in cases of commitment to institutions the child was frequently returned to jail to await the convenience of the United States marshal in taking him to the institution. The requirement of bond for release by the Federal courts is also a factor in increasing the time of detention, since it is often difficult for the children to furnish bond; and even in cases where bond was furnished it was sometimes two or three days before it was secured. In the largest number of the 260 Federal court cases in which detention was reported—91, or 35 per cent—the child was detained less than two weeks; but a considerable number were held for longer periods, as shown in the following list.

Total _____ 260

Less than 2 weeks	91
2 weeks, less than 1 month	32
1 month, less than 2	31
2 to 3 months	27
4 to 5 months	11
6 to 7 months	5
Length of detention not reported	63

Eighty-eight children were reported detained by juvenile and other State courts; all but 1 of the 35 for whom length of detention was reported were detained less than two weeks.

It is of interest to compare the length of detention with the length of time between apprehension and disposition. Of the 197 children before Federal courts in whose cases this comparison was possible, 66.5 per cent were held only part of the time between apprehension and final disposition, and 33.5 per cent were detained for the entire period. In a majority of the latter cases the time between apprehension and disposition was less than four months. Table 9 shows the duration of detention for cases before the United States district courts.

TABLE 9.—*Time between apprehension and disposition and duration of detention; children arrested in 1918 and 1919 for violating postal laws, and brought before United States district courts.*

Time between apprehension and disposition.	Children violating postal laws and brought before U. S. district courts.							
	Total.	Reported as to detention.						Not reported as to detention.
		Total.	Not detained.	Detained.				
				Total.	Entire time.	Part time.	Length of detention not reported.	
Total.............................	676	326	66	260	66	131	63	350
Less than 2 weeks...................	90	40	12	28	13	7	8	50
2 weeks, less than 1 month..........	66	30	3	27	11	9	7	36
1 month...........................	107	60	4	56	11	25	20	47
2 to 3 months......................	131	70	8	62	20	34	8	61
4 to 5 months......................	55	29	13	16	8	6	2	26
6 to 7 months......................	40	23	10	13	2	9	2	17
8 to 9 months......................	17	8	3	5	....	5	....	9
10 to 11 months....................	11	6	1	5	....	4	1	5
1 year or over.....................	27	10	1	9	....	7	2	17
Not reported......................	132	50	11	39	1	25	13	82

The duration of detention was reported in only 35 of the 88 juvenile and other State court cases. In 25 of these 35 cases the child was detained the entire time, the period being less than two weeks in 24 cases, and two weeks but less than a month in 1 case.

SOCIAL HISTORY.

Information regarding social history—including previous delinquency records, school attendance, employment, home conditions, and mode of living—was available from the post-office records in comparatively few cases. The information obtained from the Post Office Department was supplemented, however, from court and institutional records. Reports were obtained as to previous delinquency for only 391 of the 1,108 children, information as to school attendance for 573 children, employment prior to arrest for 718, mode of living for 365, and home conditions for 351 children.

Previous delinquency records.

For the purpose of this study a previous delinquency record has been taken to mean that the child had been arrested previously, since reports on the post-office records are made in terms of the number of arrests. Of the 391 children for whom information was reported as to whether or not they had been previously delinquent, 187 had been arrested 'previously, and 204 were first offenders. Of the 187, 81 had been arrested once; 24, twice; 11, three times; 3, four times; and 4, five times or more; the number of arrests was not reported in 64 cases, though the child was known to have been arrested at least once previously. Sixty of the 377 children for whom data with reference to previous institutional commitments were available were reported to have been committed to institutions prior to the postal violation, and five of these children had had more than one such commitment.

Over half—54.3 per cent—of the 186 first offenders for whom disposition by Federal, juvenile, or other State court was reported, were committed to institutions—Federal, State, or private—and to jails. This was 16 per cent less than the percentage (70.3) of those committed who were known to have been arrested previously. Over three-fourths—78.1 per cent—of the first offenders before United States district courts were committed to institutions, as compared with only one-sixth—16.7 per cent—of the first offenders before juvenile and other State courts. The proportion placed on probation was larger for first offenders than for children previously arrested. The dispositions are shown in table 10 for the 344 cases in which court action was reported, and in which information was obtained with regard to whether the child had been arrested previously.

TABLE 10.—*Disposition of case, previous delinquency record, and type of court; children arrested in 1918 and 1919 for violating postal laws.*

Disposition of case.	Children violating postal laws whose previous delinquency records were reported.						
	Total.	First offenders.			Arrested previously.		
		Total.	Before United States district courts.	Before juvenile and other State courts.	Total.	Before United States district courts.	Before juvenile and other State courts.
Total......................	[1] 344	186	114	72	158	[2] 105	53
Commitment to institution.....	212	101	89	12	111	81	30
Probation.......................	68	48	2	46	20	6	14
Other disposition...............	64	37	23	14	27	18	9

[1] Exclusive of 11 children who were first offenders and 7 children who had been arrested previously in whose cases no court action was reported
[2] Includes 8 children before U. S. district courts, whose cases were later transferred to juvenile courts.

School attendance.

Of the 573 children for whom information with reference to school attendance was obtained, only 163 were reported to be attending school at the time of their arrest. Included in these are some cases of boys or girls arrested during vacation but reported as attending school during the school term; doubtless this was also true of a number among the 410 reported as not attending school. Three children under 10 years of age. 7 who were 10 or 11 years of age, and 15 aged 12 or 13 years were reported as not attending school, making a total of 25 under 14 years of age not attending. Table 11 gives the school attendance according to age distribution.

TABLE 11.—*Age at apprehension and school attendance; children arrested in 1918 and 1919 for violating postal laws.*

Age at apprehension.	Children violating postal laws.			
	Total.	Attending school.	Not attending school.	School attendance not reported.
Total..	1,108	163	410	535
Under 10 years................................	38	9	3	26
10 to 11 years.................................	70	27	7	36
12 to 13 years.................................	150	37	15	98
14 to 15 years.................................	308	53	99	156
16 to 17 years.................................	532	34	283	215
Not reported..................................	10	3	3	4

Employment.

Regulations regarding employment of children in the postal service.—The postal laws and regulations contain little specific reference to the employment of children, but the following excerpt, in connection with the fact that letter carriers and postal clerks are required by civil-service rules to be 18 years of age or over, indicates that it is not the intention of the post-office authorities that boys under 16 years of age be employed as special-delivery messengers in cities:[11]

At city delivery offices postmasters should employ substitute carriers and clerks, preferably the former, instead of boys, as special-delivery messengers, where the volume of such business is sufficient to warrant these employees in taking up the work and the conditions are otherwise favorable; but boys 16 years of age or over may be so employed when, in the judgment of the postmaster, circumstances require it or he is of the opinion that the efficiency of the service will be promoted thereby.

Number employed and type of employment.—Three hundred and sixteen of the 1.108 children were reported employed prior to arrest, 402 were not employed, and no report concerning employment was obtained in 390 cases. It was impossible to make a detailed classi-

[11] Postal Laws and Regulations, 1913, sec. 864, par. 1, Washington, D. C.

fication as to the type of employment for those outside the postal service, as they were grouped together under employment other than postal. A considerable proportion of the postal violations by juveniles may be accounted for by the temptations offered by their employment in positions where they had access to mail. Of the 316 working children, 166—52.5 per cent—were employed by the Post Office Department; of these, 95, or 57.2 per cent, were special-delivery messengers; 42, or 25.3 per cent, were clerks or substitute clerks; and 29, or 17.5 per cent, were in other types of postal service. Employment other than postal was reported for 143, or 45.3 per cent; and for 7, or 2.2 per cent, the kind of employment was not reported.

TABLE 12.—*Age and employment at time of apprehension; children arrested in 1918 and 1919 for violating postal laws.*

Employment at time of apprehension.	Children violating postal laws.						
	Total.	Under 10 years.	10–11 years.	12–13 years.	14–15 years.	16–17 years.	Age not reported.
Total......................	1,108	38	70	150	308	532	10
Total employed.................	316	....	6	14	72	222	2
In postal service............	166	....	1	1	31	132	1
Special-delivery messenger..................	95	....	1	1	18	75	....
Clerk.....................	42	....	....	....	8	34	....
Other postal service....	29	....	....	....	5	23	1
In other than postal service.	143	....	5	12	38	87	1
Employed, occupation not reported.................	7	....	....	1	3	3	....
Not employed.................	402	26	45	88	116	123	4
Not reported.................	390	12	19	48	120	187	4

Ages of those employed.—A total of 20 children under 14 years of age—the minimum working age under the majority of State child-labor laws—were reported as being employed. Some of these children may have been employed only part time or during vacation, but detailed information was obtained for very few cases. Only 2 were employed in the postal service, 17 were otherwise employed, and the kind of employment was not reported in 1 case. Reference to Table 12 will show that almost half the employed children between the ages of 14 and 16 years and three-fifths of those between 16 and 18 years of age were in the postal service. Although the general policy of the Post Office Department is not to employ children under 16 years of age, 20 per cent of the children offending against postal laws who were employed in the postal service were under that age—20 of the 95 as special-delivery messengers and 13 of the 71 in other kinds of postal service.

The number of juvenile postal employees reported as violating postal laws was greater in 1919 than in 1918 by 40 cases, the largest increase being in the number of special-delivery boys arrested, owing to the prevalence of " stubbing " in some localities during that year.

Type of employment and type of offense.—The types of offenses committed by the 166 postal employees were in all cases suggested by their type of service. The most frequent were larceny of mail and " stubbing." Over half—56.5 per cent—of the entire number of cases of larceny of mail by children employed at time of apprehension involved postal employees. The detail is given in the following list:

Total _____		166
Larceny_____		91
Of mail_____	87	
Of postal funds or property_____	1	
Other _____	3	
" Stubbing "_____		58
Embezzlement_____		8
Breaking and entering and larceny, post office_____		3
Forgery_____		2
Larceny of mail and forgery _____		2
Having stolen property in possession_____		1
Other _____		1

Larceny of mail was the offense most frequently committed by those in other than postal-service occupations; 62 of the 143 so employed committed that offense. Of the 246 children charged with post-office breaking and entering and larceny—the offense with which the second largest number of children were charged—111 were known not to be employed, no employment information was obtained for another group of 111, and 21 were known to be employed outside the postal service.

Home conditions and mode of living.

In 351 cases some information was available regarding the home conditions, and in 365 the mode of living was known. The records of the Post Office Department have been supplemented by the various institutional and court records secured. Social histories were obtained in the cities visited for those cases referred to the juvenile courts for action. One of the phases of the problem of the child offender tried by a Federal court is brought out in the comparative amount of social history obtained by Federal and juvenile courts. Because of lack of probation service very little preliminary social investigation is made in the Federal courts, except in the few courts where the judge arranges informally for it. The records of the United States attorneys and the court dockets give almost no social information; the amount obtained depends largely upon the policy of the inspectors in charge of the divisions or of the inspectors handling the cases. Investigations by the inspectors are primarily to obtain facts regarding the details of the offense and are more comparable with police investigations than with investigations by juvenile-court probation officers. However, many inspectors attempt to obtain some social information and report it to the United States attorney with a view to promoting a better understanding of the case.

Postal cases referred to juvenile or other State courts having probation systems are investigated as are other delinquency cases, and reports in such cases contain information relating to family history and home conditions. In cases committed to institutions by juvenile courts the social history is sent to the institution, but the commitment papers sent by the United States district courts give only the fact of arrest and such other facts as may be entered in the court docket. Because of this absence of social history in cases before the Federal courts, it is impossible to estimate the number of cases in which the home conditions would probably have warranted probation had there been provision for such disposition. Sufficient information to permit of analysis was obtained only in regard to the status of the parents, which was reported for 351 cases as follows:

Total children	351
Parents living together	188
Mother dead, father in home	12
Father dead, mother in home	40
Stepmother, father in home	12
Stepfather, mother in home	21
Both parents dead	20
Mother in home, father deserting	8
Father in home, mother deserting	2
Separated or divorced	18
Mother in home	10
Other	8
Home otherwise broken	14
Father in home, mother away [12]	1
Mother in home, father away [13]	13
One parent dead, other deserting	2
One parent dead, other not reported	11
One parent dead, other away [14]	3

[12] Whereabouts of mother was not reported.
[13] Includes six cases in which whereabouts of father was not reported.
[14] Includes one case in which father boarded away from home.

TABLE 13.—*Age at apprehension and mode of living; children arrested in 1918 and 1919 for violating postal laws.*

Age at apprehension.	Children violating postal laws whose mode of living was reported.					
	Total.	Mode of living.				
		Parental home.	Relative's home.	Own home, married.[1]	Living independently.	Other.
Total.............................	365	296	31	4	11	23
Under 10 years.......................	7	6	....	....	....	1
10 to 11 years.......................	27	23	3	....	....	1
12 to 13 years.......................	53	48	2	....	1	2
14 to 15 years.......................	124	99	15	....	3	7
16 to 17 years.......................	151	117	11	4	7	12
Not reported........................	3	3	....	....	....	....

[1] All girls.

For 365 children—344 boys and 21 girls—mode of living was reported. Of these, 296 were living in the parental home, at least one parent being present; 31 were in the homes of relatives; 4 girls were married and living in their own homes; 10 boys and 1 girl were living independently, 4 of these under 16 years of age. The 23 reported as living in some other manner included 6 runaways or transients, 1 in a home for dependent children, 1 away at school, 3 living with foster parents, and 1 girl living with a man to whom she was not married.

CHAPTER III. CHILDREN COMMITTED TO INSTITUTIONS.

The institutions to which the largest number of juveniles violating Federal laws are committed by the United States district courts are the National Training School for Boys (located in the District of Columbia) and certain State reformatories with which the Department of Justice contracts to receive Federal prisoners. Proportionately fewer commitments are made in cases referred to juvenile and other State courts, and the children are sent to State industrial schools or to private institutions, few being committed to State reformatories.

Two serious problems are presented by the types of institutions being used for Federal commitments of juveniles: First, the age limits of offenders received at these institutions; second, the inaccessibility of the institutions to a great majority of the courts.

The National Training School for Boys receives boys through the age of 17 years, and is the one Federal institution for juveniles only which receives violators of the Federal laws from outside the District of Columbia.[1] While the fact that this institution receives only juveniles is favorable, the great distance from most of the United States district courts creates a serious problem, not only in the expense to the Government of sending a boy to it but also in the effect of committing him to an institution so far from home. Doubtless some commitments to this school from distant States are made because the judges prefer an institution for juveniles, regardless of distance.

The State reformatories receive boys and men between the ages of 16 and 30. Where such institutions hold contracts to receive Federal cases, boys under 16 years of age and of 16 and 17 years are being confined in institutions with older men. Legally, these State reformatories are supposed to receive only first offenders, but both those visited reported that this rule was not being strictly enforced.

---

[1] The National Training School for Girls, also in the District of Columbia, is a Federal institution for juveniles, but girls outside the District are seldom committed to this institution and those committed from the Juvenile Court of the District of Columbia are committed for offenses under the juvenile-court law. During the war 15 girls were sent to the school from a southern State on the charge of immorality within the 5-mile zone of an Army camp. All but three of these girls were transferred to the woman's reformatory of another State within a few days, as the National Training School for Girls was not fitted to care for that type of case. These girls have not been included in this study, because the offense arose from a war situation, and no records of like cases were available from the other sources consulted.

Hence, besides being with older men, the boys are often thrown with so-called hardened criminals.

Except the New York State Reformatory at Elmira, which receives Federal prisoners from the State of New York only, the institutions receive commitments from outside the State in which the reformatory is located.

NATIONAL TRAINING SCHOOL FOR BOYS.

Number of boys committed and types of offenses.

Two hundred and forty-seven boys arrested during 1918 and 1919 for violations of Federal laws were reported committed to the National Training School for Boys, including 21 cases not committed until 1920. The number of commitments of children arrested during 1918 was larger than for 1919, 141 for the former year and 106 for the latter. Of the boys committed, 187 were white and 60 were colored.

Boys are also committed to this institution from the Juvenile Court of the District of Columbia for offenses under the juvenile-court law, but these commitments were not comparable with those included in this study and are omitted.

Of the 247 boys, only 4 were committed from the District of Columbia, 1 by the Supreme Court of the District (which has the powers of a United States district court), and 3 by the juvenile court, to which the cases had been referred by the United States attorney of the District on preferred charges; the remaining 243 boys were committed by United States district attorneys in 24 different States. The extreme distances from which many children were committed are evident from the following list:

Total	247	Mississippi	8
		Missouri	5
Alabama	26	New Jersey	3
Connecticut	2	New York	19
Delaware	1	North Carolina	18
District of Columbia	4	Ohio	10
Florida	16	Oklahoma	3
Georgia	18	Pennsylvania	7
Illinois	4	South Carolina	17
Kansas	8	Tennessee	12
Kentucky	9	Texas	9
Louisiana	18	Virginia	8
Maryland	5	West Virginia	14
Michigan	3		

The number of boys committed for postal violations is only slightly larger than the number committed for other offenses—132, as compared with 115. Of the latter, interstate-commerce offenses were the most frequent, there being 74 cases. The numbers committed for the various offenses other than postal are listed as follows:

Total	115

Interstate-commerce violations	74
Internal-revenue violations	12
National defense act violations	7
Railroad offenses (during time when railroads were under Federal control)	7
Larceny of United States property	5
Forgery (to defraud the Government)	3
Other [2]	7

Of the postal offenses, larceny of mail and post-office breaking and entering and larceny were the specific charges for which the largest number of boys were committed, there being 63 commitments for the former and 39 for the latter. The numbers committed to the National Training School for Boys for the various types of postal offenses were as follows:

Total [3]	132

Larceny of mail [4]	63
Breaking and entering and larceny, post office	39
Forgery	10
Wrongful use of mails	6
Embezzlement	3
Larceny of postal funds or property	3
Attempted robbery	2
Breaking and entering, post office	2
Detaining or destroying mail	2
Larceny of mail and forgery	1
" Stubbing " special-delivery letters	1

The following are instances of some of the less serious offenses by juveniles against Federal laws, for which they were tried and committed by Federal courts:

(1) A 14-year-old boy was committed to the National Training School for Boys for burning a haystack which was on United States property.

(2) Another 14-year-old boy was committed to the National Training School for larceny of bicycle tires belonging to the United States.

---

[2] Includes one case each of deserting the Army, trespassing on United States property, purchasing such property unlawfully, embezzlement, destroying war material, and violation of the war-savings and drug acts.

[3] No post-office record could be found for 10 of these cases. Two cases not included here were reported by the Post Office Department, but there was no record of the children's having been received at the school, and doubtless the order of commitment was changed and the change not reported to the postal authorities.

[4] Larceny of mail from lock boxes—23 cases—and of parcel-post packages—12 cases—were the most numerous of this general class of offenses.

(3) A third boy stole a bottle of whisky from a box car. He was charged with violating the interstate-commerce act and committed for three years.

(4) Taking a ride on a hand car which was railroad property was the offense for which a 16-year-old boy was committed to the National Training School for two years. It was his first offense.

Ages of boys committed.

Boys are received by the National Training School through the age of 17 years. As will be seen by the following list, over four-fifths of the 247 boys committed for Federal offenses during the two years of the study were between the ages of 14 and 17 years, inclusive; 44 boys were under 14 years, and 1 boy was 18 at commitment, having become 18 after his arrest.

	Number.	Per cent distribution.
Total	247	100. 0
Under 10 years	1	.4
10 to 11 years	18	7.3
12 to 13 years	25	10.1
14 to 15 years	93	37.7
16 to 17 years	108	43.7
18 years	1	.4
Not reported, but under 16 years	1	.4

Term of commitment and parole.

Commitments to this institution from the United States district courts are, with few exceptions, for definite periods of time, which may terminate before or after the completion of the child's minority. Therefore in this institution, which is primarily for juveniles, boys often remain beyond the age of 21 years, especially in cases where no parole is earned or where parole is violated and the boys are returned.[5]

Of the 247 boys committed for Federal offenses, only 11 were committed until they should reach majority, and only 3 for indeterminate periods. The variance in terms of commitment is due to the different policies of the judges in sentencing for maximum or for minimum terms. The largest number of boys (79) received sentences of two but less than three years. One boy barely 14 years of age was committed for seven years for robbing a post office—his first offense, so far as known. Of the boys under 14, only 1 was committed for less than a year and the remainder for various terms between two and five but less than six years. Table 14 shows these terms by age at commitment.

---

[5] Report of Board of Trustees of the National Training School for Boys for the Fiscal Year Ended June 30, 1919, p. 4. Washington, D. C., 1920.

TABLE 14.—*Term of commitment, by age at commitment; children committed to National Training School for Boys for Federal offenses in 1918 and 1919.*

Age at commitment.	Children committed to National Training School for Boys.											
		Term of commitment.										
	Total.	Less than 1 year.	1 year, less than 2.	2 years, less than 3.	3 years, less than 4.	4 years, less than 5.	5 years, less than 6.	7 years, less than 8.	During minority.	Indeterminate.	Not reported.
Total.............	247	9	42	79	43	23	12	1	11	3	24
Under 10 years........	1			1							
10 to 11 years..........	18	......	2	7	5	2	......	......	1	......	1
12 to 13 years..........	25	1	1	4	9	4	3	......	3	......	......
14 to 15 years..........	93	3	15	32	14	6	7	1	5	2	8
16 to 17 years..........	108	5	24	34	15	10	2	......	2	1	15
18 years...............	1		......	[1] 1							
Not reported, but under 16 years..........	1					1					

[1] Became 18 years of age between apprehension and commitment.

The length of commitment dated from the day the order was made by the court, regardless of the date upon which the boy actually arrived at the institution. As boys were committed to the school by courts located at great distances from it, the interval between court disposition and admission to the school varied, being in 34 cases one month or over. The intervals between commitment and admission were as follows:

Total..............	247	2 months..............	7
		3 months..............	1
Less than 1 week..............	80	4 months..............	1
1 week, less than 2..............	68	5 months..............	1
2 weeks, less than 1 month........	63	7 months..............	1
1 month..............	23	Interval not reported............	2

Of the boys who waited two months or more, eight were from Alabama, one was from Illinois, one from Kentucky, one from Ohio, and one from Tennessee.

Often the boy is detained after court commitment until arrangements can be made for the United States marshal of his district to accompany him to the institution. Twenty-four boys were returned to jail after commitment, while five who had not been detained in jail pending hearing were so held thereafter.

Boys may earn parole by the end of a year from the date of commitment, upon satisfactory record according to the requirements of the school. This study was made early in 1920, and therefore very few of the boys sentenced in 1919 were eligible for parole. Only 14 of the 247 boys were reported as paroled; in 13 of these cases the offense was committed in 1918, and in 1 in 1919. At the time of the study, 41 boys had been discharged, and 36 were reported to have escaped.

Detention prior to commitment.

The records of the National Training School show detention of the boys prior to commitment, but the accuracy of the figures is qualified by the fact that this information is obtained only from the boys' statements in the initial interviews at the school. Of the boys committed, 192—77.7 per cent—were reported as having been detained part or all of the time between apprehension and disposition; 176, or 91.7 per cent of those detained, were held in jails; the remaining 16 were detained as follows: 9 in a juvenile detention home or a shelter maintained by the Society for the Prevention of Cruelty to Children, 3 in a house of detention (not reported whether or not a special juvenile detention home), 1 in an industrial school, 1 held by the juvenile court (place of detention not reported), and in 2 cases the type of detention was not reported. Ninety-five of the 132 boys committed for postal offenses were detained previous to commitment, 82 of the 95 reporting jail detention. Ninety-seven of the 115 committed for other offenses reported detention; 94, or all but 3, were detained in jails, the 3 reporting detention in a juvenile detention home.

Three-fifths of those detained in jails were under 16 years of age. The age distribution of the 176 boys reporting jail detention is shown as follows:

	Number.	Per cent distribution.
Total	176	100. 0
Under 16 years	105	59. 7
Under 10 years	1	
10 to 11 years	13	
12 to 13 years	28	
14 to 15 years	63	
16 to 17 years	71	40. 3

The long periods of detention reported were due partly to the length of time between apprehension and commitment in Federal courts and partly to the difficulty in obtaining bonds. In all but 9 of the 192 cases in which the boy was detained, length of detention was reported. In 52.5 per cent of the 183 cases, the boy was detained for one month or over. Length of detention is shown below:

	Number.	Per cent distribution.
Total	183	100.0
Less than 1 month	87	47.5
Less than 2 weeks	54	
2 weeks, less than 1 month	33	
One month or over	96	52.5
1 month	43	
2 months	25	
3 months	12	
4 months	9	
5 months	3	
6 months	3	
10 months	1	

Previous delinquency records.

The results of the absence of probation in the Federal courts are shown in the number of boys committed to the National Training School upon their first offense. many of whom would doubtless have been placed on probation by a juvenile court. Over half (136) of the 247 boys committed reported commitment upon their first offenses; 66—over one-fourth—reported one previous arrest; 27—one-tenth—more than one but less than five; and 6 reported five or more previous arrests. The information secured with reference to previous arrests is as follows:

	Number.	Per cent distribution.
Total	247	100.0
No previous arrests	136	55.1
1 previous arrest [1]	66	26.7
More than 1, less than 5 arrests [2]	27	10.9
5 or more arrests [3]	6	2.4
Number of arrests not reported [4]	12	4.9

Since these figures are based on the boys' statements upon entering the school, the proportion reported as previously arrested is undoubtedly an understatement of the facts. Eighteen reported previous institutional records, and 3 had served previous terms in city jails.

[1] Eight with previous institutional records.
[2] Seven with previous institutional records.
[3] Three with previous institutional records.
[4] Three having several previous terms in jail.

School and employment records.

School and employment records previous to commitment were also taken from the boys' statements upon admission to the school. Of the 184 boys who reported on school attendance, 146, or 59.1 per cent, were not attending school; 24 of these were under 14 years of age, 56 were 14 but under 16, and 66 were 16 but under 18. Nine of these boys reported that they had never attended school; of these, 3 were 12 but under 14 years of age, 2 were 14 but under 16, and 4 were 16 but under 18. Only 38 stated that they were attending school.

It was impossible to tabulate the types of employment, other than postal service, because of the indefiniteness of the information. The number of boys reporting that they were employed prior to commitment was 131; 55 reported that they were not employed, and 51 did not report as to employment. Of the 53 boys under 14 years of age, 24—not quite half—were reported as employed, but none were employed in the postal service.

Sixty-nine of the 132 boys committed for violating postal laws were employed, only 11 of these being in postal service of some kind; 43 were not employed; and for 20 the employment was not reported. Of the 115 boys who had been committed for other offenses, 72 were employed, 12 were not employed, and 31 did not report whether or not they were employed. Table 15 gives the data on the employment of the boys.

TABLE 15.—*Employment prior to commitment, by age at apprehension; children committed to the National Training School for Boys for postal and for other Federal offenses in 1918 and 1919.*

Age at apprehension.	Total.	Children committed to National Training School for Boys.											
		For postal offenses.								For other Federal offenses.			
		Total.	Employed prior to commitment.				In other employment.	Not employed.	Not reported as to employment.	Total.	Employed.	Not employed.	Not reported as to employment.
			Total.	In postal service.									
				Total.	Special-delivery messengers.	Clerks and other postal employees.							
Total	247	132	69	11	5	6	58	43	20	115	72	12	31
Under 14 years	53	32	13	.....	.....	.....	13	15	4	21	11	4	6
14 to 15 years	99	61	30	5	3	2	25	23	8	38	24	7	7
16 to 17 years	94	39	26	6	2	4	20	5	8	55	37	1	17
Not reported	1	.....	.....	.....	.....	.....	.....	.....	.....	1	.....	.....	1

Social history.

Very little is known of the social histories of the boys coming to the school, as the commitment papers did not include these facts. Each boy upon entrance to the institution was questioned as to his parents' status and his home environment, and the records showed only the facts thus obtained—in most cases very meager. It was known that 132 boys came from homes where the parents, or the parent and step-parent, were living together; 24 reported both parents dead; 68, one parent dead; and 16 stated that their parents were separated or divorced, 3 of the latter having one parent in a hospital for the insane. Seven did not report as to status of parents.

TWO STATE REFORMATORIES.

Number of boys committed and types of offenses.

The New York State Reformatory at Elmira receives Federal commitments from the State of New York only, and consequently fewer juveniles were committed to that institution than to the Iowa State Reformatory at Anamosa. Ten boys were committed to the New York reformatory during the period covered by this study, and 29 to the Iowa reformatory. Five of those sent to the New York reformatory were committed for offenses against postal laws and 5 for other offenses, 2 of the latter having been committed for violations of the interstate-commerce act, 1 for grand larceny, and 2 for offenses not specified. Twenty-two boys were committed to the Iowa reformatory for postal and 7 for other Federal offenses; the latter included 1 committed for internal-revenue violations, 3 for interstate-commerce violations, and 3 for whom the type of offense was not reported. All but one of those committed to both institutions were committed by United States district courts.

The following list shows the localities from which the boys were committed to the Iowa reformatory, and the number from each:

Total	29
California, southern district	1
Illinois, northern district (Chicago)	13
Maryland	2
Ohio	6
Washington	1
West Virginia	6

The fact that boys were sent to the Iowa institution from States as far distant as California, Washington, West Virginia, and Maryland, shows the lack of suitable arrangements for the commitment of juveniles to institutions within easy access of their homes and the courts committing.

Ages of boys committed.

No boys under 16 years of age were committed to the New York reformatory, and only 3 under that age were committed to the Iowa institution. The largest number (24) were 17 years of age, 11 were 16, 3 were 15, and 1 was 18, having attained this age between arrest and commitment. The following list shows the age distribution of those committed to these institutions:

Total	39
New York State Reformatory, Elmira	10
16 years	1
17 years	8
18 years	1
Iowa State Reformatory, Anamosa	29
15 years	3
16 years	10
17 years	16

Term of commitment, and parole.

The terms of commitment to both these institutions were for definite periods, except in two cases of commitment during minority to the Iowa reformatory. Of the 10 boys committed to the New York reformatory, 1 was committed for a term of five years, 1 for two years and six months, 3 for two years, and 5 for one year but less than two.

Commitments to the Iowa reformatory were in general for shorter terms, there being 12 for periods of six months or less. The longest term was for three years, there being 6 of that length; 4 boys were committed for two years, 5 for one year, and 2 during minority.

Conditions affecting parole are the same for the Federal as for State cases, except that in the case of Federal offenders a parole, after recommendation by the superintendent and the board of parole for the institution, must be approved by the Attorney General of the United States. Parole is earned through good conduct while in the institution. In addition, no prisoner at the New York reformatory may be paroled until he has a position in the line of work for which he has trained while in the institution and approved by the parole officer in the district to which he is going.

Three boys were paroled from the New York institution and five from the Iowa institution. The boys serving short sentences of six months or less would not of course be eligible for parole.

Detention prior to commitment.

Detention pending hearing was reported in the case of only one boy committed to the New York institution. The records of the Iowa institution did not give any facts regarding detention prior to commitment; but information from other sources, such as post-office and jail records, showed that seven boys committed to the Iowa reformatory were detained, six of them in county jails, the place of detention being not reported for one boy. All seven were postal offenders and are included in the discussion under detention in the section on postal offenses.

Previous delinquency records.

As in the case of boys committed to the National Training School, a majority (23) of those committed to the two reformatories were first offenders. One boy was committed for one year and one month for breaking into a freight car and stealing a bottle of milk—his first offense. Because the bottle of milk was stolen from a freight car in interstate shipment the case was taken to the Federal court, where there were no facilities for placing him on probation, had the judge desired to do so. Of the 15 reporting previous arrest, 7 reported only one, 3 reported two, and 4 reported three or more. For 1 boy the number of previous arrests was not reported; and for another there was no report as to whether or not he had been previously arrested. One boy had previously served terms in two institutions.

School and employment records.

All but 7 of the 39 boys committed to the two reformatories reported that they were employed prior to commitment. All 10 committed to the New York institution were employed in occupations other than postal service. Of the 22 postal offenders committed to the Iowa institution, 12 were in postal service as special-delivery messengers or temporary substitute clerks at the time the offense was committed; 1 was in the Navy; 5 were laborers or mechanics; for 1 the type of employment was not reported, and 3 reported no employment. Three of the 7 committed for other offenses were employed, and 4 reported no employment.

Only one of the seven boys who reported no employment stated that he was attending school prior to commitment, there being no report on this point for the other six.

Previous to the completion in December, 1919, of the Woman's Reformatory at Rockwell City, Iowa, the Iowa State Reformatory had a woman's department, and six girls under 18 years of age were committed there for violation of the section of the national defense act relating to immorality around Army camps. These girls came from Alabama, Florida, and South Carolina. Three of the girls were 16, and three were 17 years of age. All were committed for a definite term of one year, and the three who had not been discharged were transferred to Rockwell City in December, 1919.

CHAPTER IV. CHILDREN VIOLATING FEDERAL LAWS IN EIGHT LOCALITIES.

NUMBER OF CASES IN EACH LOCALITY.

In order to obtain information concerning the extent of the problem and the various methods of procedure in the United States district courts as well as the juvenile and other State courts, eight localities were selected for special study, as follows: District of Columbia, Maryland, Pennsylvania (eastern district), New York (eastern and southern districts), Massachusetts, Indiana, and Illinois (northern district).[1]

Selection of these localities was made from information received from the Post Office Department supplemented by data from the National Training School for Boys. The places selected were those in which there were the largest number of cases coming under the scope of this study and which were representative of different parts of the country and of the different policies in handling Federal cases involving juveniles.

In this section of the report particular attention is called to the disposition made of juvenile cases other than commitment to the three institutions included in the study, and to the length of time between the child's arrest and the final disposition. Short-term commitments to jail, placing the offender in the custody of the United States marshal for a day, fines, a few commitments to local industrial schools and private institutions, and informal probation were dispositions made frequently by the Federal courts.

The total number of cases reported for these eight localities was 417, of which 328 involved postal offenses, and 90 other offenses. These figures are underestimates of the problem in each locality, because of inability to obtain information as to the exact number of juveniles committing offenses other than postal, owing to absence of age data in the records of the United States attorneys and the Federal courts. The postal cases reported probably include all such

---

[1] The territory included was as follows: (1) District of Columbia; (2) Maryland (entire State); (3) eastern district of Pennsylvania: Berks, Bucks, Chester, Delaware, Lancaster, Lehigh, Montgomery, Northampton, Philadelphia, and Schuylkill Counties; (4) eastern district of New York: Kings (Brooklyn Borough), Nassau, Queens (Queens Borough), Richmond (Richmond Borough), and Suffolk Counties; (5) southern district of New York: Columbia, Dutchess, Greene, New York (Bronx and Manhattan Boroughs), Orange, Putnam, Rockland, Sullivan, Ulster, and Westchester Counties; (6) Massachusetts (entire State); (7) Indiana (entire State); (8) northern district of Illinois: Boone, Carroll, Cook (Chicago), Dekalb, Dupage, Grundy, Jo Daviess, Kane, Kendall, Lake, La Salle, Lee, McHenry, Ogle, Stephenson, Whiteside, Will, and Winnebago Counties.

cases, because of the check through the first source—the reports of the post-office inspectors. Table 16 gives for each district the number of cases, the types of offenses, and the types of courts hearing the cases.

TABLE 16.—*District, type of offense, and type of court; children in eight selected localities arrested in 1918 and 1919 for violating Federal laws.*

District.	Total.	Children in selected localities violating Federal laws.							
		Children violating postal laws.				Children violating other Federal laws.			
		Total.	Before United States district court.	Before juvenile or other State court.	No court action taken.	Total.	Before United States district court.	Before juvenile or other State court.	No court action taken.
Total....................	418	328	180	130	18	90	64	23	3
District of Columbia.........	34	27	10	15	2	7	5	2	....
Maryland....................	35	24	[1] 16	1	7	11	4	7	....
Pennsylvania, eastern district....................	[2] 29	23	10	10	3	6	2	3	1
New York, eastern district...	19	13	3	9	1	6	5	1	....
New York, southern district.	112	62	30	30	2	50	38	10	2
Massachusetts..............	[3] 57	57	5	49	3	....	....	....	....
Indiana....................	[4] 24	21	15	6	....	3	3	....	....
Illinois, northern district....	108	101	91	10	....	7	7	....	....

[1] Includes 1 child before the United States district court, whose case was later transferred to the juvenile court.
[2] Includes 2 cases outside the city of Philadelphia.
[3] Includes 31 cases outside the city of Boston.
[4] Includes 6 cases outside the city of Indianapolis.

DISTRICT OF COLUMBIA.

Number and types of cases.

Because of the form of government in the District of Columbia, all violations of the law are under Federal jurisdiction, yet the large majority are not comparable with violations of Federal laws in other localities. Because of the opportunities offered it might be expected that the problem of juvenile offenders against Federal laws would be more serious in the District of Columbia than in other localities. This does not seem to be the case, however, as only 34 cases were reported by the Post Office Department, the Supreme Court of the District of Columbia (having the jurisdiction of a United States district court), and the juvenile court. This number included 27 postal cases and 7 of other types—4 of forgery of Government checks and 3 of larceny of United States property.

Types of courts and ages of children.

Half the cases (17) were referred to the juvenile court on preferred charges of larceny or "taking the property of another." Two cases were dismissed by the United States attorney without further prosecution. All the juveniles referred to the juvenile court were under 16 years of age, and only 2 under 16 were heard before the supreme court. Although the age limit of the juvenile court is 17 years, of the 13 children 16 years of age or over who were before the District Supreme Court, 9 were under 17 and might have been referred to the juvenile court, so far as age was concerned. The age distribution of the cases before the juvenile court and the Supreme Court of the District of Columbia was as follows:

Total	34
Before supreme court	15
15 years	2
16 to 17 years	13
Before juvenile court	17
Under 10 years	2
10 to 11 years	1
12 to 13 years	4
14 to 15 years	10
No court action	2
15 to 16 years	2

Dispositions.

Disposition other than commitment to institutions or jails was made in 9 cases by the supreme court and in 14 by the juvenile court. Legal provision for probation is made for the supreme court, and in 4 cases sentence was suspended and the boy placed on probation; 1 boy was dismissed by the United States commissioner after preliminary hearing. At the time of this study final disposition had not been made in 4 cases. The dispositions by the juvenile court in the 14 cases not committed to institutions were as follows:

Total	14
Placed on probation	1
Placed on probation with suspended sentence	6
Committed to Board of Children's Guardians (sentence suspended)	1
Dismissed	6

One boy was committed to the National Training School for Boys by the Supreme Court of the District of Columbia, and 3 by the juvenile court. Four of the boys before the former court were committed to a penitentiary and 1 was sentenced to the Washington Asylum Hospital and Jail.

Time between apprehension and disposition; detention.

A much longer time elapsed between apprehension and disposition in a majority of the cases before the supreme court than in those handled by the juvenile court. Only 2 of the supreme-court cases, but 16 of the juvenile-court cases, were disposed of in less than one month from time of apprehension, 12 of the latter being disposed of in less than two weeks.

Information with regard to detention was obtained in only 14 cases, there being 13 children reported detained and 1 reported not detained. Two other children were reported remanded to jail, but it was not known whether they were actually detained. Of the 13 detained, 8 were held at the House of Detention (for women and children) by order of the juvenile court, 4 were held in jail by order of the supreme court, and 1 was detained by order of the Federal authorities but was released without court action. One of the boys was first detained by the juvenile court, and when the case was later taken to the supreme court he was placed in jail to await grand jury action.

MARYLAND.

Number and types of cases.

Thirty-five children were reported for the District of Maryland as violating Federal laws. Of these, 24 violated postal laws and 11 committed other offenses, including 7 arrested for interstate-commerce violations, 1 for selling liquor to a sailor, 1 for shooting craps on a Government reservation (Navy camp), 1 for forgery, and 1 for whom the type of offense was not reported.

Types of courts and ages of children.

Of the 35 cases reported,[2] 20 were dealt with by the United States district court, 8 by the Baltimore juvenile court, and in 7 cases reported by the Federal authorities no court action was taken. The 5 children committing offenses outside Baltimore were before the United States district court, which meets in Baltimore.

All interstate-commerce cases (7) in which arrests were made by inspectors of the Baltimore & Ohio Railroad were taken by the railroad company before the juvenile court.

All but 3 of the 20 children before the United States district court were over 14 years of age. Three of the 8 children before the juvenile court were under the age of 14, 4 were reported to be 14 but under 16 years of age, and the age of 1 child was not reported. Of the 7 children for whom no court action was reported, 1 was 13 years of age, 2 were 15, 1 was 16, 2 were 17, and for 1 the age was not reported.

Dispositions.

Commitments to public institutions were made by Federal authorities in 8 of the 20 cases tried by them, and in a ninth case arrangements were made by which the child was sent to a private institution. In 5 of the 10 cases disposed of in other ways, the child was fined; 2 children were dismissed, 1 being found "not guilty," the other being fined on another charge; in 4 cases the boy was com-

---

[2] One case before the United States district court was later transferred to the juvenile court.

mitted to the city jail for one day—doubtless to conform with the law that sentence must be imposed after conviction in Federal cases, probation not being provided for. Three children were committed to State reformatories—2 of them to the Iowa reformatory and 1 to the Connecticut reformatory at Cheshire; 5 were committed to the National Training School for Boys; and in 1 case the child was sent to a private institution in Baltimore.

Of the boys committed, 6 were 15 years of age at commitment and 3 were 17. Of those fined, 1 was 14 years of age, and the others were 16 or 17 years. Three of the boys committed to jail for one day were 16 or 17 years of age, and one was 15.

Of the 8 boys before the juvenile court 1 was committed to St. Mary's Industrial School, 1 was fined, 1 dismissed, and 5 were placed on probation. The proportion of cases in which dispositions other than commitments were made was larger in the juvenile than in the Federal court. Three of the 5 children placed on probation were under 14 years of age, and 2 were 14 years old. Two of the 3 not placed on probation were 14 or 15 years of age, and the age of the third was not reported.

Time between apprehension and disposition; detention.

The problem of the long period of time between arrest and disposition as found in the Federal courts generally is somewhat lessened in the district of Maryland, because Baltimore is the only place of meeting of the court, which is in almost constant session except for two months in the summer. This makes it possible for cases to be brought up for trial more quickly than in districts where the court meets only at stated times. Disposition was made in 8 of the cases before the United States district court within a month after arrest, 3 cases were disposed of in one month but less than two, 2 in two months, 2 in four months, and 3 in six months; the length of time was not reported in 2 cases, as the date of arrest was not given. All the 8 cases before the juvenile court were disposed of in less than two weeks; 6 of them on the day the arrest was made.

Six of the 35 children were reported as having been detained pending hearing, 4 in jail and 2 in private institutions. No detention was reported in 2 cases; 4 children were remanded to jail in default of bond, but further report as to whether they were actually detained was not made. No report as to detention was made in 23 cases, including the 8 handled by the juvenile court.

EASTERN DISTRICT OF PENNSYLVANIA.

Number and types of cases.

Of the 29 cases reported in the eastern district of Pennsylvania 23 involved postal offenses and 6 offenses of other types. All except 2 were Philadelphia cases. The six boys arrested for offenses other than postal included two accused of fraudulent claims for pay at the Hog Island shipyard, one of selling narcotic drugs, one of deserting the Navy, one of wearing the United States uniform unlawfully, and one of wearing a Boy Scout's uniform with Army trimmings.

Types of courts and ages of children.

In Philadelphia 11 boys were dealt with by the Federal authorities, and 12 by the juvenile division of the municipal court; 7 of the postal offenders taken to the juvenile court were referred directly by the arresting officers, and no record of these cases was made by the inspector. In four cases no court action was taken. Of the two cases outside Philadelphia, one was handled by the United States district court in session at Lancaster, and the other was referred to the court of quarter sessions, a State court.

All six boys under 14 years of age were taken before the juvenile court, as were also five who were 14 to 15 years of age, and one aged 16 years. Of the 13 boys before the Federal court, 1 was 15 years, and 12 were 16 or 17 years of age. The boy referred to the court of quarter sessions was aged 17 years.

Dispositions.

In this district juvenile Federal offenders are seldom committed to institutions. The juvenile court follows its usual procedure in delinquency cases, and the Federal authorities prefer to continue cases and place the children on probation informally. One boy was sent by the Federal court to the National Training School for Boys, and one child was committed and one returned to an institution by the juvenile court. The dispositions were as follows:

Total	29
Before United States district court	12
Committed to National Training School	1
Informally placed on probation	7
Dismissed	2
Disposition not reported	2
Before juvenile or other State courts	13
Committed to institution	1
Placed on probation	2
Returned to institution	1
Restitution ordered	1
Dismissed	8
No court action taken	4

Informal probation was made possible through arrangements with the municipal court of Philadelphia, of which the juvenile court is a division. The United States district attorney frequently sent child offenders, immediately after arrest, to the house of detention. These cases were seldom brought before the juvenile-court judge, the offenses being usually of a minor character. The superintendent of the home, acting as a probation officer, placed the child on probation or discharged him, just as he would do in the case of children violating State laws. This policy was pursued by the district attorney even with boy and girl offenders over 16 years of age.

Time between apprehension and disposition; detention.

Because so many cases were placed on probation in this manner or were handled through the United States attorney's office, more prompt action was taken than is usually possible in Federal cases. Of the eight cases handled by Federal authorities in which dates of arrest and disposition were reported, three were disposed of in less than two weeks, two in one month, and three in two months.

The house of detention in Philadelphia is used frequently by the Federal authorities, as well as by the juvenile court. Only four boys were reported to have been detained in jail, none of these being so held in Philadelphia. Three of them were detained in jail in Illinois on another charge for one month previous to removal to Philadelphia to answer for the postal offense for which they were wanted there, and the fourth boy was detained in a county jail in Pennsylvania.

EASTERN AND SOUTHERN DISTRICTS OF NEW YORK.

Number and types of cases.

The largest number of juveniles violating Federal laws in any of the localities studied was reported in the eastern and southern districts of New York. The total number of cases in these two districts was 131—75 postal cases and 56 Federal cases of other types. The large number of offenses other than postal was due to war conditions, as 38 were violations of the national defense act and two other war-time acts[1]—16 cases of unlawful wearing of a uniform and 22 cases which involved procuring liquor for or selling liquor to soldiers or sailors. These war-time cases were more prevalent in New York than in the other localities studied.

Three interstate-commerce violations were reported, 5 cases of larceny of United States property, 1 scheme to defraud the Government, 1 assault with intent to commit felony on board an American vessel, 1 trespass upon Government property, 3 violations of the drug act, and 1 case of interference with and destruction of war material; in 3 cases the offense was not reported.

The number of cases in the southern district (including Manhattan and Bronx Boroughs) was 112, and the number in the eastern district (including Brooklyn and Queens Boroughs) was 19.

[1] 39 Stat., 166; 40 Stat., 76, 821.

Types of courts and ages of children.

Cases in both districts were heard by the Children's Court of New York City, being taken directly to this court by the authorities making the arrests. Forty-eight were reported as heard in the Boroughs of Manhattan, Brooklyn, and Queens by the children's court, 1 was heard by a court of quarter sessions, and 1 was heard by a magistrate's court; 76 were taken before the United States district courts; in 5 cases no court action was taken—4 were dismissed without prosecution and the fifth was transferred to the eastern district of Pennsylvania, no further report being made.

Figures showing the ages of the children taken before the different courts indicate that the policy is to refer the younger children to the children's court. Of the 8 boys reported before the United States District Court in Brooklyn, 1 was 15 and the others were 17 years of age. Of the 10 children before the children's court in the Boroughs of Brooklyn and Queens, the 2 youngest were 10 and 12 years, respectively, the others being 14 and 15 years of age. The children's court has jurisdiction only over children under the age of 16 years.

This policy is further borne out by the following age figures for the children before the courts of the southern district (including Manhattan):

Total	112
Before the United States district court	68
10 to 11 years	1
12 to 13 years	1
14 to 15 years	15
16 to 17 years	51
Before the children's court and other State courts	40
Under 10 years	3
10 to 11 years	7
12 to 13 years	8
14 to 15 years	15
16 to 17 years	7
No court action	4
Under 10 years	2
16 to 17 years	2

Dispositions.

The number of cases before the United States District Court of the Southern District which were disposed of otherwise than by commitment was somewhat larger than the number of cases resulting in commitments to institutions—33 as compared with 26. Seventeen of the 33 children were placed in the custody of the United States marshal for one day, a sentence no doubt passed by the court because of the lack of probation facilities and the inadvisability of committing the boys to an institution. Nine cases were dismissed; 1 of these involved a girl whose case was dismissed "because she was only 16 and had been in jail three days." Sentence was postponed in 3 cases, in 2 of which the boy was ordered to report weekly to a priest, and in the third the boy was discharged in the custody of his mother during the time of continuance; 1 boy was fined; and 3 cases were nol-prossed. Of the 26 children committed to institutions, 17 were committed to jail for short terms of 60 days or less—15 of them to the Tombs prison and 2 to the Essex County Jail in New Jersey; 8 boys were committed to the National Training School for Boys, and 1 to the New York State Reformatory at Elmira. No bill of indictment was returned by the grand jury in 2 cases, and in 7 cases disposition had not been made at the time of this study.

The dispositions made by the United States District Court for the Southern District of New York were as follows:

Total	68
Committed to institutions	26
National Training School for Boys	8
New York State Reformatory	1
Jail	17
Other dispositions made	33
Custody United States marshal for 1 day	17
Dismissed	9
Fined	1
Nol-prossed	3
Other	3
No bill of indictment returned	2
Disposition not reported	7

In contrast, 32 of the cases handled by the children's court did not result in commitments, and only 5 children were committed; in 1 case the disposition made was not reported. Two cases before other State courts were placed on probation. This larger proportion of noncommitment cases was due, of course, to the facilities available for probation and to the legal provision for dismissing cases or suspending sentence. In 26 of the 32 noncommitment cases the child was placed on probation, 5 cases were dismissed, and in 1 sentence was suspended. The 5 committed were sent to local institutions for children—2 to the New York Catholic Protectory, 2 to the Jewish Protectory and Aid Society, and 1 to the New York Juvenile Asylum.

Comparing dispositions made by the United States district court and the children's court for the same types of offenses, it is evident that the Federal authorities recognized that in some types of cases commitment to institutions is not always warranted; many cases were disposed of in such ways as were possible under the law without commitment to institutions, these dispositions being the best available substitutes for suspended sentence and probation.

Of the 8 cases before the children's court involving the procuring of liquor for, or selling liquor to, men in uniform, 7 resulted in probation and 1 in commitment to a private institution for a short period. Of the 14 children before the United States district courts for the same offense, 1 was placed in custody of a priest; 1 in custody of his mother, sentence being postponed; the cases of 2 were dismissed; 5 were placed in custody of the marshal for one day; 3 were committed to the Tombs prison for 1 day, 5 days, and 30 days, respectively; and in 2 cases the disposition was not reported.

Similarly, among the boys arrested for wearing uniforms unlawfully, the 3 before the children's court were dismissed. In 1 of the 13 cases before Federal courts sentence was postponed, the boy to report to a priest regularly; in 6 the child was placed in the custody of the marshal for one day; 14 children were placed in the Tombs prison, all for one week or less; and 2 were committed to the National Training School for Boys.

Time between apprehension and disposition; detention.

In these two districts the United States district courts are in session continuously, and for this reason there was little difference between the Federal and the State courts as to the length of time between arrest and disposition. The 3 cases in which final disposition was not made for a year or more were continued from term to term and then nol-prossed. Twenty-six of these 76 cases before the United States district courts were heard and disposition was made in less than one week from the date of arrest.

The length of time between apprehension and disposition for the 125 cases in which court action was taken is shown in the following list:

Total	126
Before United States district courts	76
Less than 1 week	26
1 week, less than 2	9
2 weeks, less than 1 month	7
1 month	6
2 months	6
3 to 7 months	4
1 year and over	3
Time not reported [a]	15
Before the children's court and other State courts	50
Less than 1 week	21
1 week, less than 2	21
2 weeks, less than 1 month	4
3 months	1
Time not reported	3

[a] Date of arrest was not reported in 5 cases; no disposition had been made in 5; date of disposition was not reported in 1; and 4 cases were continued from time to time, the child being on informal probation and final disposition not having been made.

Local ordinances of New York City require that no children under 16 years of age shall be placed in jail, and because of this ruling the children under 16 arrested for violating Federal laws were detained in the shelter maintained by the New York Society for the Prevention of Cruelty to Children and used by the children's court as a juvenile detention home. Boys over 16 were detained in the Tombs prison and in the Brooklyn city prison. Detention was reported in a total of 91 cases; 50 children were detained in jail, 38 in the shelter, and 3—all 15 years of age—for part of the time in the shelter and for the remainder in jail. Detention periods were comparatively short; 18 were detained for only one day or less, and only 4 for one month or over. Length of detention in the shelter or in jail is given below for the 91 cases in which the child was reported detained.

Total	91
Shelter maintained by Society for Prevention of Cruelty to Children	38
1 day or less	11
More than 1 day, less than 1 week	13
1 week, less than 2	11
2 weeks, less than 1 month	2
1 month or more	1
Both shelter and jail	3
1 week or less	2
Not reported	1
Jail	50
1 day or less	7
More than 1 day, less than 1 week	19
1 week, less than 2	13
2 weeks, less than 1 month	7
1 month or more	3
Not reported	1

MASSACHUSETTS.

Number and types of cases.

No cases of juveniles committing Federal offenses other than postal were reported in Massachusetts, there being 57 children reported as violating postal laws. Of these, 26 were from Boston, and 31 from outside that city. Information was obtained from the Post Office Department in all except one case, which was reported by the Juvenile Court of Boston. Supplementary information from court records was obtained for only 14 of the Boston children, the 3 in Cambridge, and the 7 in Quincy.

Types of courts and ages of children.

Because of the absence of probation facilities in the Federal courts the policy in the district of Massachusetts is to refer children violating Federal laws to the juvenile and other State courts having jurisdiction of juvenile cases. Of the 57 cases, 49 were thus referred, 5 were handled by the Federal authorities, and in 3 no court action was reported.

Of the 36 children reported from Boston, Cambridge, and Quincy, 28 were referred to juvenile courts, 1 to a municipal court, 2 to a State court in Suffolk County, 4 were handled by the Federal authorities, and no court action was reported in 1 case. All but 1 of the 21 cases reported outside these three cities were before State courts having jurisdiction over children's cases. The 5 boys whose cases were handled by the Federal authorities were all 16 or 17 years of age.

The age distribution of the children referred to juvenile and other State courts is as follows:

Total	49
Under 10 years	1
10 to 11 years	8
12 to 13 years	7
14 to 15 years	18
16 to 17 years	14
Age not reported, but under 16 years	1

Dispositions.

One of the three boys in whose cases no court action was reported was returned to the Connecticut Reformatory, from which institution he had escaped. Of the four cases handled by the Federal authorities in Boston, one was nol-prossed after indictment by the grand jury, one was dismissed by the United States commissioner upon the request of the United States attorney, one was continued by the commissioner for a month and a half pending the good behavior of the child and was then dismissed without further court action, and in one case the final disposition was not reported.

In 18 of the 29 cases from Boston, Cambridge, and Quincy, which were referred to juvenile and other State courts and reported as to disposition made, the boys were placed on probation, 6 being given a suspended sentence also; 1 boy was committed to the Massachusetts Reformatory; 3 were committed to the Industrial School for Boys at Shirley; 1 was sent to the Lyman School for Boys (a State training school); 1 was returned to the Home for Destitute Catholic Children; 1 was committed to the care of the Massachusetts State Board of Charity;[5] 3 were returned to the Suffolk School for Boys (a county institution for truants and delinquents, since closed); and in 1 case the disposition was not reported.

Nine children before State courts outside the three cities named were placed on probation, while 8 were committed to institutions,

---

[5] Now the Massachusetts Department of Public Welfare.

2 were returned to institutions without court action, and 1 case was dismissed by Federal and 1 by State authorities.

Time between apprehension and disposition.

The problem of the length of time between apprehension and disposition in cases of children violating Federal laws is not serious in Massachusetts, because almost seven-eighths of the cases were referred to the State courts, disposition being made for all but 10 of these within two weeks after arrest. Of the 5 cases handled by the Federal authorities, 1 was continued by the United States commissioner for almost two months and was then dismissed; the case which was nol-prossed was carried on the court records for a year before final disposition was made; 1 case was pending for a month; and in the 2 other cases the date of disposition was not reported.

INDIANA.

Number and types of cases, types of courts, and ages of children.

The territory included under the jurisdiction of the United States District Court of Indiana comprises the entire State. From this district 24 cases were reported, 18 of which were presented to the United States District Court in Indianapolis; the remaining 6 cases were heard before State, circuit, and county courts outside Indianapolis. Only 3 children were reported arrested for offenses other than violations of postal laws, including 2 arrested for interstate-commerce violations and 1 for embezzlement of funds.

Eleven of the 18 children dealt with by the United States district court were known to have lived outside Indianapolis. All the 11 children had to be taken away from their place of residence for court hearing.

All but 6 of the children were 16 and 17 years of age; 5 were between 14 and 16 years, and 1 was 13 years of age.

Dispositions.

In Indiana the United States district judge handles juvenile cases informally, usually following the policy of continuing cases from term to term pending the good behavior of the child, and then having the case nol-prossed. Only 5 commitments were made by the district court; 4 were to the county jail in Indianapolis (3 for 6 months and 1 for 1 day only), the fifth being a sentence of 10 years to the United States Penitentiary at Atlanta, Ga. Following the usual procedure of continuing juvenile cases pending good behavior, this boy, who was 17 at the time of arrest, had been allowed to return to his home; but upon report by his mother that he was continually in trouble, he was returned to the court and the penitentiary sentence was imposed. He had become 18 years of age before final disposition. The offense of which he was guilty was embezzlement of funds from the American Railway Express Co., which was taken under Federal control during the war.

Four boys were fined, and the cases of 8 children—7 boys and 1 girl—were nol-prossed after continuance, the children having been required to report to the court on dates set in the order for continuance; 1 case was nol-prossed because it was found that the wrong person had been indicted. In only 1 of the 6 cases reported before State courts was the child placed on probation. Three children were committed to the Indiana Reformatory, and 2 to the Indiana Boys' School.

Time between apprehension and disposition; detention.

The policy of continuing cases in the Federal court makes the time between apprehension and final disposition much longer than was found in other localities. But these cases are comparable with cases placed on probation by State courts, the nolle prosequi amounting to a dismissal order following a satisfactory probation period. In 3 of the 8 cases in which continuance pending good behavior was reported the child was practically on probation for 11 months, in 3 for 1 but less than 2 years, in one for 2 years, and in one case the length of time was not reported. The case of the boy mentioned above who was committed to the county jail for one day had been continued for a year before this final disposition was made. In 3 of the remaining 10 cases less than a month elapsed between arrest and final disposition; no report on this point was made in 3 cases.

In 4 cases before the State courts, disposition was made within one week from time of arrest; the interval was not reported in the 2 remaining cases.

Six children were reported detained pending trial, all in the county jail. No detention was reported in 6 cases, and in 12 cases no report was given as to detention. Federal prisoners were separated from other prisoners in the Marion County jail at Indianapolis, but no separation of juveniles from adults was made.

NORTHERN DISTRICT OF ILLINOIS.

Number and types of cases.

The problem of juvenile Federal offenders in the Northern District of Illinois appears to be largely confined to the city of Chicago, though 18 counties are included in that district. Of the 108 cases reported, all but 6 involved residents of Chicago, and in these 6 cases the place of residence was not reported.

Almost all the Federal offenses committed were against the postal laws. Only 3 cases were reported of larceny from interstate commerce, 1 of unlawfully wearing a uniform, and 1 of selling liquor to sailors; in 2 cases the offense was not reported. "Stubbing" seemed to be more prevalent in Chicago than in any of the other cities visited. This practice doubtless accounted for the large number of juvenile Federal cases in Chicago during the two years, as half the postal offenders were arrested on that charge.

Types of courts and ages of children.

In Chicago juvenile Federal cases were dealt with almost exclusively by the Federal authorities, only eight having been referred to the juvenile court and two to the boys' court[6] during the two years.

A large majority of the boys from this district were 16 or 17 years of age, 81 being reported in that age group. Twenty-one were 14 or 15 years of age, 3 were under 14, and the ages of 3 were not reported though they were known to be under 18 years. Three of the 8 boys referred to the juvenile court were 11, 13, and 14 years of age, respectively; 4 were 15, and 1 was 16 years of age. Both boys referred to the boys' court were 17 years of age.

Dispositions.

Including the jail commitments, in almost half the 98 cases before the United States district court the boy was committed to an institution—2 boys to the National Training School for Boys, 14 to the Iowa State Reformatory at Anamosa, 4 to the St. Charles School for Boys at St. Charles, Ill., and 23 to county jails in Chicago and the vicinity. These jail commitments were mostly for 30 days, but some were for shorter or longer periods. Commitments to the Iowa reformatory were also for short terms, the longest being for 1 year, and the others for 60 days, 3 months, or 6 months. That the largest number of commitments were to county jails may be due to the distance from Chicago of the two institutions receiving juveniles from this district on Federal commitments—the National Training School for Boys and the Iowa State Reformatory. The jails in the counties immediately surrounding Chicago were used more commonly than Cook County jail (Chicago), though a few children were committed to the latter.

Of the 55 boys before the Federal court who were not committed to institutions, 6 were sentenced to remain in the custody of the United States marshal for a day, and 2 for 1 hour; fines were imposed upon 5; and 4 were dismissed, 3 by the United States commissioner and 1 after being held as a witness. One of the 3 dismissed by the commissioner was first released on bail for 60 days and was required to report to him periodically during that time.

---

[6] The Boys' Court of the Municipal Court of Chicago has jurisdiction over all cases of boys between the ages of 17 and 21 years.

In 18 cases presented to the grand jury, no indictment was returned, and the case was dismissed with no further prosecution; 4 of these boys were reported to have been held in jail by order of the United States commissioner for 30 days before the presentation of the case to the grand jury, not only as punishment but also as an object lesson to other boys. Up to the time when the records were obtained for this study, the final disposition had not been made in 20 cases; some of these cases were being continued from time to time, others had not come to trial.

Seven of the eight boys referred to the juvenile court were placed on probation, and one was committed for 30 days to the Chicago and Cook County School for Boys. One of the two before the boys' court was committed to the Cook County House of Correction, and one was placed on probation.

The 23 boys committed to jails, the 2 sent to the National Training School, and 11 of the 14 sent to the Iowa State Reformatory were 16 years of age or over.

Time between apprehension and disposition; detention.

In only 24 cases before the United States district court was final disposition reported to have been made in less than one month from the date of arrest. The periods between apprehension and disposition were as follows:

Total		108
Before the United States district court		98
Less than 1 month	24	
Less than 1 week	4	
1 week, less than 2	8	
2 weeks, less than 1 month	12	
1 month	20	
2 months	12	
3 to 5 months	10	
6 to 10 months	7	
1 year and over [7]	3	
Not reported	22	
Before the juvenile court or the boys' court		10
Less than 1 week	3	
2 weeks, less than 1 month	1	
2 months, less than 3	6	

Detention in county jails was the only method used for the 59 juveniles detained by order of the Federal authorities; only 11 boys were reported not detained, and for 35 cases no information regarding detention was obtained. In a number of the last cases the records stated that the boys were remanded to the county jail in default of bond, but no report was obtained as to whether they were actually

---

[7] Two of these cases were given a hearing within 10 days and were continued to report to the United States attorney.

detained; bond may have been furnished early enough to prevent actual detention.   Three of the boys before the juvenile court were detained at the Juvenile Detention Home, and 1 before the boys' court was detained at a police station.   The largest number of boys detained were held for less than one week; 20 of the 34 so reported were detained for one day only.   The length of detention for the 62 detained was as follows:

Total	62
Less than 1 week	34
1 week, less than 2	6
2 weeks, less than 1 month	8
1 month, less than 2	4
2 months	4
3 months	1
Time not reported [8]	5

Previous delinquency records.

Information as to whether or not the boys reported in this district were first offenders was obtained for only 42 of the 108 children. Twenty-one, including 7 of the 8 before the juvenile court and the 2 before the boys' court, were first offenders, while 21 had been previously arrested.   Of these, 9 were arrested once previously, 5 twice, 2 three times, 2 four times, and 3 were known to have been arrested but the number of times was not reported.   Nine of the 21 previously arrested had been committed to institutions.

Twelve children before the United States district court were known to be first offenders, but in spite of this fact 10 were committed to institutions—8 to a reformatory and 2 to institutions for delinquent children; 2 were sentenced to one day in the custody of the United States marshal.   Six of the 7 first offenders before the juvenile court were placed on probation, the seventh being sent for 30 days to the Chicago and Cook County School for Boys.   Of the 2 boys referred to the boys' court—both first offenders—1 was placed on probation, and 1 was committed for 30 days to the Chicago House of Correction.

ILLUSTRATIVE CASES.

The following brief histories of three boys, two of them brothers, who had previously been before the juvenile court, are cited to illustrate the need of facilities for social investigation in the Federal courts, the complicated procedure, and the long periods between arrest and disposition during which the child, if not subjected to the injurious influences of jail detention, is left in the community without supervision.   Under juvenile-court procedure full informa-

---

[8] Includes three cases before the juvenile court and one before the boys' court.

tion concerning the social history could have been obtained, and prompt action have been taken for the correction of the child's delinquent tendencies and the protection of the public.

A 15-year-old boy was arrested by the Federal authorities on February 5, 1919, on a charge of stealing mail from hall letter boxes. A few months prior to this trouble the boy was before the juvenile court, and the investigation made at that time revealed that the mother was dead and that the father had neglected the family. There were six children in the family, the youngest of whom was in an institution for the feeble-minded. An 11-year-old girl was keeping house. Previous to her death the mother had been obliged, because of the father's neglect, to support the family. The father reported the boy to be incorrigible, running the streets at night and associating with boys who had a bad influence over him. On a later visit the probation officer found the boy boarding with a married sister. After the boy was arrested by the Federal authorities he was detained in jail for more than a month. The court procedure was as follows:

February 5. Arrested, and in default of bond placed in jail.
February 27. Indicted by United States grand jury.
March 6. Plea of not guilty entered. Bail fixed at $1,000.
March 11. Bail reduced to $500. Bonds filed for $500, and boy released from jail.
May 9. Cause set for trial May 12.
May 12. Bench warrant issued. Cause continued for trial to May 14.
May 14. Cause continued to May 16.
May 16. Trial proceeds.
May 19. Verdict of guilty by jury, with recommendations. Motion for new trial. Cause continued to June 2.
June 2. Motion for new trial. Cause continued to June 7.
June 7. Motion for new trial. Cause continued for sentence to September 15.
September 15. Cause continued to November 17 for disposition.
November 17. Cause continued 60 days to January 16, 1920, for disposition. No further action reported on docket.

Two brothers, 15 and 16 years of age, were indicted in February, 1919, on the same charge—that of stealing mail from hall letter boxes. The first boy had been arrested prior to indictment, but his brother was not arrested until May. The parents were dead. One boy lived with his maternal grandparents; the other, with his sister, had been living with the paternal grandparents, but had been turned out of the home and at the time of the trouble was living with an uncle. Both boys had been before the juvenile court for previous offenses, one having been dismissed by that court and the other having been placed under suspended sentence to the State industrial school. Subsequent to the Federal cases, the probation officer of the juvenile court reported that the boy had left his uncle's home and had not returned. Court procedure was as follows:

February 4. First boy arrested; placed in jail.
February 6. Removed from one county jail to another.
February 14. Released from jail.
February 27. Both boys indicted and bench warrant issued for the one not arrested. Bond set for first boy, $1,500.
March 6. Plea of not guilty entered for the first boy.
May 9. Cause continued for trial to May 16.

May 12. Bench warrants issued.

May 14. Cause continued for trial to May 16.

May 16. Second boy arrested.

May 16. First boy—plea of " not guilty " withdrawn, and plea of " guilty " entered.

May 17. Second boy—plea of " guilty " entered.

May 17. Trial of both boys proceeds.

May 19. Motion for new trial entered. Cause continued for hearing to June 2.

June 2. Motion for new trial. Cause continued to June 7.

June 7. Motion for new trial. Cause continued for sentence to September 15. Order entered canceling bond of first boy. Defendant released on own recognizance.

September 15. Cause continued to November 17.

November 17. Both boys fined $5, no costs.

December 30. Fine paid.

CHAPTER V. GENERAL CONCLUSIONS.

NUMBER OF CHILDREN VIOLATING FEDERAL LAWS.

This study has shown that throughout the United States during a two-year period 1,145 children under 18 years of age were arrested for violation of postal laws.[1] From the eight districts and the three institutions visited, 211 children were reported arrested during the same period for other Federal offenses—a number which undoubtedly represents only a small proportion of the total arrests for such offenses in the United States. During the two-year period, the yearly average number of children included in the two groups was 678; if complete data were available for the entire country the total yearly average under 18 years of age would without doubt be found to be nearly 1,000 and might exceed that figure. Of these, it appears that the majority are under the age of 16 years and that some are under 10 years of age.

Of the 1,145 children arrested for postal offenses, 1,091 were boys, there being only 54 girls. No girls were reported as violating other Federal laws.

The Federal offenses most frequently committed by juveniles are apparently violations of postal laws and regulations. Violations of interstate-commerce laws appear to come next in frequency; 94 of the 211 children known to have committed offenses other than postal had violated interstate-commerce laws.

With the exception of Idaho and Nevada, postal cases were reported from every State, the District of Columbia, Alaska, and Porto Rico. The largest numbers were reported from Illinois, New York, Massachusetts, California, and Pennsylvania, over 50 cases being reported for each.

Of the eight districts studied, Chicago and New York reported the largest number of cases, including postal and other types of offenses. For offenses other than postal violations, boys were reported committed to the National Training School from 21 States and the District of Columbia.

The largest numbers of children violating postal laws were reported as residing in communities of less than 10,000 population and in cities of over 500,000 population, 34.7 per cent of the 1,108 postal offenders reported by the Post Office Department residing in the former type of communities and 21.7 per cent in the latter.

---

[1] Including 1,108 reported to the Post Office Department and 37 not included in the records of the department but reported from other sources as violating postal laws.

Fifteen per cent of the children violating postal laws and reported by the Post Office Department were employed in the postal service, 33 being under 16 years of age. Adherence to the policy laid down by the Post Office Department, that young children, whose judgment and ability to withstand temptation are not fully developed, should not be employed in positions where they are intrusted with delivery of mail or with postal funds, would reduce the number of offenders against Federal laws.

Of the 1,356 cases included in this study, 121 were reported only by the National Training School for Boys or by the New York and Iowa State reformatories, and all these were tried by United States district courts or by courts in the District of Columbia.[2] Of the remaining 1,235 cases, 758, or 61.3 per cent, were tried by United States district courts; 375, or 30.4 per cent, were taken before juvenile and other State courts; 8 cases were tried first by United States district courts and were then transferred to juvenile courts; court action was not reported in 15 cases; and in 79 cases no court action was taken.[3]

METHODS USED IN CHILDREN'S CASES BY FEDERAL AUTHORITIES.

The fundamental concept of the juvenile-court movement is that children should not be held criminally responsible for their misconduct, but that they should be afforded protection, care, and training, within or outside an institution and should be safeguarded from contact with adult offenders. This principle has not been applied in the Federal courts, in which the chancery procedure has not been substituted for the criminal in children's cases, nor the criminal procedure modified. Thus, the proceedings are formal and frequently include several preliminary hearings followed by grand-jury action and public trial, while long delays are often occasioned by crowded calendars, absence of continuous session, and the distance of the court from the child's place of residence. Further difficulties are found in lack of facilities for discovering what kind of child is being dealt with, his past experience and his possibilities of development, and in the inability of the court to suspend sentence, place on probation, and supervise the child in the community. During the long periods frequently occurring between the apprehension of the children and the disposition of their cases, the children must often be kept in detention—and jail detention is the form most frequently

---

[2] For the purpose of comparing the numbers heard by Federal and by State courts these cases have been excluded, since their inclusion would overweight the proportion tried in Federal courts.

[3] Cases were included as having had court action if a preliminary hearing was held by the United States commissioner, regardless of the action taken by him. Cases dismissed by the United States attorney without further hearing were considered as having had no court action.

used by Federal courts. Holding children of tender years in jail, where they are terrified by the experience and subjected to contact with adult criminals, leaves an impression not conducive to normal development or good citizenship, that is difficult if not impossible to eradicate.

Moreover, the Federal courts are at present limited with reference to the institutions to which they may commit children. The national training schools for boys and girls, in the District of Columbia, are the only Federal institutions especially adapted to the care of delinquent children. Federal authorities in distant States are frequently reluctant to send children so far away from home, such a disposition often inflicting great suffering on both parents and child. On the other hand, the institutions nearer home with which the United States Government has made arrangements for the care of Federal offenders are frequently institutions designed primarily for adult offenders and are conducted as prisons with cell blocks and prison discipline. The younger children committed to these institutions are subjected to a program not adapted to their training and are in contact with older offenders. The officials sometimes make an effort to modify the régime in favor of a young child—keeping him in the office of the institution during the day, for instance—but such practices can be only sporadic and of doubtful success.

An essential feature of the juvenile-court system is that a finding of delinquency does not constitute a conviction of crime, and that juvenile records, therefore, do not stand as criminal records. In the Federal courts the children found to have committed the offenses with which they are charged thereby stand convicted of crime, and suffer throughout life from the disqualifications consequent upon a criminal record.

Many judges, commissioners, attorneys, and post-office inspectors were found who recognized that the usual procedure was not adapted to the handling of children's cases; and, moreover, the statement was sometimes made that grand juries were very unwilling to return indictments in these cases. Under a more or less rigid legal system, when there exist in any particular case unusual circumstances, such as the extreme youth of the offender, one of three courses may be followed: (1) The imposition of the penalty fixed by law, sometimes in spite of doubt in the minds of the authorities as to whether such disposition is in accord with real justice; (2) the dismissing or nol-prossing of the case or refusal to indict, the authorities taking no steps to correct the offender or to safeguard society; and (3) the use of various expedients not specifically provided by law, which it is hoped will more nearly achieve justice, the correction and training of the offender, and the protection of the community. Many instances of the adoption of such expedients have been cited in this repcrt. They range from immediate reference of the case to juvenile courts by post-office inspectors and United States attorneys to the use of informal probation by the Federal authorities themselves, prior to the hearing or pending continuance on condition of good behavior. They also include short-term jail sentences and such nominal sentences as small fines and sentences to one day in the custody of the United States marshal. Except the reference to juvenile courts, none of these methods of handling children's cases is satisfactory, because the authorities have no facilities for ascertaining the necessary facts about the child and his environment, nor the means for the intensive supervision and reconstructive work essential to treatment of delinquents in the community.

Following is a comparison of the usual procedure in a well-organized juvenile court and in a United States district court, leaving out of consideration expedients sometimes used by Federal authorities:

JUVENILE-COURT PROCEDURE.	UNITED STATES DISTRICT-COURT PROCEDURE.
1. Initiation of case.	
Complaint and summons, except in cases of summary arrest.	Arrest upon warrant, or summary arrest. (In some cases arrest follows instead of preceding indictment.)
2. Period between initiation and court action.	
Prompt court action (within a few days or a week).	Frequently weeks or months elapse before final court action.
3. Care pending court action.	
Release to parents on personal recognizance, or detention in detention home for children.	Release on bond or detention in jail.
4. Preliminary investigation.	
Thorough investigation, including: Physical examination. Mental examination. Personal history (schooling, recreation, habits, companions, etc.). Home conditions. Family history.	Investigation confined mainly to ascertaining whether or not child committed the offense.
5. Court action.	
Hearing—private, informal, without jury.	Preliminary hearing before commissioner. Presentment to grand jury, or direct to court on information filed. Trial—public, formal, often with jury.

JUVENILE - COURT PROCEDURE — Continued.	UNITED STATES DISTRICT-COURT PROCEDURE—Continued.

6. *Disposition of case.*

Dismissed or filed, if child not in need of protection or discipline, *or*	Dismissed, or nol-prossed, *or*
Probation, *or*	Fine, *or*
Placement in care of child-placing agency, *or*	Jail sentence, *or*
Commitment to special institution for care of juvenile delinquents.	Commitment to National Training School (District of Columbia), *or*
	Sentence to reformatory or penitentiary (State or private institutions for delinquent children are available to a few United States courts).

7. *Follow-up care.*

For children on probation by trained probation staff.	No provision.

8. *Effect of adjudication.*

Juvenile-court record does not constitute a criminal record.	Conviction of crime.

POSSIBILITIES FOR MORE ADEQUATE TREATMENT.

Two possibilities suggest themselves for providing a procedure better adapted to the handling of Federal cases involving children: First, a definite system of reference to State courts, preferably at the beginning of the case; and second, the establishment of a Federal probation system, accompanied by certain other modifications of the Federal procedure in children's cases, so that an informal chancery procedure will be possible.

Reference to State courts.

Juvenile-court organization is constantly being extended, and State-wide systems are being developed, under which rural as well as urban communities have available court organizations especially adapted to children's work. Even where juvenile courts are not fully developed, the State courts having jurisdiction over children's cases have the advantage of prompt action and usually have some means for probationary supervision.

The practice of referring children's cases to juvenile or other State courts is already followed to a considerable extent. Almost a third of the cases reported by the Post Office Department during the two-year period were so referred. In one district, children violating Federal laws were frequently sent, immediately after arrest, to the house of detention maintained by the juvenile court. The superintendent of the home, who had the power to place juvenile delinquents on informal probation, dealt with these Federal offenders in the same manner as with juvenile court cases.[4]

A regular system of reference of children's cases to State courts, under uniform rules, would be much more effective than the method now followed at the discretion of the authorities in some districts.

Modification of Federal procedure in children's cases.

Prior to December, 1916, Federal judges had always used their discretion in placing offenders on probation.[5] In that month the Supreme Court of the United States held that Federal judges had no legal power to place offenders on probation except in the District of Columbia. Immediately thereafter, in February, 1917, a bill providing for probation, for adults as well as for juveniles, was passed by both Houses of Congress but did not receive the President's signature. In the course of hearings on probation bills introduced in the House of Representatives in 1920, the author of one of the bills presented letters from 49 Federal judges, of whom 43 were in favor of the plan. One judge wrote:

I have your letter of December 12 asking me for my opinion as to the wisdom of a probation system in the Federal courts. It is indeed not only wise but an absolute necessity for any effective administration of justice. At present in the case of juvenile offenders a judge's position is most unsatisfactory. The Supreme Court has forbidden any suspension of sentence, and except through a colorable evasion of the judge is bound to deal sentence then and there. If he imprisons the juvenile for a period he does two bad things; he does his best to take away any chance which the offender may still have for recuperation by throwing him into the worst possible surroundings, and he takes away his only hold over him, as his jurisdiction terminates when the sentence has expired. The result violates the judgment of all competent penologists, I think. We need in the first place some power to suspend sentence.

The judge goes on to express his opinion that voluntary probation officers could be obtained to carry out the work of supervision.[6]

The bills introduced in 1920 were not enacted into law, and in April, 1921, a bill (H. R. 4126) was introduced relating to the parole of United States prisoners and providing for a probation system in the United States courts. This bill was also referred to the Committee on the Judiciary, and hearings were held on May 31. It differs from the 1920 bill, referred to in the letter cited above, principally in respect to compensation of probation officers. The latter bill provided that the judges appointing a probation officer might determine whether a salary was to be paid and the amount of the salary, and that salaried officers should be under civil-service regulations. The

---

[4] See p. 50.

[5] See p. 5.

[6] "Probation system in the Federal courts: automatic parole." Hearings before the Committee on the Judiciary, House of Representatives, 66th Cong., 2d sess. Serial No. 20, p. 8. Government Printing Office, Washington, 1920.

bill now before Congress provides that probation officers shall serve without pay. The main provisions relating to probation are as follows:

1. *Appointment of probation officers.*—Courts of the United States having original jurisdiction of criminal actions, except in the District of Columbia, shall appoint as many probation officers, male or female, as occasion may require, such officers to serve without compensation.

2. *Cases in which probation may be applied.*—After a plea of guilty or nolo contendere, or after conviction, the imposition or execution of sentence may be suspended and the defendant placed upon probation in any case except those involving treason, homicide, rape, arson, kidnaping, or a second conviction of a felony.

3. *Period of probation.*—Original period of probation, together with extension thereof, shall not exceed five years.

4. *Conditions of probation.*—Probationer shall be provided with a written statement of the terms and conditions of probation; he shall observe the rules prescribed for his conduct and report as directed. He may be required to pay a fine, to make restitution or reparation, and to provide for the support of any person or persons for whose support he may be legally responsible.

5. *Preliminary investigations.*—Investigations shall be made by the probation officers in all cases referred to them by the court. They shall make recommendations to the court to enable it to decide whether or not the defendant ought to be placed on probation.

6. *Supervision of probationer.*—Probation officers shall keep informed concerning the conduct and condition of each probationer under their supervision. They shall use suitable methods to aid persons on probation and to bring about improvement in their conduct and condition. They shall keep records of their work and report to the court from time to time concerning all cases in their care.

7. *Release from probation.*—Upon expiration of the term of probation, or when directed by the court, the probation officer shall report to the court, with a statement of the conduct of the probationer. The court may discharge the probationer from further supervision, or may extend probation.

8. *Modification of the terms of probation, and revocation of the probation order or of suspension of sentence.*—At any time during the probationary term the court may modify the terms and conditions of probation, or may terminate probation, discharging the probationer, or may cause the probationer to be arrested and brought before the court. At any time after the probation period, but within the maximum period for which the defendant might originally have been sentenced, the court may cause the defendant to be arrested and brought before the court. In either case, upon causing the probationer to be brought before the court, probation or suspension of sentence may be revoked and sentence imposed.

The bill applies to adults as well as to juveniles, and does not take cognizance of the peculiar problems involved in the handling of children's cases. Moreover, it does not provide for paid probation service, which has been found to be essential to effective work with children. But the passage of the bill would enable the Federal courts to utilize the professional probation service which has been developed in connection with State courts. To the extent to which such cooperation between Federal and State courts could be effected the provisions of the bill would make it possible for United States district courts to be informed concerning the character of the children before them and the kind of disposition that would best protect the interests of the children and the general public. The courts would also have means of supervision and constructive help for children placed on probation.

Except for such amelioration as probation officers might be able informally to effect, there would still remain the disadvantages involved in the length of time between apprehension and final action, jail detention, formal procedure and public trial, and the disqualifying effects of a criminal record. It would doubtless be possible, through cooperation with the State courts, to secure to the children the benefits of special facilities for detention pending hearing and for intensive study through such diagnostic clinics as exist for the purpose of giving physical and mental examinations. Such cooperation with the States might also make available for the use of the Federal authorities more institutions especially designed for the care of delinquent children who can not safely remain under supervision in the community.

The difficulties of delayed hearings, formality and publicity, and criminal record could not be met except by further specific legislation.

It is evident that the possibilities of adapting Federal court procedure to children's cases are limited, and that because of the relatively small number of such cases before any one Federal court, cooperation with State courts and utilization of their resources seem to be essential. It is probable, therefore, that the simplest, most practicable, and least expensive plan for the proper handling of children's cases involving violations of Federal laws would be the first suggested in this chapter—the development of a definite system of reference to State courts, at least for certain types of Federal cases involving children.

Whatever plan may be adopted, the same fundamental principles governing court procedure in children's cases must be followed if the children are to be saved the suffering and disastrous results involved in the criminal procedure in juvenile cases. Perhaps of equal importance from the standpoint of public welfare, child offenders whose cases are now dismissed or nol-prossed, or who receive nominal sentences through a desire to avoid unjust or harsh punishment, could then be given the protective care that would prevent future delinquency.

THE FORGOTTEN ADOLESCENT

A STUDY OF THE PRE-TRIAL TREATMENT OF BOYS CHARGED WITH CRIME IN NEW YORK CITY

———

A PUBLICATION OF

THE NEW YORK LAW SOCIETY
36 West 44th Street
New York City
1940

This study and its publication were
made possible by a grant from
Carnegie Corporation of New York.
Carnegie Corporation is not, however, the author, owner, publisher,
or proprietor of this publication,
and is not to be understood as
approving by virtue of its grant any
of the statements made or views
expressed therein.

TABLE OF CONTENTS

THE FORGOTTEN ADOLESCENT

A Study of the Pre-Trial Treatment of Boys
Charged with Crime in New York City

INTRODUCTION

Criminologists and lawyers may disagree on many issues but
they agree that in any effort to improve the administration of
criminal justice and advance the prevention of crime, the
problem of the young offender is crucial. This insight led to
the creation and development of the juvenile court with its
specialized procedure, humane approach and emphasis on treatment and rehabilitation. Whatever the imperfections of juvenile
court practice, the institution is one of the great achievements
of modern times. But the jurisdiction of the juvenile court
is rigidly circumscribed by an age limit which in New York
is fixed by statute at sixteen. In consequence, thousands of
immature persons above that age are annually caught in
the toils of the criminal law in New York City alone. Their
plight has been called to public attention on many occasions
during the past few years: more than a decade ago by the
Brooklyn Bureau of Charities, in 1931 by an able study prepared for the State Crime Commission and, more recently, by
two challenging volumes published in 1938, The Adolescent
Court and Crime Prevention[1] and Youth in the Toils.[2]
The issue has been and is of lively concern to social workers
and others interested in the welfare of youth and the improvement of law administration. In Brooklyn, an Adolescent Court
has been established as a part of the Magistrates' Courts. But
evaluation of the work of the Brooklyn court is still in the
controversial stages. Elsewhere in the City nothing of lasting
importance has been done.

Sensing a typical case of lag between the perception of social
need and the adaptation of legal machinery to fill the need,

---

[1] By Magistrate Jeanette G. Brill and Dr. E. George Payne (N. Y.,
Pitman).

[2] By Leonard V. Harrison and the late Pryor McNeill Grant, under
the auspices of the Delinquency Committee of the Boys Bureau formed
by the Association for Improving the Condition of the Poor and the
Charity Organization Society (N. Y., Macmillan).

The New York Law Society determined to reexamine the field, with particular reference to the legal problems involved in making the adaptation. In view of the Society's special interest in procedure, it was resolved to study the impact of the criminal law upon male adolescents[3] above the juvenile court age and below twenty-one, up to the time of trial—leaving to others the more complex penological issues involved in the ultimate disposition and treatment of those found guilty. In this respect we have been concerned with a much narrower problem than the American Law Institute which has undertaken an evaluation of the entire structure of criminal justice as it affects the adolescent group and has advanced far-reaching proposals for reform.

At the outset of our inquiry we faced the difficulty that on a number of basic questions, such as bail, the only quantitative data available was that for 1929 contained in the Report of the Crime Commission referred to above. Fortunately, the Citizens Committee on the Control of Crime, Inc., had collected case histories on every felony and serious misdemeanor charge for which an arrest was made for the year ending June 30, 1938. This material, indispensable to any statistical analysis of the problem, was generously made available by the Committee. A study of 2,793 adolescent cases included within this data and additional research, made possible by the consent of the New York City Department of Correction to examine its files, enabled us to reconstruct the statistical picture from almost contemporary records. We found that—as we had suspected—there has been some but relatively little change in the situation as it was described by the Crime Commission almost ten years earlier. For example, the Crime Commission pointed out that 90% of adolescents charged with felonies and serious misdemeanors were committed to detention jails at some stage of the proceedings against them although 75% ultimately were not imprisoned. Our statistics indicate that 78% of such adolescents were committed to jails at some point although 64% ultimately were not institutionalized.

---

[3] Female adolescents present a separate problem and one to which we have not addressed ourselves specifically. Our statistics indicate that among the adolescents charged with more serious crimes, they constitute 3.2% (see Table J, *infra*, p. 59), a percentage too small to affect any inference we may have drawn from those statistics.

Quite as important as this statistical survey, in persuading us of the need for change, was the simple observation of what happens to a youth charged with crime in this City from the time of his arrest until his trial—if, indeed, his case ever reaches the stage of an actual trial. As with many social problems, a careful observation of the existing state of affairs leads to understanding of an evil and points to a solution; the facts amenable to statistical tabulation merely enlarge the picture by indicating the magnitude of what is involved. Hence, in the report which follows, our major concern has been to describe once again the existing procedure for dealing with male adolescents who run afoul of the law, to examine its legal foundation and to set forth suggestions for its improvement. The results of our statistical study are set forth in detail in an Appendix.

Neither in our description nor in our recommendations do we purport to be breaking new ground. We have, however, desired to reach an independent judgment and, having done so, we set forth the results of our inquiry in the hope that we may be of assistance to those working in the field who rightly ask that at long last something constructive and permanent be done for the City as a whole.

PRE-ARRAIGNMENT PROCEDURE

A criminal prosecution may be initiated either by summons or arrest. The Code of Criminal Procedure restricts the use of the summons to misdemeanor and summary offense cases.[4] To facilitate the use of the summons, the Inferior Criminal Courts Act of New York City directs the Board of City Magistrates to prepare and issue summonses in blank, attested in the name of the Chief City Magistrate, to members of the police force for purposes stated in regulations adopted by the Board with the concurrence of the Police Commissioner.[5] Such a summons when filled in, countersigned by a police officer, and served upon the person to whom it is addressed, has the same effect as if it were issued individually and directly by the Chief Magistrate. In pursuance of regulations adopted under this section, members of the New York City

---

[4] New York Code of Criminal Procedure, Section 150.
[5] Inferior Criminal Courts Act of the City of New York, Sections 116 and 118.

Police Department are empowered to issue summonses in certain classes of cases involving petty offenses.[6]

In 1937, of the 42,500 adolescents between the ages of sixteen and twenty-one arrested or summoned,[7] 29,150 were charged with offenses with respect to which blank summonses may be issued. On the basis of Police Department statistics, we estimate that a blank summons was issued in every such case.[8] In the remaining 13,350 cases, including the summary offenses of disorderly conduct, vagrancy, gambling and jostling, the great majority of misdemeanors and all felonies, the adolescent's first contact with the law was an arrest in practically every instance.[9]

---

[6] For an enumeration of the offenses see New York City Police Department, Manual of Procedure (1937), Article 2, subdivision 92.

[7] According to the Annual Report of the Police Department of the City of New York for 1937 (p. 102), 941,789 persons were arrested or summoned. On the basis of tables therein contained (pp. 90-113), we estimate that of these persons, 16,000 were charged with felonies or serious misdemeanors. 3,600 of the 42,500 adolescents arrested or summoned in that same year were charged with the latter offenses. It is thus seen that while adolescents account for only a small part of all arrests made or summonses issued, less than 4.5%, they account for a very substantial part—about 22.5%—of arrests arising out of charges of the commission of felonies or serious misdemeanors.

For the crimes included within the term *serious misdemeanor,* as used in this report, see note 12, *infra.*

[8] The total of 42,500 is taken directly from the consolidated table in the Annual Report (1937) entitled "Total Number of Arrests by Age Groups" (p. 102). The term "arrests" is used as a general term to include cases initiated through the Police Department by summons and arrest. From the tables which follow (pp. 103-113), in which there is a breakdown of specific crimes by ages, we arrived at the figure 29,150. We found that for the year, 1937 all charges against adolescent defendants for which blank summonses could·be issued fell either into the category of traffic violations, motor vehicle law violations or violations of corporation ordinances. And from a general table (p. 11) in which all cases reported are broken down by general criminal classifications and then divided by individual arrests and persons summoned, we found that in all traffic, motor vehicle law and corporation ordinance cases, blank summonses were issued. This last table is not subdivided by age groups.

[9] There were 3,609 adolescents arrested for disorderly conduct, 1,400 for the summary offense of gambling, 802 for vagrancy, 58 for jostling, and approximately 515 for other summary offenses. Among the misdemeanors, the distribution was as follows: Gambling—1,015, petty larceny—810, simple assault—258, shoplifting—303, possessing dangerous weapons—146, unlawful entry—87, possessing burglar's tools—50, and others—635. Felonies accounted for approximately 3,340 arrests. The remaining 325 arrests included violations of parole, federal offenses and fugitives from justice.

When a summons is issued, the adolescent's only contact with the police is at the time of service. On the other hand, if arrested, and the crime charged is a felony, he remains in the custody of the police from the time of arrest until he is brought to court.[10] Where the crime charged is a misdemeanor or a summary offense, the arrestee may be released on posting of "station house bail",[11] but unless he can do so, he must remain in the custody of the police until brought to court. Our first aim is to determine the nature and incidents of this police custody.

Following an arrest, the officer proceeds with the boy on foot to the precinct station house. In an "emergency" the boy is handcuffed and transported in a police van.

On arriving at the station house, the adolescent is "booked" and searched. A person charged with a felony or serious misdemeanor[12] or disorderly conduct arising out of jostling or an attempt to "pickpocket" is then fingerprinted and photographed after which he is accompanied to the detectives' room for a thorough questioning.[13] Of the 395 adolescents in Man-

---

[10] Subdivision 70, Article 9 of the New York City Police Department, Manual of Procedure (1937) provides in part: "The police will be responsible for prisoners in their custody while transporting them to court, while prisoners are being arraigned, while prisoners are being tried, and at all times while prisoners are in court outside of the Detention Pens."

[11] New York Code of Criminal Procedure, Section 554. The Annual Reports of the Police Department contain no data on the frequency of release on station house bail.

[12] Serious misdemeanors where used in this report refer to those misdemeanors enumerated in Section 552, New York Code of Criminal Procedure, and include, possessing a dangerous weapon, possessing burglars' tools, receiving stolen property, unlawful entry of a building, aiding escape from prison and unlawfully possessing or distributing habit-forming narcotics.

[13] Rule 378 of the Rules and Regulations of the New York City Police Department states in part: "Persons arrested charged with felony or thievery, or with any of the misdemeanors or offenses mentioned in section 552 of the Code of Criminal Procedure . . . shall be taken without unnecessary delay to the precinct detective office for the purpose of identification." As it reads the rule may be interpreted to exclude questioning other than that which is necessary to identify the arrestee. No rule of the department or provision of the Manual of Procedure specifically provides for questioning arrestees to obtain confessions or other evidence. The detective's examination has become associated in the public mind with the "third degree". See Reports, National Commission on Law Observance and Enforcement, Lawlessness in Law Enforcement—Police (1931) 90 and 93.

hattan who were defended by the Voluntary Defenders Committee of the Legal Aid Society, 71 or 18% claimed to have been "beaten" by the police.[14] Some of the adolescent inmates at the New York City Reformatory whom we interviewed made similar claims; more of them charged only that they had been questioned very vigorously. While these charges may properly be viewed with some skepticism, it nevertheless remains true, as was asserted by a prominent committee of the Association of the Bar of the City of New York, that the practice of *in camera* detectives' examinations is conducive to the application of third degree methods.[15]

If accused of a felony or serious misdemeanor, the adolescent must pass through the "lineup" at headquarters in advance of being taken to court.[16] Since the lineup is conducted every morning at nine, all such arrestees are detained overnight in a station house. Those charged with minor crimes are not brought to headquarters for this purpose, but if the time of arrest was such that they could not be brought to court immediately after booking, they too are detained overnight.

In the fifty-one precincts possessing detention facilities, adults and adolescents are confined in the same quarters. The cells are small and equipped with a bunk, toilet and wash basin. The "joint-tight" solid wooden bunk is considered the most desirable by the State Commission of Correction and many precincts now possess them. The obsolete steel bunk is

---

[14] In that year the cases of 1,276 defendants of all ages were handled by the Committee, and in 201 or 15.7% of the cases there were claims of police beatings. The percentage of such claims has diminished since 1935, when there were claims in 405 cases, or 26% of the 1,554 cases handled, and 1936 when there were claims in 313 cases, or 19.4% of the 1,606 cases handled. "Police beatings" in the context in which it is here used includes any kind of alleged battery inflicted by the police during the time the defendant is in their custody.

[15] Reports, Association of the Bar of the City of New York (1928) 253.

[16] Rule 378 of the Rules and Regulations of the New York City Police Department reads in part: "All such persons (those charged with felonies or misdemeanors enumerated in Section 552 of the Code of Criminal Procedure) who have been arrested, and are still in custody of the police, shall be delivered at Manhattan Headquarters of the Detective Division not later than 8 A. M. the next day." We have been informed that some arrestees charged with felonies and serious misdemeanors are taken to court on the day of arrest without being brought to the lineup.

still used in some and the old-fashioned iron latticed bunk in a few. No bedding is supplied to males. Generally, the cell quarters are clean and in good order, but in a number of places they are in need of complete repainting and repair. Many of the precincts have sufficient accommodations to avoid doubling up except in the case of a raid.[17] However, in a few, facilities are so inadequate that doubling up must be resorted to even on normal nights. The Police Department's Manual of Procedure[18] provides for an expenditure not to exceed ten cents for food to be supplied from a neighborhood restaurant for persons without funds at mealtimes. The records of the State Commission of Correction indicate that there has been general compliance with this requirement but that an occasional precinct has failed to conform. Persons with funds may send for food at their own expense.

In the morning those required to pass through the lineup are transferred to headquarters. The others are taken to a district magistrate's court. In either event the trip is made in a police van. Those entering the van have been previously handcuffed in pairs. No special arrangements are made for transporting adolescents so that young boys in trouble for the first time may find themselves placed together with hardened adult offenders. The police van, commonly referred to as the "Black Maria", has become a symbol of disgrace in the public mind. Many young persons placed therein and handcuffed for the first time must experience extreme personal degradation.

At headquarters the group is first placed in a screened-off section of the lineup room. Here adolescents and adults are crowded together indiscriminately. In turn each one ascends a stage, upon which a powerful spotlight is directed, and while standing, assumes various profile and full-face positions to enable the audience of detectives to observe him closely. Although the detectives cannot be seen from the stage, their presence is very much felt by the person under observation. One of the boys interviewed put his own reaction in these words: "I don't

---

[17] Although adults and adolescent "prisoners" are housed in the same quarters, each prisoner is supposed to be housed in a separate cell. Article 13, subdivision 2 of the Manual of Procedure (1937) reads: "Only one prisoner will be detained in a cell overnight."

[18] Article 13, subdivision 4.

know why, but I suddenly got very scared. Everything inside of me sort of curled up." Most of the boys who have not been through it before,[19] and even many who have, must share his reaction.

After the lineup, the members of the group are finally taken to court. This means that the boy is again handcuffed and huddled into the "Black Maria" in indiscriminate association with older offenders.

It is clear that the present procedure following arrest and before arraignment is as unsympathetic a method of handling adolescents as could well be devised. At almost every point adolescents are thrown into association with adults charged with crime. Whatever the charge which led to their arrest, they are handcuffed and transported in the "Black Maria". Those charged with serious offenses may, on occasion, be subjected to fairly harsh treatment by detectives. Whether or not they are, they probably fear that they will be and most of them are forced to undergo the disturbing experience of the lineup. Finally, facilities for overnight detention in station houses are such that no special account can be taken of the needs of the immature. It is, of course, recognized that public security requires that in the more serious misdemeanor and felony cases, prosecution should be initiated by arrest rather than by summons. But public security does not require that in the time between arrest and arraignment all adolescents should be exposed to the disagreeable incidents we have described.

MAGISTRATES' COURTS

The courts of first contact for arrestees are, with one minor exception,[20] the Magistrates' Courts. These courts occupy a uniquely important position and their methods of handling adolescents are of great significance.

---

[19] Of the 2,793 adolescent cases studied for this report, only 560, or one out of five, had records of previous arrests. See Table H, *infra,* p. 58.

[20] The exception arises in a case where the Grand Jury hands down an indictment although there has been no preliminary examination in the magistrates' courts. (See New York Code of Criminal Procedure, Section 252.) This occurs infrequently. Of 2,793 adolescents prosecuted for felonies or serious misdemeanors from July, 1937, through June, 1938, 146 (5.2%) were proceeded against on indictment without a preliminary examination.

The Felony Court

From police headquarters a person charged with a felony or serious misdemeanor is taken to a felony court[21] for arraignment. Felony courts[22] have been established in Manhattan, Brooklyn, Bronx and Queens.

On his arrival at the court, the accused is placed in a detention pen to await the call of his case. This pen, known as the "bull pen", is in the Manhattan court a large room, barred at the windows and doors, with wooden benches adjacent to the walls and a toilet in one corner. Judged by any standards this detention pen is an extremely unsatisfactory place. The detention pen in the Bronx Felony Court is equally bad. There are, however, better quarters in the Brooklyn and Queens Felony Courts because these courts are housed in newer buildings. But in all these pens men and boys of all ages, starting with sixteen, and of all types, both first and repeated offenders, are detained together. The intermingling which takes place, as we have said, first at the police stations, next in the police vans, then at police headquarters, is continued in the bull pens.

The general practice seems to be that at a time which may be as long as an hour before the call of the defendant's case on the calendar, he is taken from the bull pen, where he may already have been waiting from a half-hour to three hours, to a "cage" situated in the court room. In the Manhattan Court the cage is a rectangular enclosure wired on the sides and at the top. It contains, adjacent to the wall, a bench, which accommodates approximately ten persons. The occupants of

---

[21] Section 145 of the Inferior Criminal Courts Act of the City of New York (in effect July 1, 1936) creates in the magistrates' courts a felony court with separate parts in New York, Bronx and Kings Counties, it being provided that the chief magistrate may create other parts as the need arises. Section 147 provides that where such courts are established all persons arrested for a felony or any of the misdemeanors enumerated in Section 552 of the Code of Criminal Procedure must be arraigned and examined before a magistrate holding the felony court.
For the distribution by age and original charge of 2,793 adolescents charged with felonies and serious misdemeanors, whose cases were studied in connection with this report, see Table G, *infra,* p. 56.

[22] The Manhattan Felony Court is located on Centre Street in the Criminal Courts Building, a building the age of which is attested by the fact that it is to be replaced shortly by a new one. The Brooklyn Court in the new Central Courts Building, 120 Schermerhorn Street, was erected in 1931. The Bronx Court is housed in a very old building, 3rd Avenue and 161st Street, while the Queens Court, Catalpa Avenue and Fresh Pond Road, is housed in a relatively new building. There is no branch of the Felony Court in Richmond.

the cage are, of course, within easy view of everyone in the
court room, and the sessions of these courts, for one reason
or another, are extremely well attended. The cage in the
Bronx Felony Court has no seating accommodations but instead contains the stairs leading to the detention pens. The
accused persons stand on these stairs while awaiting the
call of their cases. Those standing at the top of the stairs
can be seen by the public in the court room. The Queens
Felony Court has a slightly different type of cage. It is a par-
titioned-off section of the court room open at the top in which
the defendants, unseen by those in the court room, stand while
awaiting the call of their cases. The Brooklyn Felony Court
functions without a cage.

On the calendar call, the court attendant announces the name
of the defendant and the name of the arresting officer, including the precinct to which the latter is attached. The defendant
is released from the cage and approaches the clerk's table in
front of the judge's bench. The complaint is read aloud to him.
The attendant then turns to the defendant, informs him of his
right to counsel,[23] asks whether he pleads guilty or not guilty
and whether he desires to "waive examination".[24]

---

[23] Section 188 of the New York Code of Criminal Procedure provides: "When the defendant is brought before a magistrate upon an
arrest, the magistrate must immediately inform him of the charge
against him, and of his right to the aid of counsel in every stage of
the proceedings and before any further proceedings are had." The
Legal Aid Society has a representative only in the Manhattan Felony
Court, and the defendant is told that if he cannot afford an attorney,
the magistrate will assign their representative as counsel. In the latter
instance, the defendant is given an opportunity to consult with his
assigned counsel before pleading and the hearing is usually adjourned
to a later date.

[24] Section 190 of the New York Code of Criminal Procedure provides: "The magistrate, immediately after the appearance of counsel,
or if none appear and the defendant require the aid of counsel, must,
after waiting a reasonable time therefor, proceed to examine the case,
unless the defendant waives examination."
The practice of asking the defendant how he pleads is not provided
for in the Code of Criminal Procedure. Section 198 provides that if
the defendant chooses to make a statement, *only* the following questions
may be put to him:
"What is your name and age?"
"Where were you born?"
"Where do you reside, and how long have you resided
there?"
"What is your business or profession?"
"Give any explanation you may think proper, of the circumstances in the testimony against you, and state any facts
which you think will tend to your exculpation. [*sic!*]"

The examination or hearing in a Magistrate's Court is not unlike that in any other court of law. Its object in this instance is to determine by an examination of the witnesses whether a *prima facie* case of the commission of the alleged crime can be established. The magistrate, after hearing all the evidence, can either discharge the accused, hold him for the Grand Jury or the Court of Special Sessions, or order the substitution of a charge over which he has summary jurisdiction.[25] By and large, these hearings are conducted carefully and in an orderly manner. There is prevalent, however, a general atmosphere of noise and confusion due to the fact that the physical facilities are inadequate for the great number of people who have business there. Under these circumstances the public expression of Society's grievance against the defendant, unaccompanied as it is by any systematic proffer of understanding assistance, threatens a profound and unnecessary shock to a young and impressionable boy. The unwisdom of this practice is emphasized by the fact that in almost one out of every five cases adolescent defendants are exonerated in this court.[26]

The District Courts

The arraignment and hearing of persons charged with committing a summary offense or ordinary misdemeanor[27] takes

---

[25] There are many minor offenses, not rising to the "dignity of crimes" over which magistrates have summary jurisdiction. (See Peo. *ex rel.* Burke v. Fox [1912], 205 N. Y. 490, 494.) Among these offenses are disorderly conduct, vagrancy, begging, intoxication, violation of corporation ordinances.
Under Sections 130 and 131 of the Inferior Criminal Courts Act of New York City a magistrate may, with the consent of the defendant, sit as a Court of Special Sessions for the trial and determination of certain misdemeanor charges such as Sabbath breaking, sanitary law violations, coin receptacle frauds and railroad law violations.

[26] Of 2,647 adolescents arraigned in the Felony Court, from July, 1937, through June, 1938, 18.4% were dismissed, 58.2% were held for the Grand Jury, 15.7% were held for the Court of Special Sessions, 6.3% were disposed of as wayward minors, 1% were convicted of other summary offenses, and .2% were acquitted of other summary offenses. See Table D, *infra*, p. 52.

[27] By ordinary misdemeanor we mean one not embraced within Section 147 of the Inferior Criminal Courts Act of New York City, which provides that arraignment for felonies and the very serious misdemeanors enumerated in Section 552 of the Code of Criminal Procedure must be in a Felony Court. For the misdemeanors covered by Section 552, see note 12, *supra*. Among the ordinary misdemeanors are included petty larceny, gambling, simple assault and indecent exposure.

place in one of the many district magistrates' courts scattered throughout the city.[28] In these courts the accused persons who have been taken into custody by arrest are detained in a bull pen of the same type used in the Felony Courts. If the court room contains a cage it too is utilized in the same manner with the accused being put there for a short interval of time prior to the call of his case on the calendar.[29] While the treatment of adolescents in the District Court parallels that in the Felony Court in these respects, as well as in the absence of segregation and in the public hearing, it is fair to say that the District Court presents a less serious problem, precisely because all of the persons arraigned, adults as well as adolescents, are charged with relatively minor offenses. The process is likely, therefore, to involve less terror and degradation for the adolescent and the danger of his intermingling with adults, though genuine, is unlikely to be so grave. On the other hand, bull pens and cages remain bull pens and cages, regardless of the crime charged. And the importance of adopting a protective attitude toward young persons may reasonably be regarded as even more important when they are charged with relatively trivial wrong-doing than when they are suspected of serious crimes. Moreover, many of the cases in the District Court, involving such complaints as disorderly conduct, may point to a maladjustment likely to develop rapidly into patterns of genuine criminality unless a proper readjustment is achieved.

---

[28] See Sections 101 and 106 of the Inferior Criminal Courts Act. Females charged with (a) keeping a disorderly house, (b) wayward minor, (c) prostitution under Section 350, Multiple Dwelling Law, (d) prostitution under subdivision 4, Section 887, Code of Criminal Procedure, and (e) larceny (shoplifting) as a misdemeanor are arraigned in the Ninth District Court known as the Women's Court. The territorial jurisdiction of this court includes the entire City of New York. There is a Night Court in Manhattan and the Bronx for the arraignment of men charged with summary offenses and ordinary misdemeanors. Recently such a court has been established in Brooklyn with a territorial jurisdiction to include Queens.

[29] In these courts, the magistrate is prone to assume the roles of both prosecutor and defense counsel inasmuch as a representative from the district attorney's office is present only for unusual cases, the Legal Aid Society has no representative and rarely, if ever, is counsel assigned. Hearings are short and usually held on the same day that the accused is arraigned. If the hearing is adjourned, or sentence is reserved, or the defendant is held for Special Sessions, the magistrate may parole the defendant in another's custody or release him on his own recognizance, or set bail.

The District Court, with its limited facilities and varied business, is obviously ill-adapted to rendering this constructive social service.

Bail and Parole

When a person is arrested for committing a crime, if it be a felony or serious misdemeanor, the court *may* fix bail, and if it be a misdemeanor other than a serious one, the court *must* fix bail pending trial.[30] And the New York State Constitution[31] provides that when bail is required, it shall not be excessive. Magistrates are given the power to set bail or place the defendant on parole until his appearance is required unless the individual has previously been convicted of a felony or twice convicted of certain serious misdemeanors. In such cases, under Section 552 of the Code of Criminal Procedure, bail may only be set by a judge of one of the higher courts, and under Section 103 of the Inferior Criminal Courts Act, the magistrate may not parole the defendant even though he is reasonably satisfied that he would appear.

The "purpose of requiring the defendant to give bail after arrest is to secure his presence at the trial"[32] The elements which in general "may properly be taken into consideration by the court in determining the amount of bail" have been said to be the "nature of the offense, the penalty of the offense, the probability of the willing appearance of the defendant or his flight to avoid punishment, the pecuniary and social conditions of the defendant and his general reputation and character, and the apparent strength of the proof as bearing upon the probability of conviction".[33] The same elements would presumably be regarded as relevant in determining whether to release on parole rather than to require any bail. But these

---

[30] Section 553 of the New York Code of Criminal Procedure provides: "If the charge be for any crime other than as specified in Section 552, he may be admitted to bail before conviction as follows:
    1. As a matter of right, in cases of misdemeanors.
    2. As a matter of discretion in all other cases."

[31] Article 1, Section 5.

[32] People *ex rel.* Rothensies v. Searles, 229 A. D. 603, 343 N. Y. Supp. 15 (1930).

[33] *Ibid.*

elements are of unequal significance and the enumeration is not exhaustive. Under ordinary circumstances, the age, character and family situation of the defendant have far more bearing on the danger of flight than has the nature of the offense charged. Neither the requirement of bail nor pre-trial detention in default of bail is a punitive device. The problem is to obtain—by the method least burdensome or damaging to the defendant—reasonable assurance that he will appear for trial.

The consideration of parole and bail in these terms should permit the development of a wholesome policy of keeping as many youthful defendants as possible out of our pre-trial detention prisons. Yet the data we have compiled, like that for 1929 reported in the Crime Commission's study,[34] clearly indicates that no such policy has been developed. In the year ending June 30, 1938, 78% of all adolescent defendants between the ages of sixteen and twenty-one charged with felonies and serious misdemeanors in the boroughs of Manhattan, Brooklyn and Queens[35] were committed to detention prisons[36] because they were unable to post bail required for their release, or at least to post it without some delay.[37] Yet 1,431 or 64% of the

[34] "Originally 90 per cent of them (adolescents) could not obtain bail, and at no time during the procedure were more than 22 per cent at liberty." Report, pp. 84-85. For the derivation of these figures, see p. 167.

[35] The data on detention were obtained from an examination of the files of the Department of Correction, the jurisdiction of which does not include the detention prison in the Bronx. Identification of cases for the purpose of this study was effected by a recanvassing of the records of the Citizens Committee for Manhattan, Brooklyn and Queens. The result of this recanvass gave us 2,227 cases or 100 less than the number contained in our data of final dispositions for those boroughs in Table C (I), a discrepancy which may be accounted for by the necessity of sifting through the records of more than 10,000 cases.

[36] Detention prisons are to be distinguished from penal institutions. Our figures on detention are concerned with commitment to the former institutions from arraignment to final disposition.

[37] 1,758 adolescents, or 78% of the 2,227 whose cases were studied, were committed to detention prisons. (See Table A, *infra*, p. 46.) 1,137, or 64.7% of the 1,758, were detained for the entire duration of their cases. 621, or 35.3%, were released after being detained for some part of the duration of their cases. (See Table B, *infra*, p. 50.) Of the former group, the median duration of detention was 34.3 days, and 25% were detained for more than 57.2 days before their release. Of the latter group, the median was 3.1 days, but 25% were detained for more than 8.9 days.

adolescents charged with such offenses in these boroughs ultimately were discharged, acquitted, given suspended sentences, or placed on probation.[38] The result was that of these 1,431 boys who were not ultimately sent to prison or otherwise institutionalized, 74% were nevertheless at this initial stage of the proceeding incarcerated in a city jail awaiting disposition of their cases. This picture becomes even more significant when it is remembered that four out of every five adolescents had no record of previous arrests.[39]

The conclusion is inevitable that no concerted effort has been made to solve the problem of insuring the appearance of adolescent defendants charged with felonies or serious misdemeanors when they are wanted in court without subjecting most of them to some period of detention in jail. Individual magistrates may, of course, have made such an effort. But the fact is that no satisfactory result has been achieved.

The Brooklyn Adolescent Court

The preceding description of the operation of the Felony and District Magistrates' Courts demonstrates their failure to meet the peculiar needs of the adolescent. A partial step towards coping with this problem has been taken in the establishment of the Brooklyn Adolescent Court, to which we have previously referred.

This court came into existence on January 1, 1935, as a special part of the Magistrates' Courts pursuant to a resolution

---

[38] The disposition figure given above, like the detention figure, is taken from Table A, *infra,* p. 46. It is to be noted that the ratio of adolescent defendants not institutionalized to those institutionalized as shown in Table A is substantially the same as that shown in Table C (I), *infra,* p. 51, for the same boroughs. It is thus seen that the difference of 100 cases between the net totals of Tables A and C (I) introduces no significant error. The apparent discrepancy between 771 commitments in Table A for 2,227 cases and 766 in Table C (I) for 2,327 cases can be explained by the fact that the data in Table A includes the sentences for a number of the 51 cases included in Table C (I) as convictions with sentences unrecorded. Table C (I) was based solely on data in the files of the Citizens Committee whereas Table A was based on data obtained from the Department of Correction as well.

[39] See note 19, *supra.*

adopted by the Board of Magistrates.[40]   It was accorded jurisdiction over male adolescents under nineteen years of age
charged with felonies, misdemeanors and summary offenses not
heard in such specialized divisions of the Magistrates' Courts
as the Traffic, Homicide and Municipal Term Courts.

Before examining the operation of this court it should be
noted that no change has been made in the arrest procedure in
Brooklyn.   Up to arraignment, an adolescent arrested in Brooklyn is handled no differently from an adolescent arrested in
Manhattan.

Adolescents charged with a felony or serious misdemeanor
are first taken before the regular Felony Court in Brooklyn.[41]
Here there is an initial sifting by the presiding magistrate who,
on the basis of a short preliminary hearing, determines whether
to transfer the defendant to the Adolescent Court or to dispose
of his case according to the regular procedure.   If the magistrate in the Felony Court determines that the defendant should
be handled by the Adolescent Court, he is taken there on the
same or the following day.   In all other cases, defendants are
initially arraigned in the Adolescent Court.

Hearings in the Adolescent Court are conducted in chambers
and are closed to the general public.   Parents and witnesses are
required to wait in the court room itself until the case is called.
Defendants are detained in a large room in the basement of the
court house.

A case is commenced by the attendant going through the
same routine used in arraigning a defendant in the regular
magistrates' courts.   The magistrate then asks the defendant to
tell his story.   If the defendant protests his innocence, an
examination is conducted.   Since January 1, 1940, an Assistant

---

[40] When, in 1936, the Inferior Criminal Courts Act of the City of
New York was amended to provide for the establishment in the Magistrates' Courts of a Felony Court for arraignment and examination of
all felonies and serious misdemeanors (note 21, *supra*) it was provided
that "nothing in this section (Section 147) contained shall be construed
as to prevent the arraignment and examination in the adolescent court
of offenders between the ages of 16 and 18 charged with such felonies
. . . or misdemeanors."

[41] When the Adolescent Court was first organized, all defendants between sixteen and eighteen were initially arraigned there.   The practice
was changed on February 1, 1938, but we are informed that the original
practice may again be put into effect.

District Attorney is present in court each day, so that it is
now possible, if the defendant is ready to proceed, to have an
examination either on the day of arraignment or the following
day. If the boy admits his guilt, or the magistrate believes
him guilty after a hearing, the case is discussed with the
Assistant District Attorney and the attending probation officer
who has already had a short interview with the boy. On the
basis of this discussion, the magistrate decides whether to substitute a charge of being a wayward minor,[42] a summary
offense defined by the Code of Criminal Procedure to include
various types of "dissolute" and "immoral" behavior by adolescents between the ages of sixteen and twenty-one, or order
the substitution of another charge over which he has summary
jurisdiction, or hold the defendant for the Grand Jury or the
Court of Special Sessions.

After a wayward minor charge has been substituted there is
a relatively complete investigation by the Probation Department
of the defendant's social background and psychological attri-
butes. On the basis of this investigation the judge determines
whether to place the boy on probation, commit him to Coxsackie
or Children's Village, or (and this happens very rarely) hold
him for the Grand Jury or the Court of Special Sessions.

Pending the outcome of the investigation, the boy may either
be paroled, released on bail, or if unable to furnish bail, committed to the Raymond Street Jail. According to the latest
report[43] of the Adolescent Court most defendants held for investigation are paroled.

---

[42] Section 913a of the Code of Criminal Procedure defines a wayward
minor as "any person between the ages of 16 and 21 who either (1) is
habitually addicted to the use of drugs or intemperate use of liquor,
(2) habitually associates with dissolute persons, or (3) is found of his
or her own free will in a house of prostitution or assignation or ill
fame, or (4) habitually associates with thieves, prostitutes, pimps or
procurers or disorderly persons, or (5) is willfully disobedient to the
reasonable and lawful commands of parent, guardian or other cus-
todian and is morally depraved or is in danger of becoming morally
depraved."
The Annual Report of the Brooklyn Adolescents' Court for 1938
does not indicate the frequency with which wayward minor charges are
substituted. Our data, covering felony and serious misdemeanor cases
arraigned in the Adolescents' Court from July, 1937, through June, 1938,
show that wayward minor charges were substituted in 11.7% (53 out
of 451) of those cases.

[43] See Annual Report (1938) at p. 26.

From the time the Adolescent Court was established until some time in 1938 four judges were assigned to the court. The judges presided in rotation for a period of two weeks each. After a report[44] by the Division of Probation of the State Department of Correction criticizing this arrangement, the court was reorganized so that one judge was assigned permanently. However, since the spring of 1939 assignments to this court have been on the same basis as assignments to the regular magistrates' courts.

It can be seen that this court is designed not only to improve methods of pre-conviction handling but also to effect changes in the policy of ultimate treatment. It is the latter purpose that is served by the device of reducing the original charge in a "deserving" case to that of being a "wayward minor", with the result that the Adolescent Court can retain jurisdiction of the boy and control his ultimate disposition. Reduction of the charge is based on the court's judgment as to the desirability of treating the defendant in this way rather than subjecting him to the processes of the ordinary criminal courts, not on an evaluation of the sufficiency of the legal evidence to warrant holding him to answer for the crime charged. The procedure, therefore, involves an extra-legal assumption by magistrates of summary jurisdiction over persons whose behavior may actually constitute a felony or misdemeanor beyond their jurisdiction.[45] The desirability of "legalizing" this procedure or extend-

---

[44] Report of A Study of the Adolescents' Court of the Magistrates' Courts of New York City (1936) 25, 26.

[45] If during the course of a hearing in a felony or misdemeanor case, it eventuates that the evidence only justifies a summary offense charge, i.e., a charge over which a magistrate has summary jurisdiction, the presiding magistrate may dismiss the original charge and order a new complaint drawn up charging the commission of a summary offense. Peo. v. McCabe (1932) 144 Misc. 702, 259 N. Y. Supp. 734. But the statutes confer no power upon a magistrate to order such reduction on any grounds other than the insufficiency of the evidence to establish "probable cause" for requiring the defendant to stand trial on the more serious charge and its sufficiency to warrant a charge of the lesser offense. Otherwise, he is confined to dismissing the charge or holding the defendant for the Grand Jury or Court of Special Sessions. See Peo. v. Warden (1932) 259 N. Y. 430, 433; Peo. v. McCarthy (1929) 250 N. Y. 258, 264. Moreover, a wayward minor charge, which is a summary offense, cannot be established by a plea of guilty but only "upon competent evidence after a hearing" as required by Section 913b of the Code of Criminal Procedure. Peo. v. Brewster

ing it to other boroughs without "legalization" depends upon two major factors: (a) the desirability of permitting judges, in their discretion, to treat adolescents technically guilty of felonies or misdemeanors by methods approximating those employed in the Children's Court; (b) the desirability, if this practice is approved, of entrusting the discretion to magistrates rather than to judges of some other court or rank or to some other agency. We are not prepared to pass judgment on this phase of the problem presented by the Adolescent Court which we regard as beyond the scope of the present study. We do believe, however, that in relation to pre-conviction problems, the Brooklyn Adolescent Court has introduced improvements of definite value.

The housing of the court in a separate building means that adolescents do not associate with adults. Closed hearings in chambers shelter a boy from the disagreeable effects of formal hearings in open court although this is to a great extent offset by the fact that all those charged with felonies and serious misdemeanors are first arraigned in the Felony Court. The utilization of parole pending disposition in nearly all cases of defendants whose charges have been reduced to "wayward minor" represents another improvement. This is reflected in the fact that among those under nineteen years of age not ultimately imprisoned, commitment to a detention prison was less frequent from the Brooklyn Adolescent Court than from courts elsewhere in the city.[46] Finally, the close co-operation between the Probation Department and the judge in the Adolescent

---

(1931) 232 App. Div. 1, 248 N. Y. Supp. 599, aff'd 256 N. Y. 558. In the Brooklyn Adolescent Court no hearing is held on the wayward minor charge.

Speaking of the Brooklyn Adolescent Court, Magistrate Jeanette G. Brill has said: "We pay no attention to it [the penal code] at all insofar as reducing a felony to a wayward minor is concerned." Proceedings, Governor's Conference on Crime, The Criminal and Society (1935) 277-278. But the question of jurisdiction has not been tested in the higher courts.

The statistics for the year ending June 30, 1938, show that the practice of reducing a charge to being a wayward minor obtains in Bronx and Queens as well as in Brooklyn. Indeed, the percentage of reductions in the Queens Felony Court (26.8) was larger than in the Brooklyn Adolescent Court (11.7). However, no special court has been established in Queens and the practice has not received the public attention that it has in Brooklyn.

[46] The comparative figures were: Brooklyn Adolescent Court, 54.3%; Brooklyn Felony Court, 72.6%; Queens Felony Court, 64.8%; and Manhattan Felony Court, 77.4%.

Court provides one of the necessary foundations for an even more extended use of parole.

DETENTION PRIOR TO FINAL DISPOSITION

There is no specialized institution in New York City for the detention until the final disposition of their cases of adolescents who have not been paroled or released on bail. It has therefore been necessary to confine them in various prisons, some of which have long been deemed obsolete and none of which was designed with an eye to the special needs of youth.

In Manhattan, defendants charged with an offense or misdemeanor within the jurisdiction of the magistrate for ultimate disposition are detained overnight in either the West Side (Seventh District) or Harlem (Fifth District) Jails.[47]

Defendants charged with a misdemeanor with respect to which magistrates have jurisdiction only to conduct a preliminary examination are also detained in these district jails until their examination is completed. If they are held for trial at the Court of Special Sessions, they are then transferred to the City Prison, Manhattan, familiarly known as the Tombs.

All defendants arraigned in the Manhattan Felony Court are detained in the Tombs.

In Brooklyn and Queens all defendants, irrespective of the crime charged or the court in which they were arraigned, are committed to the Brooklyn or Queens City Prisons; these institutions, as well as those enumerated above, are under the jurisdiction of the New York City Department of Correction.

In Bronx and Richmond[48] defendants are committed to their respective county jails, each of which is under the jurisdiction of the County Sheriff.

It is to be noted that whenever defendants have to be transferred from a court to a ·jail not adjoining it, or from one jail to another, a Department of Correction van or, in the

---

[47] If convicted, they may be detained in one or the other of these jails pending investigation by a probation officer. Moreover, a workhouse sentence for a period of less than five days is spent in these jails.

[48] Richmond was excluded from the scope of this study in view of its relatively negligible case load (see p. 36) and the absence of statistical data in the files of the Citizens Committee on the Control of Crime, Inc.

Bronx and Richmond, the Sheriff's van is used. These vehicles are large, enclosed trucks with screened vents along the top of each side. Before being placed in this van, the accused are handcuffed. Again there is no segregation of adolescents or of first offenders.

West Side and Harlem District Jails

The West Side and Harlem District Jails in Manhattan are dark, damp, dreary places. They have the familiar barred small cells, each of which contains two cots—minus mattresses—suspended from the walls. In the normal course of events, boys between the ages of sixteen and twenty-one are housed on a separate tier at both jails. Occasionally, following an unexpected police dragnet, a large number of vagrants is committed to the West Side Jail from the Manhattan Night Court with which it is connected. At such times it is not only necessary to dispense with the attempted "segregation" of adolescents on a separate tier but cots must be placed in the corridors to house the sudden influx of inmates.

The toilet and washing facilities are hopelessly inadequate and in need of repair. Each jail contains two showers to serve an average daily prison population of approximately two hundred.

Meals are served in the corridors in the Harlem Jail or on the tiers in the West Side Jail, where small tables are placed with four stools to each table.

There is no planned activity for the inmates during the course of the day, eighteen to twenty hours of which are spent in the cells. In the remaining three or four hours they are allowed into the corridors on the main floor in the Harlem Jail or on the tiers in the West Side Jail,[49] where some sit around talking and others play cards or checkers. The West Side Jail also has a small library containing some sixty old books and twenty magazines.

Opinion seems to be unanimous among administrators and other informed persons that the West Side and Harlem Dis-

---

[49] At present the semi-outdoor garage of the West Side Jail is being converted into a recreation place so that some of the inmates, probably the Workhouse help and material witnesses, will occasionally be able to get some fresh air.

trict Jails in Manhattan are unsuited for the detention of a large and heterogeneous population. A recent report by the State Correction Commission characterizes the conditions of housing at the West Side Jail as "indefensible from the standpoint of decency and humaneness", a verdict which applies with equal justice to the Harlem Jail. Yet every week in the year ten to twenty boys are confined in those institutions from one to three days pending trial.

City Prison, Manhattan (The Tombs)

The Tombs, which was built in 1897, consists of a main prison with two annexes, North and South, and has a normal capacity for 553 persons. First offenders under twenty-one years of age are housed in the North Annex and second offenders under that age are housed in the South Annex.

In these annexes, the cell blocks, composed of stone and brick, constitute a building within a building. The cells are arranged on tiers and each tier has a narrow gallery facing the outside wall. The cells open on this gallery.

There are 72 cells in the North Annex and 52 cells in the South Annex. The cells are in incredibly poor condition and receive very little sunlight. Each cell contains two old rusted iron cots suspended from a wall, an open flush toilet in one corner and a wash basin in the other. All plumbing, both in and out of the cells, is exposed. It is virtually impossible to keep the walls, exposed plumbing or the cots clean. For many years it has been recognized that the annexes as well as the main building are in a hopelessly wretched state, and this recognition is responsible for the present construction of a new Tombs, to which we later refer (p. 39).

As each boy is admitted he is given a towel, pillow case, two sheets and two blankets; one blanket has to serve as a mattress. Linens and the towel are changed weekly.

The average daily number of boys in the North Annex is about sixty-five. About thirty adult men who have been committed to the New York City Penitentiary on Riker's Island sleep in the North Annex of the Tombs but work during the day at the Women's Detention Home. They leave the Tombs in the morning and come back in the late afternoon. There are opportunities, of course, for occasional contact between these men and the younger inmates. Moreover, their presence necessitates the doubling up of a number of boys in the small cells.

In sharp contrast to the deplorable physical conditions has been the attempt to develop a program, approximating that of a correctional institution, under which the boys can spend a substantial part of the day outside their cells in wholesome activity. The following program is now in use:

7:30 to 9:00 A. M.	Breakfast in the cells and cleanup
9:00 to 9:30	Physician's visiting hours
9:30 to 10:50	School
10:50 to 11:05	Indoor recreation
11:05 to 11:30	Lunch in the cells
11:30 to 12:30	Indoor recreation
12:30 to 2:00 P.M.	Outdoor recreation
2:00 to 3:45	Lecture and movies
3:45	Return to cells
4:00	Dinner in the cells
9:00	Lights out

The indoor activities take place on the main floor, which consists of three corridors. The school, conducted by a young keeper who is a college graduate, is not compulsory, but most boys attend for otherwise they must remain in their cells. The curriculum consists mainly of elementary English, history and geography. Most of the boys spend the indoor recreation periods playing cards or checkers, sitting around and talking, and reading books borrowed from a library which contains about seventy volumes. Others, adept at drawing or mechanical work, are encouraged to devote their recreation periods to these activities; and a little cheer has been added to the jail by a dozen drawings hung on the wall and bookcases constructed out of odd boxes. The lecturer in the afternoon period may be a minister, or someone sent out by the Board of Health or by a City Museum. The lecture is usually accompanied by educational movies or slides.

For the outdoor recreation period, the boys are taken to the prison yard where they may play a variety of soft ball games.

The keeper in charge of the North Annex stated that since the program has been in effect, the boys are less sullen, do less swearing, and are not so apt to make their crimes the main topic of conversation. This is encouraging, but the work of the Department of Correction is necessarily handicapped by the woefully limited physical facilities.

There is a social service bureau in charge of a volunteer worker. Sometimes legal aid arrangements are made for needy boys to whom counsel was not assigned by the court. In addition, if the parents or relatives of a boy are uninformed as to his predicament, the bureau attempts to get in touch with them. Occasionally, clothes are obtained for an unusually poor boy.

No program has been arranged for the boys housed in the South Annex, other than to permit them to stand or walk around the narrow galleries outside their cells most of the morning and in the afternoon until 3:30.

City Prison, Brooklyn (Raymond Street Jail)

This prison was built in 1850 and rebuilt in 1910. It is composed of a main building and an annex or wing. The normal capacity of both buildings is about 469 persons.

Boys from sixteen through eighteen years of age who are being held by the Brooklyn Adolescent Court are housed in the annex which formerly was the Women's Wing. Consisting of three tiers, it has a total of sixty-six steel cells with two cell blocks of eleven cells each on a tier. The cells, unlike those in the North Annex of the Tombs, get a reasonable share of air and sunlight since their rear, composed solely of bars, is close to the outside windows. In addition, they are clean, comparatively bright and freshly painted. Each cell is equipped with a cot and spring, a toilet and a wash basin in good condition. There is a daily morning inspection of the cells. Upon his admission a boy is given two blankets, two sheets, one pillow and slip, and one towel. As at the Tombs, one blanket serves as a mattress and the linen and towel are changed weekly.

Prisoners from Riker's Island who work in this jail are also assigned quarters in the Wing. Consequently there are accom-

modations for a maximum of fifty-four boys and it is sometimes necessary to keep a boy temporarily in the Main Building, described below, even though he is being held by the
Adolescent Court.

There is some planned activity in the Wing but it is greatly
restricted by inadequate facilities. During the morning, there is
an hour period for school and a one and one-half hour period
for recreation on the main floor of the wing. In the afternoon
the boys are permitted out in the yard for an hour and this is
followed by another hour of indoor recreation. They spend
their indoor recreation periods playing cards or checkers or
just sitting around and talking. There is a library of a hundred and fifty books, a gift from the Kings County Grand
Jurors Association, of which some boys avail themselves,
although a glance at the titles included would create doubts
as to their appeal to boys in this age group. Once a week
on Wednesdays, lectures are given and movies shown in the
chapel. These are also attended by the older boys from the
Main Building. There is a social service bureau similar to
the one at the Tombs.

In the Main Building there are eight tiers in each of the
two stone cell blocks. In one of the blocks, boys from
sixteen through eighteen years of age, who are being held by
courts other than the Adolescent Court, are kept on one tier,
those from nineteen to twenty-one on another, and those from
twenty-one to twenty-three on a third. The cells are dreary,
bleak and airless. Some were in the process of being
painted, though crudely, at the time this jail was visited. The
toilets seem to need repair.

The only recreation in this building consists of a walk
around the main corridor of the cell block for an hour and a
half in the morning and again in the afternoon. The inmates
walk in one direction for three-quarters of an hour, a bell
rings, they automatically turn around and walk for three-
quarters of an hour in the opposite direction. Their feet
never seem to leave the ground as they walk. They just
shuffle along, shoulders drooped, faces expressionless even when
they are talking.

City Prison, Queens

The City Prison, Queens, was erected in 1895 and consists of a main building and an annex. The main building has five tiers of cells constructed on a pit-like basis around one central corridor. There is thus no opportunity for real segregation of the adolescent inmates in this building, though segregation is attempted by housing them on the top tier. This jail is definitely brighter and more airy than either the Tombs or the Main Building of the Raymond Street Jail. The toilets and sinks appear to be in good condition. The cells are generally clean and neat. There are twenty-eight cells on each tier with two cots in each cell. Since the average daily population on the top tier numbers about fifteen, it is rarely found necessary to place two boys in a cell. Sometimes a newcomer, who is depressed or frightened, is placed in the same cell with an inmate who, the Warden believes, will help him to make an adjustment.

There are no facilities for indoor recreation. Nor are the boys permitted out in the yard because, according to the Deputy Warden, there is a steady stream of trucks entering and leaving at all hours. From eight to eleven in the morning and one to four in the afternoon the inmates may congregate on the galleries of the tiers, where they are left to their own devices. There is a library of one hundred and fifty books, supplied by the Public Library, which is maintained on the main floor. Every Wednesday books are changed and on that day the inmates are allowed on the main floor to return their old books and to borrow new ones. They may exchange books with each other. There is no social service bureau.

On December 1, 1939, the annex, at one time the Women's Prison, was reopened as part of a plan to remove all adolescents from the Main Building in the Raymond Street Jail in Brooklyn. At the present writing, the Wing of the latter institution is being renovated to permit the complete segregation of the Workhouse help from the adolescents and the latter have been temporarily transferred to the Queens Annex. Ultimately, Brooklyn defendants under twenty-one without previous felony records will be housed in the Queens Annex and the remainder will be kept in the Raymond Street Wing.

The Annex is completely removed from the Main Building. On each of the three floors there are four cell blocks with an average of six cells in each block. At the entrance to each block there is a solid steel door, kept locked at all times. The cells open on a corridor which is bounded by the outside wall. At present the inside wire mesh screens on the windows of these corridors are kept closed and locked because of the defective condition of the outside iron bars. In consequence, there is little ventilation and sunlight. Improvement is contemplated in the near future by renovating the outside bars so that the screens can be kept open. The cells are freshly painted, each one containing an open toilet and a wash basin. There are two beds suspended from a wall. Each boy is given two blankets, one of which serves as a mattress, a pillow, pillow case, two sheets and a towel. There is a bathtub in each section.

There are accommodations for forty boys with one in a cell. In the present transitional period, many more Brooklyn boys are detained in Queens than will eventually be the case and it has been necessary to put two boys together in many of the cells. The remaining cells are assigned to prison help and material witnesses who are confined in separate cell blocks.

Meals are served in the cells. The boys are let out of their cells and into the corridor for about three hours in the morning and again in the afternoon. There is no program of activities and the only recreation consists in strolling around the corridor or in playing cards. Some type of program is now in preparation but its effectiveness will be limited by the lack of available space other than the corridors.

Bronx County Jail

This seven-story jail, the most modern in the city, was completed in December, 1937. Adolescents under twenty-one years of age are housed on the fifth floor, entirely separated from any other group. A central corridor divides the floor into North and South sections, each section containing two cell blocks. Each cell block consists of a row of twelve cells, a prisoners' walk and a jailers' walk. These walks, which are five and one-half feet wide and seventy-two feet long, are separated along their entire length by a row of steel bars extending from the floor to the ceiling. In the prisoners' walk are six collapsible small shelves, used as tables, attached to the row of steel bars, with two seats, likewise attached, for each shelf. The ventilation, heating and sunlight are excellent throughout.

Each cell is eight feet long and six feet wide, entirely constructed of steel, and opens toward the windows of the outside wall. There is one bed in each cell, attached to the wall, and for each bed a mattress of rubber composition enclosed in ticking. An indirect light is recessed in the wall above the cot. There is an open toilet in one corner and a wash basin in the other. In addition, each cell block is equipped with a shower and extra toilet. Upon admission to the institution, each boy is supplied with a blanket, pillow, pillow case, two sheets and a towel. The linen and towel are changed weekly.

There is no program of activities. From eight in the morning until eight in the evening the boys are locked *out* of their cells and left to their own devices in the prisoners' walk. This idleness is only broken by the midday and evening meals, an hour's walk around the roof in circular formation when the weather permits, religious services on the appropriate Sabbath Day in the chapel, which is of extraordinary beauty, and a half-hour visit three times a week. When the radio system with four amplifiers for each cell block is in order, it is operated between five and eight in the evening.

In evaluating these prisons as institutions for detention of adolescents, the following criteria would, we think, be generally accepted: (1) the effectiveness with which adolescents are segregated from adults; (2) the wisdom with which members of the adolescent group are classified; (3) the decency and physical adequacy of sleeping quarters; (4) the adequacy of physical facilities for educational and recreational group activities; (5) the existence and effectiveness of an educational and recreational program.

Judged by these standards it is obvious that the detention facilities used in the City are defective in various respects. Only in the Bronx and in the Queens Annex is there complete and effective segregation. Except for the separation of first offenders in the Tombs there is no significant classification. Only in the Bronx, and perhaps in the Raymond Street Wing, can the sleeping quarters be regarded as adequate. In no case are there adequate facilities for educational and recreational group activities—not even a common mess hall. Only in the North Annex of the Tombs has there been a genuine if handicapped attempt to develop a program and to utilize persons with the requisite training to carry out such a program.

It is paradoxical and foolhardy to require that young boys presumptively innocent, more than half of whom will not be sent to prison after trial,[50] spend a considerable period of time in jail before trial under such unfavorable conditions. And that the time is considerable is shown by the fact that of those adolescents committed in the year ending June 30, 1938, 50% were incarcerated more than sixteen days and 25% were detained more than forty-four days.[51]

Delay

The length of pre-trial detention results, of course, from the time consumed in the various stages of the proceedings. Appended to this report is a table[52] indicating the lapse of time from one stage to another and comparing the data for 1937-8 with that gathered by the Crime Commission for 1929. The large number of cases, in which the interval from arrest to trial is a month or longer, suggests that greater dispatch may be possible. Whether the delay which now occurs serves a useful purpose and, if not, whether it is caused by the prosecution or by the defendants themselves or their counsel are deeper questions which the statistical findings do not answer. The questions can only be answered by a critical study of the practice of the District Attorney's office in selecting cases for expeditious trial and disposition and in dealing with requests for adjournment by defense counsel. But this much is clear: If pre-trial detention can be avoided except in cases where it is

[50] See Table C (I), *infra*, p. 51. For detailed correlations of final dispositions by original charge of 2,793 adolescents charged with felonies and serious misdemeanors in Manhattan, Bronx, Brooklyn and Queens, see Table E, *infra*, p. 53.

[51] See Table B, *infra*, p. 50.

[52] See Table F, *infra*, p. 55.

genuinely necessary and if proper places of detention can be obtained, delay will present a much less serious problem even in cases where it is admittedly unjustified.

CONCLUSIONS AND RECOMMENDATIONS

The marked contrast between the methods applied in the Children's Court in dealing with young people under sixteen and those employed in dealing with persons above this age has led the American Law Institute to propose the creation of specialized tribunals and institutions for the individualized treatment of adolescents above the Children's Court age and under twenty-one. But until this far-reaching reform is adopted, individuals who are above the age limit of the Children's Court and are nevertheless immature rather than adult will be drawn into the ordinary processes of the criminal law. To some extent at least the criminal law now takes account of their immaturity *after* conviction, by providing special reformatories[53] and perhaps, also in various forms of administrative[54] and judicial leniency. But the ordinary criminal law takes no account of their immaturity *before* conviction. This is the striking fact which this study reveals, a fact which is all the more striking when it is remembered that *before* con-

---

[53] Thus, Section 2184a, New York Penal Law, provides that any male person over sixteen and under nineteen years of age who has been convicted of any crime, except one punishable by death or life imprisonment, may be sentenced to the New York State Vocational Institution instead of to a state prison or a penitentiary. See also New York Penal Law, Sections 2185 (Elmira Reformatory), 2186 (county penitentiary or jail); Inferior Criminal Courts Act of New York City, Section 132 (New York City Reformatory).

[54] In adolescent as in adult cases, the primary instrument of administrative mitigation is the acceptance of a plea of guilty to a lesser offense than that charged. Seventy per cent of the felony indictments against adolescents from July, 1937, through June, 1938, were finally disposed of in this way. The percentage of reduced plea dispositions for all defendants, including adults, was 47.7. See TWELVE MONTHS OF CRIME IN NEW YORK CITY (July 1, 1937-June 30, 1938), a report prepared by the Citizens Committee on the Control of Crime, Inc. This variation does not indicate, however, that a reduced plea is accepted with substantially greater frequency in adolescent than adult cases since only 6.6% of the indictments against adolescents were dismissed as opposed to 20% of the indictments against all defendants. Nevertheless, we believe it to be the fact that ordinarily prosecuting officials regard the defendant's youth as a favorable factor, in deciding whether to sanction a reduction in the charge and, what is even more important, in determining the extent of the acceptable reduction.

viction the law is dealing with adolescents all of whom are presumptively innocent, many of whom will be adjudged innocent, and most of whom will not be sent to prison. This anomalous condition should be remedied by the establishment of specialized pre-trial procedures for dealing with adolescents. The proposals hereinafter set forth suggest such remedies.

1. PRE-ARRAIGNMENT PROCEDURE

Many of the undesirable experiences to which an adolescent is subjected during the short period of time between arrest and arraignment—usually less than twenty-four hours—can be simply avoided.

(a) Greater Use of Summons Rather Than Arrest

By virtue of Section 118 of the Inferior Criminal Courts Act of New York City and regulations adopted pursuant thereto by the Board of City Magistrates with the concurrence of the Police Commissioner, police officers are authorized to issue summonses in certain general classes of cases involving, in the main, petty offenses. This section as well as Section 150 of the Code of Criminal Procedure precludes the use of the summons in felony cases and the policy embodied in these provisions undoubtedly extends to serious misdemeanors as well. But among the remaining misdemeanors and summary offenses, with respect to which "blank" summons regulations have been adopted, gambling has been excluded. Moreover, summonses may be issued to persons charged with disorderly conduct[55] only after they have first been arrested, and arraigned and identified at the station house. We recommend that the Board of City Magistrates and the Police Commissioner consider the desirability of authorizing the issuance of "blank" summonses, where the person is believed to be under twenty-one, in gambling cases and of eliminating the present station house arraignment prior to such service, in disorderly conduct cases, with the exception, perhaps, of jostling and consorting. The adoption of such regulations might eliminate

[55] Manual of Procedure (1937), Article 2, subdivisions 93-96 inclusive. Prostitutes, gamblers, gangsters, pickpockets, professional thieves, known criminals, and intoxicated persons are excluded.

up to 5,000 arrests a year of adolescents charged with those offenses.

(b) Arraignment Immediately After Arrest

The characteristic features of the present routine—association with adult prisoners, station house examination and detention, transfer to police headquarters for the lineup, all before arraignment in court—should give way to a system under which the arrested boy is taken immediately to court or to a detention place for *adolescents* if court is not in session. To be sure, it may be necessary as a matter of mechanics to permit the arresting officer to take his prisoner to the station house pending arrival of a vehicle to transport him to court or to the detention place; the number of cars otherwise required might be prohibitive. But in that event, a special room should be set aside at the station house for this temporary detention under the supervision of a properly qualified person and enough vehicles should be provided to make certain that the waiting period will not be more than a few hours at the most. Such an arrangement will substantially meet the problem and its feasibility is clear. It should be added that the plan we propose is not inconsistent with the practice which obtains in juvenile cases,[56] as well as in others, of permitting bail to be posted at the station house in accordance with Section 554 of the Code of Criminal Procedure. Neither is it incompatible with permitting the police to interrogate the defendant *at the place of detention* in proper cases and under proper safeguards.

(c) Fingerprinting and Photographing

Under Section 940 of the Code of Criminal Procedure, a defendant charged with a felony or serious misdemeanor must be fingerprinted and may be photographed for the purpose of ascertaining whether he is a previous offender. Since this provision serves a useful purpose, it should be retained. But the fingerprinting and photographing should not be done at the station house, but rather at the court or the place of detention.

---

[56] See subdivision 1, Section 74, Domestic Relations Court Act of New York City.

(d) Transportation

Under no circumstances should an adult prisoner be transported with an adolescent. Nor should an adolescent be handcuffed except where the circumstances of the arrest necessitate this precautionary measure in the interests of public security. A boy arrested under such special conditions should be accompanied to court alone or with other adolescents whose conduct demands similarly rigorous treatment. In these cases, wherever possible, and in all other cases an adolescent should be transported in a vehicle such as that now employed by the Society for the Prevention of Cruelty to Children instead of a patrol wagon.

2. A SPECIAL MAGISTRATE'S COURT FOR ADOLESCENTS

(a) The Need for a Special Court

To eliminate the intermingling of adolescents and adults charged with serious crimes, to devise prudent methods of reducing the number of adolescents committed to places of detention pending trial, to improve physical facilities and to shelter the defendant from conditions which degrade him,—in short, to approximate for adolescent cases in their pre-trial stages the approach and techniques of the juvenile court, it is essential to establish a special Magistrate's Court.

The concentration of adolescent cases in a special court would have the further advantage of facilitating the participation, at an early stage of the proceedings, of the Legal Aid Society and of other social agencies which may be willing to cooperate with that organization in performing the important function of providing adequate legal defense where it cannot otherwise be obtained.

If a separate adolescent court served no other purpose, its existence would be justified by the assistance which such centralization would give to judges in coping with the problem inherent in the fact, to which we have previously referred,[57] that 78% of all adolescent defendants, more than four-fifths

---

[57] See pp. 14-15, *supra.*

of whom are first offenders, and 74% of those who are not finally institutionalized are committed to a detention jail. A separate adolescent court will enable any magistrate sitting in that court to focus his attention upon releasing as many adolescents as possible either on their own recognizance or in the custody of a guardian or third person. If the judges assigned to the court specialize in adolescent cases, as we think they should, even greater concentration of attention will be achieved. Such specialized attention will *set the foundation for* a substantial attack on the very serious problem of reducing the number of adolescents incarcerated before final adjudication and shortening the period of their commitment, where such detention is unavoidable. While the creation of the court will make this attack possible, its success will not depend on the judges alone. The proper performance of the judicial task requires that the court be implemented by a probation division, adequately staffed and otherwise equipped, to investigate the background of individual defendants for the information of the court and perhaps even to supervise adolescents who, for want of a responsible guardian, could not otherwise be released without bail. But the creation of the court will provide an incentive to the development of such a probation division and may stimulate private social agencies to cooperate in obtaining background information, in supervising individual adolescents and in helping to provide bail when it is required and cannot otherwise be obtained. Even with existing public and private budgets, it should be possible by unified cooperative effort greatly to improve the existing situation.

(b) Night Sessions

The proposed separate adolescent court should hold night as well as day sessions. The provision for immediate arraignment following arrest, suggested above, would thereby be given added substance. Moreover, night sessions will facilitate the release on bail or parole, or the earlier dismissal in proper cases[58] of a large number of boys who would otherwise be compelled to spend a night in a detention jail.

---

[58] In the year ending June 30, 1938, 486 or 18% of the adolescents arraigned for felonies and serious misdemeanors were discharged in the Magistrates' Courts. See Table D, *infra,* p. 52.

(c) Closed Hearings

The desirability in cases involving immature defendants of closing hearings to the public has been demonstrated in the Children's Court and the Brooklyn Adolescent Court. The same practice is followed in the Women's Court. It should certainly be adopted, in the absence of exceptional circumstances, in the proposed Adolescent Court. The statutory guarantee of a public trial is inapplicable to examinations in the Magistrates' Courts. Section 203 of the Code of Criminal Procedure provides: "The magistrate may also exclude from the examination every person except the clerk of the magistrate, the prosecutor and his counsel, the Attorney-General, the District Attorney of the county, the defendant and his counsel and the officer having the defendant in custody." No legislation, therefore, is required to enable the Board of Magistrates to provide for closed hearings in adolescent cases.

(d) Proper Physical Facilities

The establishment of a special part of the Magistrates' Courts would also simplify the problem of obtaining physical facilities adequate to insure decent court surroundings and waiting rooms. These are externals, it is true, but experience has amply demonstrated the necessity of creating an environment which furthers rather than hampers the sympathetic handling of particular cases. Ideally, it would be desirable to have a separate building for each branch of the special adolescent court. Until the capital outlay is available for new buildings, there should be a thorough canvass of available facilities, including those which will be provided by the new Criminal Courts Building in Manhattan.

(e) Scope of Jurisdiction

If magistrates in the proposed court are to conduct careful and thorough proceedings, it is important that the case load be not too large. A working basis for keeping the case load within reasonable limits is suggested by the restriction as to jurisdiction over crimes now in effect in the Brooklyn Adolescent Court. All infractions and crimes now handled in the specialized Traffic and Municipal Term Courts would continue to be handled there, and the proposed court[59] would concern itself with:

1. All felonies for examination.
2. All remaining misdemeanors for examination.
3. The arraignment, *trial* and *final disposition* of offenses over which magistrates' courts have jurisdiction, such as: Disorderly conduct, degeneracy, jostling, intoxication, drug addiction and male wayward minor charges.

Accordingly, no case of an adolescent within the age span of the proposed court would be handled in a regular district court.

On this plan, we estimate the probable number of cases in each borough falling within the jurisdiction of the court to be as follows[60]:

	16-19	16-21
Manhattan	4,050	8,165
Bronx	1,040	2,100
Brooklyn	2,025	4,100
Queens	580	1,180
Richmond	115	240

It is apparent that the case load of an adolescent court with an age limit of nineteen would be approximately half that of a court with an age limit of twenty-one. But the statistics

---

[59] The jurisdiction of the proposed court would be broader than that of the Brooklyn Adolescent Court since it will also include those crimes now handled by the Homicide Court. In the main these crimes include all homicides and any violation of a motor vehicle statute or ordinance resulting in personal injuries.

[60] The estimates are based on Reports of the Magistrates' Courts and the Police Department for the year 1937. The Report of the Magistrates' Courts contains for all courts in each borough a tabulation of the arraignments by offense but not by age. The Report of the Police Department, on the other hand, allocates the total number of arrests by offense and age but not by borough.

Since the estimates desired could not be derived from either source directly, the procedure followed was to interpolate the appropriate age ratios for the projected group of crimes, as obtained from the Report of the Police Department, among the borough totals for this group of crimes, as obtained from the Magistrates' Courts Report. It should be noted that the arraignment rather than the arrest totals were used as the basic figure for the reason that the number of arraignments for the group of crimes under consideration exceeded the number of arrests by some 18%. The resultant higher figures, being more conservative, were deemed fairer estimates of the case load of the proposed adolescent court.

also show that the prospective case load of the proposed courts, if the age limit were set at twenty-one, would, in each borough, be substantially less than the case load of any district court and less or not substantially more than the case load of the Felony Court.

	Lowest No. in District Court	Felony Court	Proposed 16-21 Adolescent Court
Manhattan	9,803	9,569	8,165
Bronx	10,197 (Estimated)	1,684 (Estimated)	2,100
Brooklyn	7,361	3,974	4,100
Queens	2,379	3,870	1,180
Richmond	1,231 (Estimated) (Also handles 8,489 traffic arraignments)		240

These figures clearly show that the establishment of a special court to deal with cases falling within an age span of sixteen to twenty-one is administratively feasible and that even with greater attention to individual cases than is possible in the normal courts, it would not impose an undue burden upon the personnel of the Magistrates' Courts. We express no judgment as to whether a single court should be established for the whole city, a separate court in each borough or whether there should be some combination of boroughs, such as Queens and Brooklyn.[61] The resolution of this issue calls for a detailed canvass of man power and facilities which we have not attempted to make. It is obvious, however, that the court should be conducted by magistrates who will rotate from the adolescent part to the regular part as little as possible. Assignment of judges with an especial interest in this problem for a substantial period of time to the adolescent court will greatly

---

[61] When Sections 100 and 106 of the Inferior Criminal Courts Act of New York City are read together, it is clear that the Board of City Magistrates may establish a special City Magistrate's Court with city-wide territorial jurisdiction and that the Chief City Magistrate may divide such court into branches with jurisdiction embracing more than one borough. Cf. Peo. *ex rel.* Klein v. Warden, 266 N. Y. 547 (1935), which sustained, without opinion, the city-wide jurisdiction of the Women's Court, a special City Magistrate's Court created by Section 109 of the Inferior Criminal Courts Act of New York City. See also Cobb, INFERIOR CRIMINAL COURTS ACT OF NEW YORK CITY (1925) pp. 109, 50.

assist the development of the specialized approach to adolescent cases which it is the function of the court to achieve. Finally, it should be noted that in advocating an adolescent court we are not advocating the general adoption of the "wayward minor" procedure now employed in the Brooklyn Adolescent Court. That procedure involves, as we have said, the use of an extra-legal device to shift from the higher courts to the magistrates the power to make ultimate treatment disposition of adolescent cases. It can only be evaluated in the light of a rounded approach to the problem of ultimate treatment and that problem is beyond the scope of this study and report.

If the age limit of the proposed court is to be twenty-one, as we suggest, rather than nineteen, an amendment to the Inferior Criminal Courts Act is probably necessary. Section 147 of that act provides that all persons charged with felonies or any of the misdemeanors and offenses enumerated in Section 552 of the Code of Criminal Procedure shall be arraigned and examined by a magistrate holding a felony court as established under section 145 rather than by a magistrate holding a district court, with the proviso that "nothing in this section shall be construed to prevent the arraignment and examination in the adolescent court of adolescents between the ages of sixteen and eighteen years charged with such felonies, offenses or misdemeanors". Hence, Section 147 explicitly authorizes arraignment in an adolescent court only for persons under nineteen years of age. On the other hand, the fact that the statute refers to arraignment in a felony rather than a district court leaves room for the argument that it does not exclude arraignment in another specialized court, which the Board of City Magistrates is authorized to create under Section 100, even though it is not a felony court. To avoid this uncertainty as to jurisdiction, Section 147 should be amended to include within the proviso adolescents nineteen and twenty years of age. But if the amendment process entails delay which we do not now envisage, we urge that the Board exercise its undoubted power to make a more modest start by immediately establishing an adolescent court with an age limit of nineteen.

In recommending the establishment of an Adolescent Court we do not imply that it is unnecessary to make further distinctions within the adolescent group itself. On the contrary, it is of vital importance in the administration of the work of the court to avoid the mingling of adolescents charged with serious and trivial offenses and to prevent the association of defendants with previous convictions of relatively serious crimes and defendants without such convictions. Moreover, a substantial number of defendants between the ages of sixteen and twenty-one, though chronologically adolescents, may actually be seasoned or dangerous criminals for whom the specialized procedure we propose is patently unnecessary or inappropriate and whose contact with true adolescents involves the same or greater dangers as their contact with adults. But these problems are simply met by providing for proper segregation pending arraignment in the Adolescent Court and endowing the judge with the discretion which he should have, in any event, to direct that particular cases proceed in ordinary course in the Felony Court.

3. IMPROVED DETENTION PLACES

We anticipate that a special court for adolescents will effect a significant reduction in the number who must be detained before trial. Many cases will inevitably remain in which the defendant must, on arraignment, be committed to an institution of detention because of his inability to post bail. Moreover, under the proposed plan, there will be those who, after arrest, will be taken immediately to the detention place, when court is not in session, and if they cannot post bail or are precluded from doing so, they will be compelled to remain there at least overnight.

The facilities used in the City for the detention of adolescents—West Side and Harlem Jails and the Tombs in Manhattan, Raymond Street Jail in Brooklyn, Queens City Prison and Bronx County Jail—are of uneven merit but none of these institutions is even remotely geared to meet the special needs of youth. They are, paradoxically enough, drastically inferior to most of the institutions to which adolescents are committed if they are *convicted* of crimes and are not placed on probation. We recognize that in the City Jail now being constructed in Manhattan, to take the place of the Tombs, special provision will be made for the detention of adolescents. They will be housed separately on two of the top floors in cells of the modified outside type which will insure plenty of light and air.

Moreover, each of these floors will contain a "day room" to be used for group activities and a screened roof will be available for outdoor recreation. With the right kind of program and a staff capable of carrying it out, the establishment of this institution should work an incalculable improvement in conditions for Manhattan. But it will not solve the problem. In the first place, it is not clear that the new Tombs will or can completely eliminate the detention of adolescents in the West Side and Harlem Jails, though it is to be hoped that it will. In the second place, the new institution will not affect the situation in Brooklyn, Queens or the Bronx. In the third place, the new Tombs will be a prison and, whatever the merits of the portion of the building used for adolescents, neither it nor the boys housed in it will escape the implications of this implacable fact. For those defendants between the ages of sixteen and twenty-one who, though chronologically adolescents, are actually hardened characters, the facilities of the new Tombs will be admirable and, as we have previously said, the judge should be endowed with discretion to deal with such "adolescents" in the same way as with adults. But for the vast majority between sixteen and twenty-one, what is needed is a detention home, which is not a part of a larger prison, and which conforms to the standards recommended by the United States Children's Bureau for juvenile detention. Those standards are:

1. Sufficient space without crowding the number likely to be detained at any one time.

2. Arrangements of quarters so as to permit segregation according to character of offense, physical condition, etc. (For older children, single rooms are considered to be better than dormitories and less supervision at night is necessary when single rooms are provided.)

3. Separate bathing and toilet facilities for those suffering from infectious disease.

4. Proper lighting and ventilation.

5. Dining rooms, recreation rooms and schoolrooms.

6. Security against escape—windows may be protected by iron screenery or may be constructed of iron frames with small panes of glass.

7. Adequate protection from fire.

8. Outdoor play space.

In our opinion, the sound policy for New York City is to establish a separate detention home for all adolescents from all boroughs who do not present a serious detention problem and to utilize the new Tombs for those who do present such a problem. This will unify all adolescent detention for the entire City in two places and effect a needed classification at the same time. Such unification has the disadvantage of putting the place of commitment in many cases further from the boy's home than it would be under a plan for separate borough or county institutions. But this disadvantage is greatly outweighed by the increased opportunity to develop a satisfactory program. Unification will be particularly desirable if a single adolescent court is established for the entire City. Such a court, or any of the higher courts, should be authorized to commit defendants to either of these institutions regardless of the origin of the case or the place of arraignment.

The English Criminal Justice Bill is a persuasive precedent in support of our recommendations. That bill proposes to keep adolescents, specifically the group from seventeen to twenty-three years of age, out of the regular detention prisons during the pre-conviction stage by establishing remand centers similar to the remand homes now used for juveniles up to seventeen years of age. The measure has the support of all parties and presumably would not have been abandoned were it not for the intervention of the war. The need to provide similar facilities in New York City cannot be gainsaid. The expenditure will result in ultimate reduction of the cost of law enforcement and will return dividends to the people of the City in other and even more important ways.

The recommendations we have made are addressed to the crucial features of the present pre-trial procedure, not to proceedings in the trial courts or to the deeper issue of treatment after conviction. But their adoption will, we believe, substantially contribute towards a humane handling of the adolescent defendant in the City of New York.

SUMMARY

Our recommendations may be summarized as follows:

Pre-Arraignment

1. The Board of City Magistrates and the Police Commissioner should consider the desirability of authorizing the issuance of blank summons, where the person is believed to be under twenty-one, in gambling cases and of eliminating the present station house arraignment, prior to such service, in disorderly conduct cases.

2. On arrest, an adolescent defendant should be taken immediately to court, or to a place of detention if court is not in session.

3. Fingerprinting and photographing should not be done at the station house but at the court or the place of detention.

4. Except in unusual cases, adolescent defendants should be transported in vehicles similar to those used by the Society for the Prevention of Cruelty to Children and should not be placed in the same vehicle with adults.

5. There should be no handcuffing, except in unusual cases.

Magistrates' Courts and Procedure

1. A separate adolescent court in the Magistrates' Courts should be established with an age limit of nineteen until legislation is enacted allowing an age limit of twenty-one.

2. The assignment of judges should be for long periods of time to permit the judges to become specialists in the handling of adolescent cases.

3. The court should be implemented by a probation division adequately staffed and otherwise equipped to investigate the background of individual defendants for the information of the court and perhaps even to supervise adolescents who, for want of a responsible guardian, could not other-

wise be released without bail. Moreover, an effort should be made to stimulate private social agencies to cooperate in the performance of these tasks.

4. The proposed court should hold night as well as day sessions.

5. Hearings should be closed to the general public.

6. Plans should be made for housing branches of the new court in decent quarters.

Detention

1. A new detention home constructed and operated according to the standards of juvenile detention homes should be established in New York City.

2. Irrespective of the origin of the case or the place of arraignment, all adolescents not presenting a serious detention problem should be committed to the detention home, and those presenting such a problem should be committed to the new Tombs.

APPENDIX

INDEX TO TABLES

PAGE

TABLE A

DETENTION PRIOR TO FINAL DISPOSITION OF ADOLESCENTS, 16 TO 21 YEARS OF AGE, CHARGED WITH FELONIES AND SERIOUS MISDEMEANORS IN MANHATTAN, BROOKLYN AND QUEENS, JULY, 1937 THROUGH JUNE, 1938, CLASSIFIED BY AGE, CRIME AND FINAL DISPOSITION.

	All Crimes				Homicide			Robbery			Rape		
	Total	Per Cent	Number Detained	Per Cent Detained	Total	Number Detained	Per Cent Detained	Total	Number Detained	Per Cent Detained	Total	Number Detained	Per Cent Detained
All Dispositions—All Ages	2227	100.0	1758	78.9	14	13	92.9	336	299	89.0	165	130	78.8
Not Institutionalized—All Ages	1431	64.3	1060*	74.0	4	4	100.0	132	111	84.1	132	99	75.0
16	260		178	68.5	1	1	100.0	17	14	82.4	8	5	62.5
17	300		209	69.7	2	2	100.0	19	17	89.5	21	14	66.7
18	292		210	71.9				27	21	77.8	36	26	72.2
19	267		213	79.8	1	1	100.0	36	33	91.7	30	26	86.7
20	291		234	80.4				30	23	76.7	35	27	77.1
Age Unrecorded	21		16	76.2				3	3	100.0	2	1	50.0
Institutionalized—All Ages	771	34.6	698	90.5	9	9	100.0	200	188	94.0	33	31	93.9
16	86		79	91.9	2	2	100.0	13	12	92.3	1	1	100.0
17	142		129	90.8	2	2	100.0	22	20	90.9	5	5	100.0
18	157		145	92.4	2	2	100.0	46	45	97.8	8	7	87.5
19	192		167	87.0	1	1	100.0	60	56	93.3	5	5	100.0
20	183		167	91.3	2	2	100.0	56	52	92.9	13	12	92.3
Age Unrecorded	11		11	100.0				3	3	100.0	1	1	100.0
Disposition Unrecorded	25	1.1			1			4					

* This figure includes 159 cases in respect to which we had no definite record as to final disposition. However, since the records of these cases were found in the Department of Correction files without any notation of commitment to an institution, we assume that the defendants in these cases were not institutionalized. This assumption is justified by the fact that in the normal routine a notation of commitment to an institution would have been made on these Department records had such been the disposition.

TABLE A (CONTINUED)

	Other Sex Offenses			Felonious Assault			Burglary			Grand Larceny		
	Total	Number Detained	Per Cent Detained	Total	Number Detained	Per Cent Detained	Total	Number Detained	Per Cent Detained	Total	Number Detained	Per Cent Detained
All Dispositions—All Ages	54	34	63.0	125	95	76.0	718	598	83.3	566	409	72.3
Not Institutionalized—All Ages	43	25	58.1	101	75	74.2	462	373	80.4	381	251	65.9
16	8	5	62.5	7	4	57.1	124	93	75.0	65	31	47.7
17	9	3	33.3	17	13	76.5	121	94	77.7	82	51	62.2
18	8	6	75.0	30	22	73.3	77	62	80.5	84	56	66.7
19	6	3	50.0	17	13	76.5	74	67	90.5	69	46	66.7
20	11	8	72.7	30	23	76.7	66	57	86.4	72	59	81.9
Age Unrecorded	1									9	8	88.9
Institutionalized—All Ages	11	9	81.8	24	20	83.3	247	225	91.1	178	158	88.8
16	2	2	100.0	1	1	100.0	43	41	95.3	21	18	85.7
17	5	4	80.0	5	4	80.0	59	54	91.5	33	32	97.0
18	2	2	100.0	1	1	100.0	52	47	90.4	32	29	90.6
19	1			8	8	100.0	54	46	85.2	52	43	82.7
20	1	1	100.0	9	6	66.7	38	36	94.7	38	34	89.5
Age Unrecorded							1	1	100.0	2	2	100.0
Disposition Unrecorded							9			7		

TABLE A (CONTINUED)

	Fraud and Forgery			Extortion			Receiving Stolen Goods			Possessing Dangerous Weapons		
	Total	Number Detained	Per Cent Detained	Total	Number Detained	Per Cent Detained	Total	Number Detained	Per Cent Detained	Total	Number Detained	Per Cent Detained
All Dispositions—All Ages	22	19	86.4	7	5	71.4	26	14	53.8	61	43	70.5
Not Institutionalized—All Ages	19	17	89.5	5	4	80.0	21	12	57.1	41	26	63.4
16	2	2	100.0	1	1	100.0	2	1	50.0	7	4	57.1
17	3	3	100.0				7	3	42.9	4	2	50.0
18	4	4	100.0				3	2	66.7	5	2	40.0
19	4	3	75.0	2	1	50.0	5	3	60.0	9	5	55.6
20	5	4	80.0	2	2	100.0	4	3	75.0	14	12	85.7
Age Unrecorded	1	1	100.0							2	1	50.0
Institutionalized—All Ages	3	2	66.7	2	1	50.0	4	2	50.0	19	17	89.5
16										1		
17				1	1	100.0	2	2	100.0	2	2	100.0
18	1	1	100.0	1			1			3	3	100.0
19							1			3	3	100.0
20	2	1	50.0							10	9	90.0
Age Unrecorded												
Disposition Unrecorded				1			1					

TABLE A (CONTINUED)

	Possessing Burglar's Tools			Unlawful Entry			Malicious Mischief			Miscellaneous		
	Total	Number Detained	Per Cent Detained	Total	Number Detained	Per Cent Detained	Total	Number Detained	Per Cent Detained	Total	Number Detained	Per Cent Detained
All Dispositions—All Ages	26	22	84.6	26	18	69.2	27	18	66.7	54	41	75.9
Not Institutionalized—All Ages	16	15	93.8	19	12	63.2	23	16	69.6	32	20	62.5
16	3	3	100.0	3	3	100.0	4	4	100.0	8	7	87.5
17	1	1	100.0	4	2	50.0	5	1	20.0	5	3	60.0
18	2	1	50.0	5	1	20.0	4	3	75.0	7	4	57.1
19	2	2	100.0	4	4	100.0	5	5	100.0	4	2	50.0
20	8	8	100.0	2	2	100.0	4	2	50.0	7	3	42.9
Age Unrecorded				1			1	1	100.0	1	1	100.0
Institutionalized—All Ages	9	7	77.8	7	6	85.7	3	2	66.7	22	21	95.5
16	1	1	100.0	1			1			1	1	100.0
17	3	2	66.7	2	2	100.0				4	3	75.0
18	3	2	66.7	1	1	100.0				4	4	100.0
19	2	2	100.0	1	1	100.0				2	2	100.0
20				2	2	100.0	2	2	100.0	9	9	100.0
Age Unrecorded										2	2	100.0
Disposition Unrecorded	1						1					

TABLE B

Length of Detention.

Days	Total Number Detained	Percentage Detained	Detention for Entire Duration of Case		Detention for Partial Duration of Case	
			No.	%	No.	%
1	161	9.1	13	1.1	148	23.8
2	102	5.8	20	1.8	82	13.2
3	73	4.2	23	2.0	50	8.1
4	62	3.5	25	2.2	37	6.0
5	61	3.5	22	1.9	39	6.3
6–10	249	14.2	134	11.8	115	18.5
11–15	152	8.6	106	9.3	46	7.4
16–20	96	5.5	59	5.2	37	6.0
21–25	67	3.8	60	5.3	7	1.1
26–30	71	4.0	53	4.7	18	2.9
31–35	72	4.1	66	5.8	6	1.0
36–40	90	5.1	83	7.3	7	1.1
41–45	71	4.0	66	5.8	5	.8
46–50	66	3.8	61	5.4	5	.8
51–75	194	11.0	185	16.3	9	1.4
76–100	129	7.3	120	10.6	9	1.4
101–150	25	1.4	24	2.1	1	.2
151–200	15	.9	15	1.3		
201–300	1	.1	1	.1		
301–325	1	.1	1	.1		
Total	1758	100.0	1137	100.0	621	100.0
Per Cent of Total Number Detained				64.7		35.3

TABLE C

FINAL DISPOSITIONS OF ADOLESCENTS, 16 TO 21 YEARS OF
AGE, CHARGED WITH FELONIES AND SERIOUS MISDEMEAN-
ORS, JULY, 1937 THROUGH JUNE, 1938.

I. MANHATTAN, BROOKLYN AND QUEENS

	No.	%	No.	%
Total			2327	100.0
Total Not Institutionalized			1504	64.6
Dismissed	533	22.9		
Acquitted	126	5.4		
No bill (Grand Jury)	229	9.8		
Wayward Minor	163	7.0		
Suspended Sentence	101	4.3		
Probation	352	15.1		
Total Institutionalized			766	32.9
Total Unrecorded			57	2.4
Disposition unrecorded	6	0.3		
Convicted but sentence unrecorded	51	2.2		

II. MANHATTAN, BROOKLYN, QUEENS AND BRONX

	No.	%	No.	%
Total			2793	100.0
Total Not Institutionalized			1812	64.9
Dismissed	649	23.2		
Acquitted	147	5.3		
No Bill (Grand Jury)	269	9.6		
Wayward Minor	168	6.0		
Suspended Sentence	122	4.4		
Probation	457	16.4		
Total Institutionalized			916	32.8
Total Unrecorded			65	2.3
Disposition unrecorded	6	0.2		
Convicted but sentence unrecorded	59	2.1		

TABLE D

Dispositions in Magistrates' Courts of 2647 Adolescents, 16 to 21 Years of Age, Arraigned for Felonies and Serious Misdemeanors in Manhattan, Bronx, Brooklyn and Queens, July, 1937 through June, 1938.

		Total Number Arraigned	Dismissed	Adjudicated a Wayward Minor (Summary Offense)	Convicted of Other Summary Offense	Acquitted of Other Summary Offense	Held for Special Sessions	Held for Grand Jury	Unrecorded Cases
Homicide	No.	10	2					8	
	%		20.0					80.0	
Rape	No.	192	55	2		1	7	127	
	%		28.6	1.0		.5	3.6	66.1	
Robbery	No.	326	40	9	4		3	270	
	%		12.3	2.8	1.2		.9	82.8	
Felonious Assault	No.	139	45	4	8	2	17	61	2
	%		32.4	2.9	5.8	1.4	12.2	43.9	1.4
Burglary	No.	872	138	82			27	624	1
	%		15.8	9.4			3.1	71.6	.1
Possessing Burglar's Tools	No.	33	3	4			14	12	
	%		9.1	12.1			42.4	36.4	
Grand Larceny (Auto)	No.	385	104	39		3	39	200	
	%		27.0	10.1		.8	10.1	51.9	
Grand Larceny (Other)	No.	329	27	11	1		184	106	
	%		8.2	3.3	.3		55.9	32.2	
Receiving Stolen Property	No.	36	14	3				19	
	%		38.9	8.3				52.8	
Fraud	No.	35	5	2			16	12	
	%		14.3	5.7			45.7	34.3	
Forgery	No.	36	4				4	28	
	%		11.1				11.1	77.8	
Arson	No.	7						7	
	%							100.0	
Miscellaneous Sex Offenses	No.	79	19	3	1		29	27	
	%		24.1	3.8	1.3		36.7	34.2	
Narcotics (Felony)	No.	1						1	
	%							100.0	
Possessing Dangerous Weapons	No.	79	17	2	6		32	21	1
	%		21.5	2.5	7.6		40.5	26.6	1.3
Malicious Mischief	No.	34	4	7	3		16	4	
	%		11.8	20.6	8.8		47.1	11.8	
Unlawful Entry	No.	36	8		2		26		
	%		22.2		5.6		72.2		
Miscellaneous Felonies	No.	18	1		2		1	14	
	%		5.6		11.1		5.6	77.8	
Total	No.	2647	486	168	27	6	415	1541	4
	%		18.4	6.3	1.0	.2	15.7	58.2	.2

TABLE E

Final Dispositions by Original Charge of 2793 Adolescents, 16 to 21 Years of Age, Charged with Felonies and Serious Misdemeanors in Manhattan, Bronx, Brooklyn and Queens, July, 1937 Through June, 1938.

| | | Total Defendants | Magistrates' Courts | | | | | Special Sessions Court | | | | | | Grand Jury | County and General Sessions Courts | | | | | |
			Dismissed	Adjudicated a Wayward Minor (Summary Offense)	Convicted of Other Summary Offense	Acquitted of Other Summary Offense	Unrecorded Cases	Dismissed	Acquitted	Suspended Sentence	Probation	Committed to an Institution	Sentence Unrecorded	No Bill	Dismissed	Acquitted	Suspended Sentence	Probation	Committed to an Institution	Sentence Unrecorded
Homicide	No.	17	2											2		2			9	1
	%	100	11.8											11.8		11.8			52.9	5.9
Rape	No.	192	55	2		1		2	2		4	2	1	58	8	4	1	25	27	2
	%	100	28.6	1.0		.5		1.0	1.0		2.1	1.0	.5	30.2	4.2	2.1	.5	13.0	14.1	1.0
Robbery	No.	394	40	9	4		2	1	2			2		27	26	27	5	18	230	3
	%	100	10.1	2.3	1.0		1.4	.3	.5			.5		6.9	6.6	6.8	1.3	4.6	58.4	.8
Felonious Assault	No.	139	45	4	8	2		6	10	2		7		18	4	10		8	13	
	%	100	32.4	2.9	5.8	1.4		4.3	7.2	1.4		5.0		12.9	2.9	7.2		5.7	9.4	
Burglary	No.	906	138	82			1	4	8	6	11	17		73	22	14	47	184	288	11
	%	100	15.2	9.1			.1	.4	.9	.7	1.2	1.9		8.0	2.4	1.5	5.2	20.3	31.8	1.2
Possessing Burglar's Tools	No.	33	3	4				3	1	1	5	4		4			1		3	3 (1 died)
	%	100	9.1	12.1				9.1	3.0	3.0	15.2	12.1		12.1			3.0		9.1	9.1
Grand Larceny (Auto)	No.	408	104	39		3		12	6	2	7	14	2	41	13	8	10	58	86	5
	%	100	25.5	9.6		.7		2.9	1.5	.5	1.7	3.4	.6	10.0	3.2	2.0	2.5	14.2	21.1	1.2
Grand Larceny (Other)	No.	334	27	11	1			27	15	22	56	67	2	16	7	3	2	23	54	1
	%	100	8.1	3.3	.3			8.1	4.5	6.6	16.8	20.1	.6	4.8	2.1	.9	.6	6.9	16.2	.3

These categories include convictions for lesser offenses as well as for the crime charged.

TABLE E (CONTINUED)

		Magistrates' Courts				Special Sessions Court							Grand Jury		County and General Sessions Courts				
	Total Defendants	Dismissed	Adjudicated a Wayward Minor (Summary Offense)	Convicted of Other Summary Offense	Acquitted of Other Summary Offense	Unrecorded Cases	Dismissed	Acquitted	Suspended Sentence	Probation	Committed to an Institution	Sentence Unrecorded	No Bill	Dismissed	Acquitted	Suspended Sentence	Probation	Committed to an Institution	Sentence Unrecorded
Receiving Stolen Property No.	36	14	3								1		4	3		1	6	3	1
%	100	38.9	8.3								2.8		11.1	8.3		2.8	16.7	8.3	2.8
Fraud No.	35	5	2				2	3	1	5	5	1	3	1			3	4	
%	100	14.3	5.7				5.7	8.6	2.9	14.3	14.3	2.9	8.6	2.9			8.6	11.4	
Forgery No.	37	4					1		1	1	1	1	1	1		1	17	8	
%	100	10.8					2.7		2.7	2.7	2.7	2.7	2.7	2.7		2.7	45.9	21.6	
Arson No.	7												1				2	4	
%	100												14.3				28.6	57.1	
Miscellaneous Sex Offenses No.	81	19	3	1			2	7	5	6	10		11	2	2	1	2	10	
%	100	23.5	3.7	1.2			2.5	8.6	6.2	7.4	12.3		13.6	2.5	2.5	1.2	2.5	12.3	
Narcotics (Felony) No.	1																	1	
%	100																	100.0	
Possessing Dangerous Weapons No.	80	17	2	6		1	1	5	9	7	11		4	1		2	3	11	
%	100	21.25	2.50	7.50		1.25	1.25	6.25	11.25	8.75	13.75		5.0	1.25		2.50	3.75	13.75	
Malicious Mischief No.	34	4	7	3			7	2	1		6		2					2	
%	100	11.8	20.6	8.8			20.6	5.9	2.9		17.6		5.9					5.9	
Unlawful Entry No.	36	8		2			4	8	1	3	10								
%	100	22.2		5.6			11.1	22.2	2.8	8.3	27.8								
Miscellaneous Felonies No.	23	1		2					2		1	1	1 (Fine)	4	3			2	5	1
%	100	4.3		8.7					8.7		4.3	4.3	4.3	17.4	13.0			8.7	21.7	4.3
Total No.	2793	486	168	27	6	4	70	71	51	106	158	6	269	93	70	71	351	758	28
%	100	17.4	6.0	1.0	.2	.1	2.5	2.5	1.8	3.8	5.7	.2	9.6	3.3	2.5	2.5	12.6	27.1	1.0

TABLE F

Time Elapsing from Arrest to Final Disposition for Adolescents Charged with Felonies and Serious Misdemeanors, 1929 and 1937-38, by Steps in Procedure.

ARREST TO ARRAIGNMENT IN THE MAGISTRATES' COURTS

	1937-38		1929
1–5 days	99.0%	1–5 days	84.0%
6–10	.4%	6–10	11.0%
11–15	.19%	11–60	2.3%
16–20	.15%	60–6 months	4.2%
21–30	.19%	Over 6 months	.02%

ARRAIGNMENT TO DISPOSAL IN MAGISTRATES' COURTS

	1937-38	1929
1–5	65.3%	77.0%
6–10	15.9%	10.4%
11–15	7.3%	4.6%
16–30	8.0%	6.8%

DISPOSAL IN THE MAGISTRATES' COURTS TO
GRAND JURY DISPOSAL

	1937-38	1929
1–5	19.2%	9.3%
6–15	52.0%	46.0%
16–30	18.4%	32.1%
31–60	6.8%	9.2%
Over 60	2.31%	3.0%

INDICTMENT TO ARRAIGNMENT IN THE COUNTY AND
GENERAL SESSIONS COURTS

	1937-38	1929
1–5	85.19%	79.24%
6–10	9.17%	11.76%
11–15	2.44%	2.99%
16–20	1.48%	1.49%
21–30	.74%	1.35%
31–60	.44%	1.56%
Over 60	.50%	1.55%

ARRAIGNMENT TO DISPOSAL IN THE COUNTY AND
GENERAL SESSIONS COURTS

	1937-38	1929
1–5	24.16%	7.72%
6–10	15.91%	12.94%
11–15	12.63%	18.30%
16–20	8.62%	9.41%
21–30	14.27%	15.80%
31–60	12.93%	20.88%
Over 60	11.22%	14.90%

TABLE G

Distribution by Age and Original Charge of 2793 Adolescents, 16 to 21 Years of Age, Charged with Felonies and Serious Misdemeanors in Manhattan, Bronx, Brooklyn and Queens, July, 1937 through June, 1938.

	Total Number of Defendants	16		17		18		19		20		Age Unrecorded	
		No.	%	No.	%	No.	%	No.	%	No.	%	No.	%
Homicide	17	4	23.5	5	29.4	2	11.8	2	11.8	4	23.5		
Rape	192	10	5.2	42	21.9	43	22.4	39	20.3	58	30.2		
Robbery	394	42	10.7	56	14.2	81	20.6	116	29.4	96	24.4	3	.8
Felonious Assault	139	10	7.2	29	20.9	35	25.2	30	21.6	35	25.2		
Burglary	906	223	24.6	227	25.1	163	18.0	156	17.2	126	13.9	11	1.2
Possessing Burglar's Tools	33	5	15.2	8	24.2	8	24.2	4	12.1	8	24.2		
Grand Larceny (Auto)	408	65	15.9	95	23.3	82	20.1	86	21.1	77	18.9	3	.7
Grand Larceny (Other)	334	57	17.1	78	23.4	62	18.6	76	22.8	56	16.8	5	1.5

TABLE G (CONTINUED)

	Total Number of Defendants	16		17		18		19		20		Age Unrecorded	
		No.	%	No.	%	No.	%	No.	%	No.	%	No.	%
Receiving Stolen Property	36	3	8.3	7	'19.4	12	33.3	6	16.7	8	22.2		
Fraud	35	6	17.1	5	14.3	7	20.0	7	20.0	10	28.6		
Forgery	37	2	5.4	7	18.9	8	21.6	6	16.2	14	37.8		
Arson	7	3	42.9	3	42.9					1	14.3		
Miscellaneous Sex Offenses	81	13	16.0	17	21.0	18	22.2	12	14.8	21	25.9		
Narcotics (Felony)	1							1	100.0				
Possessing Dangerous Weapons	80	9	11.3	7	8.8	11	13.8	25	31.3	28	35.0		
Malicious Mischief	34	4	11.8	6	17.6	6	17.6	7	20.6	10	29.4	1	2.9
Unlawful Entry	36	2	5.6	9	25.0	8	22.2	6	16.7	9	25.0	2	5.6
Miscellaneous Felonies	23	1	4.3	2	8.7	2	8.7	8	34.8	9	39.1	1	4.3
All Crimes	2793	459	16.4	603	21.6	548	19.6	587	21.0	570	20.4	26	.9

TABLE H

NUMBER AND PERCENTAGE OF DEFENDANTS WITH RECORDS OF
PREVIOUS ARRESTS AMONG 2793 ADOLESCENTS, 16 TO 21 YEARS
OF AGE, CHARGED WITH FELONIES AND SERIOUS MISDEMEANORS
IN MANHATTAN, BRONX, BROOKLYN AND QUEENS, JULY, 1937
THROUGH JUNE, 1938.

	Total Defendants	Number with Records of Previous Arrests	Percentage with Records of Previous Arrests
Homicide	17	5	29.4
Rape	192	31	16.1
Robbery	394	119	30.2
Felonious Assault	139	26	18.7
Burglary	906	208	23.0
Possessing Burglar's Tools	33	12	36.4
Grand Larceny (Auto)	408	80	19.6
Grand Larceny (Others)	334	43	12.9
Receiving Stolen Property	36	4	11.1
Fraud	35	4	11.4
Forgery	37	5	13.5
Arson	7	0	
Miscellaneous Sex Offenses	81	4	4.9
Narcotics (Felony)	1	1	100.0
Possessing Dangerous Weapons	80	9	11.3
Malicious Mischief	34	0	
Unlawful Entry	36	4	11.1
Miscellaneous Felonies	23	5	21.7
All Crimes	2793	560	20.1

TABLE J

DISTRIBUTION BY SEX AND ORIGINAL CHARGE OF 2793
ADOLESCENTS, 16 TO 21 YEARS OF AGE, CHARGED WITH
FELONIES AND SERIOUS MISDEMEANORS IN MANHATTAN,
BRONX, BROOKLYN AND QUEENS, JULY, 1937 THROUGH
JUNE, 1938.

	Total No. of Defendants	Male Defendants		Female Defendants	
		No.	%	No.	%
Homicide	17	15	88.2	2	11.8
Rape	192	192	100.0		
Robbery	394	388	98.5	6	1.5
Felonious Assault	139	126	90.6	13	9.4
Burglary	906	899	99.2	7	.8
Possessing Burglar's Tools	33	33	100.0		
Grand Larceny (Auto)	408	403	98.8	5	1.2
Grand Larceny (Other)	334	302	90.4	32	9.6
Receiving Stolen Property	36	36	100.0		
Fraud	35	23	65.7	12	34.3
Forgery	37	30	81.1	7	18.9
Arson	7	7	100.0		
Miscellaneous Sex Offenses	81	81	100.0		
Narcotics (Felony)	1	1	100.0		
Possessing Dangerous Weapons	80	76	95.0	4	5.0
Malicious Mischief	34	34	100.0		
Unlawful Entry	36	36	100.0		
Miscellaneous Felonies	23	21	91.3	2	8.7
All Crimes	2793	2703	96.8	90	3.2

Correctional Treatment of Youth Offenders

By Leonard V. Harrison

Published January 1944

The Committee on Youth and Justice

COMMUNITY SERVICE SOCIETY OF NEW YORK

105 East 22 Street, New York 10, N. Y.

Foreword

RECOGNIZING the seriously blighting effects of crime upon the offender, the family and society in general, the Community Service Society maintains an active interest in all measures designed to curb delinquency and crime, particularly among youthful beginners.

The Society's first interest is in *prevention*. Through its services to individuals and families, and through its activities in the fields of health and housing, the Society lays its hand to the task of counteracting conditions which are generally conducive to delinquency. Notwithstanding the preventive endeavors undertaken by us and by all others who strive for the same ends, there is much delinquency and crime and much of it will be encountered in the future.

Without diminishing our primary interest in prevention of delinquency, we are at the same time concerned with developing improved resources, both public and private, for preventing a recurrence of anti-social behavior through the rehabilitation of youth offenders who are not restrained by existing barriers. The Society's Committee on Youth and Justice is giving special attention to the judicial and correctional phases of restoring children and adolescents who, in various stages of ignorance, heedlessness, deliberation or rebellion, either stray into trouble or boldly strike out on paths leading ultimately to reformatory and prison.

The dislocations that may be expected in the period of demobilization and post-war readjustment will, unless the experiences of the past are reversed, contribute to a rise in the volume of crime. We must do all that can be done to achieve the greatest possible reversal of the usual post-war experiences. This publication directs the reader's attention to the need for strengthening our resources in one important field, that of combating crime which is so costly to society and so destructive in the lives of youth offenders.

WALTER S. GIFFORD
Chairman, Board of Trustees

Correctional Treatment
of Youth Offenders

Introduction

This is the fourth pamphlet in a series prepared by the Committee on Youth and Justice of the Community Service Society in support of the Youth Correction Authority plan.* In the earlier documents we have disclosed serious defects in the sentencing practices of the criminal justice system and have pointed to the Youth Correction Authority plan as a constructive proposal for avoiding such defects and shortcomings in the future.

In this pamphlet emphasis is placed upon the conflicting, disorganized procedures employed in the correctional treatment of youths convicted by the criminal courts. Ten histories of youth offenders are given as illustrations of the chaotic nature of existing practices. With two exceptions the names are disguised.

The reader will wish to know what differences in procedure and in kinds of treatment would be introduced through creation of a Youth Correction Authority. At the end of this pamphlet is given a description of the powers and responsibilities of an Authority; this may profitably be consulted before a reading of the case stories. With a picture of a functioning organization in mind, the reader as he examines the cases may determine, offender by offender, what different steps a well equipped Authority would be expected to take as measures of rehabilitation in such cases.

* The other pamphlets are: Preventing Criminal Careers; Prisons Cost Too Much; Chaos in Sentencing Youth Offenders.

[5]

Front Page Criminals

Anthony and William Esposito, true names calling for no concealment, came to be referred to as the "mad dog killers" for their crimes of murder committed in a payroll holdup and in attempting to make their escape amid the noonday crowd of a Fifth Avenue shopping center on January 14, 1941. They had killed a payroll messenger and a pursuing traffic officer and had seriously wounded a taxicab driver who courageously went to the aid of the mortally wounded policeman. These murderous robbers carried on their persons a small arsenal of six loaded revolvers and 136 extra cartridges. They had bullets stuffed in every coat and vest pocket and more in boxes for reserve use. At trial, they feigned insanity and indulged in extravagant courtroom antics in the vain effort to save themselves from the electric chair.

Family Background. The Esposito brothers were shiftless and dull-witted, yet criminally cunning. Their characters had been formed in a family of unmistakable criminal propensities and more fully developed in association with congregations of criminals at reformatory and prisons. The parents had emigrated from Italy when Anthony was an infant. William was born seven years after their settlement in this country. Other members of the immediate family included an older brother, four sisters, and a youth about whose status in the family there is some doubt. The use of various surnames and given names as aliases greatly complicates accurate identification of the family relationships. The father's name might be used on one occasion, the name of a second husband on another, and the maternal family name at still another time.

The Home. An interesting account of the family scene was prepared by a staff writer of the World-Telegram in the issue of January 15, 1941 The home, frequently shifted as to location, was "always filthy, littered with trash, overrun with vermin." The mother "learned little of America or its institutions except that of begging and complaining. She could get money from social agencies and she supported herself and her family in that way for much of her life. In her home she held her children as well as she could to the strict standards of Italy. Outside the home they ran wild. Whenever they were in trouble with the authorities—legal, educational or any other kind—she tried to hide them or protect them." In her contact with one social agency the mother was regarded as uncooperative and unable or unwilling to follow any case work plan. She failed in appointments for herself and the children and refused to give information concerning the family.

Criminal Record. A good deal of information was available from the records of public penal and correctional institutions. The father had served a term of imprisonment at the state prison in Trenton, New Jersey. The eldest son had been sentenced to Sing Sing along with Anthony in 1926. Another member of the family served a sentence at an adult reformatory. The eldest sister testified that she had been convicted of shop-lifting and had served a term in prison. A second sister was convicted and fined for shop-lifting.

This family took crime and imprisonment in its stride. Social outcasts, they were impoverished and dependent, disdainful of their religious affiliations. Such was the home life in which Anthony and William were nurtured as small boys. Without in any way making excuses for the murderers, we can nevertheless raise serious questions about the administration of criminal justice which was apparently content to switch them from sordid home to penal institution and back to home again, without ever undertaking a really constructive measure of reclamation.

William's Experience

William Esposito's first recorded sally into criminal behavior came in 1927, when he was 15 years of age. With two companions, all of the same age, William waylaid, violently assaulted, and robbed a partially intoxicated man in an alleyway. For that offense he was adjudged delinquent by the Manhattan Children's Court and committed to the House of Refuge, an institution receiving, at that time, juvenile delinquents and boys from 16 to 18 convicted of misdemeanor offenses.

Commitment. The boy of fifteen was sent to an institution where for nearly two years he associated with offenders, many of them ranging up to 20 or 21 by the time of their release. What he needed most at that crucial turn in his life was association with someone better than he had known, someone who would take an interest in his development and in fortifying him with training in good work-habits. Instead he was allowed to grow accustomed to a life with offenders in performing such work as the regime of a large institution demanded. Thus he was pulled out of the frying pan of family delinquency and thrown into the fire of a large correctional institution. It was the same, later, in his prison and parole experiences. Not once did any official responsible for directing his training and rehabilitation remove him to an environment even moderately wholesome. It is possible that nothing would have succeeded in reclaiming the youngster but something of greater promise should have been tried. If society were to set out deliberately to make a confirmed criminal of a young adolescent in William Esposito's situation, would it take steps much different from those taken in his case?

Parole Violation. About five months after his parole from the House of Refuge, William was arrested for snatching a pocketbook. He was returned to the House of Refuge by the New York City Parole Commission for violation of parole. There he remained for approximately two months, at the end of which time he was released from the institution.

New Offenses. In less than two weeks William, while alone, snatched a teacher's pocketbook with contents valued at eight dollars. On the following day, again alone, he snatched another teacher's pocketbook valued at seventy-five dollars. He was not arrested until about two months later. At that time his two older brothers were serving sentences at Sing Sing and Dannemora prisons for attempted robbery. In his case the knowledge of possible punishment was no deterrent. It often fails to deter those who think they will not be caught at crime.

Arrest. William was recognized by a detective on East Fourteenth Street as a suspect wanted for the purse snatchings. As the officer approached and said, "I'm a police officer, you're under arrest, put up your hands," William wheeled drawing a revolver, and one of his companions drew a knife. William's revolver jammed. The officer grappled with him, wrenched the weapon from his hand and overpowered him. The companions fled. William insisted that he had found the weapon, a 25 calibre gun of Spanish manufacture, in a doorway a short time before his arrest.

Prison. At seventeen William was convicted of assault, first degree and sentenced to Sing Sing Prison for not less than 7½ years and not more than 15 years.

According to an official report, William was "an excellent prisoner, there were no infractions of the rules, no adverse reports." The warden recommended a chance to adjust in society and the head-keeper endorsed the warden's recommendation. Although William was a very dull individual, with an I.Q. 78 and mental age of 12½ years, he was cunning enough to sense that obedience to prison rules is a good policy for a prisoner to adopt. The prison officials were learning nothing about the real William beyond his tolerance of the prison regime against the day of his release.

Parole. In May, 1936, William, 24 years of age, was paroled. On first contact with his parole officer "he protested with a great show of earnestness that the parole officer would never have occasion to complain of his conduct." On June 19th he was arrested for "lush-working" drunks in a city park. He was discharged by the examining magistrate before whom he was arraigned.

During the next few months William's parole officer occasionally found him with another parolee and for that he was reprimanded. It should be noted also that he was unemployed. On October 17th William was arrested for assault and robbery in company with other parolees, and was held at the Tombs. The case was dismissed for lack of evidence. William denied that he knew anything about his companions who had been arrested with him. Parole supervision was continued. The parole officer conferred with the Esposito family's social worker from the Department of Welfare who observed that they were a "demanding" family. Throughout November and December, William was reported to be unemployed.

In Danger. He was kept in line for a time, owing perhaps to his own caution against return to prison on a revocation of parole. But there had been no change in him which gave evidence of rehabilitation. Genuinely protective factors were still lacking in his life and destructive factors were in the ascendant. He was harbored with a family which had known much crime, he sought out ex-prisoners for his companions, and he had no employment until January, 1937, when he was assigned to a National Youth Administration project as a junior attendant at $22 per month.

Arrest and Escape. In March, 1937, William's parole officer came upon him seated at a restaurant in company with another parolee and two other men who were wanted by the police. The officer took the two parolees into custody. Believing that a detective was on the watch behind him and his two charges, the parole officer crossed the street and William made his escape. William was at large for a little over three years until his arrest for the murders committed on January 14, 1941.

~ *II* ~

Anthony's Experience

Anthony, the older of the murderers, first appeared in court at fifteen years of age when he was adjudged delinquent in the Manhattan Children's Court for snatching a woman's handbag and was placed on probation.

Criminal Offense. At eighteen Anthony was arrested on a charge of larceny. He had been annoying a girl who struck him with her pocketbook. Following a scuffle the girl discovered that her necklace was missing and had Anthony arrested. He was convicted of petit larceny and placed on probation by the Court of Special Sessions.

Four months later, while on probation, Anthony was arrested for stealing a roll of woolen goods from a truck. He pleaded not guilty to a charge of grand larceny upon arraignment in the Court of General Sessions. Later he withdrew his original plea and entered a new pleading of guilty to petit larceny. He was sentenced to the New York City Reformatory at New Hampton for an indeterminate term not to exceed three years. The New Hampton Reformatory is maintained by the City of New York for males, aged 16 to 30 at the time of admission, who are convicted of offenses below the grade of felony, principally misdemeanors.

Escape from Reformatory. Anthony had been assigned to an honor camp operated by the New Hampton Reformatory. He made an escape in the fifth month of his sentence and remained at large until he was arrested in New York City for the commission of a new offense.

Attempted Robbery. Anthony participated in a well-planned, though imperfectly executed, robbery with his older brother and three other companions. The five men entered a Chinese restaurant at different times and seated themselves so as to be able to cover all of the exits. At a given signal they all arose, herded the customers into a washroom, and methodically robbed them of their money and valuables. In the confusion, a waiter slipped away to call the police. When the police arrived they found Anthony hidden among the customers, keeping his hands raised along with the rest. Someone pointed him out, however, and he was arrested.

Trial and Sentence. After indictment for robbery, first degree, Anthony and his brother were brought to trial in the Court of General Sessions. By consent of the Court, a juror was withdrawn, a mistrial was declared, and the two brothers were permitted to plead guilty to attempted robbery first degree. They were sentenced to Sing Sing Prison for terms of five to ten years.

Deportation Proceedings. Anthony was born in Italy and had not become a citizen of the United States. While at Clinton Prison, to which he had been transferred from Sing Sing, a deportation warrant was issued for his arrest. At 24 years of age he was paroled from Clinton to meet the warrant. First, however, he was taken into custody by the Sheriff of Orange County to stand trial for his escape, five years earlier, from the Reformatory's honor camp. He received a suspended sentence on the escape charge and was delivered to the United States authorities at Ellis Island for deportation.

After a considerable delay in prosecution of the deportation proceedings, owing to obstructive legal moves made in Anthony's behalf, the deportation order was certified. It was reported by Anthony's sisters that his mother was dying. An arrangement was made for Anthony to visit his mother and he was escorted to the home in the custody of guards of the United States Immigration and Naturalization Service.

According to an account by one of the guards, Anthony's mother was confined to a darkened room suffering from a severe paralysis. Upon seeing Anthony and his escort, the mother and sisters cried and howled in Italian. One of the sisters offered the guards some liquor to drink; another sister sent a twelve year old girl to bring bread and ham. For about five minutes the two older sisters obstructed the view of the guards. Then they left the room, apparently to replenish the bread supply. Meanwhile, Anthony had escaped through a door concealed by heavy curtains. According to the police there had been an earlier rehearsal of such a ruse leading to escape, Anthony having previously escaped from detectives in the same room and in the same way prior to the time he was taken to prison.

New Arrest. About a month later, Anthony refused to admit a police officer to the room which he was occupying under the alias James Marrow. The officer was seeking a man wanted for robbery and forced his way into the room just as Anthony was attempting to escape through a window. There was found in his possession two loaded automatics, one loaded revolver, and brass knuckles. The name James Marrow was disclosed to be false upon investigation and Anthony was indicted for criminally carrying a pistol after being convicted of a felony.

Sentence. Anthony pleaded not guilty in the Court of General Sessions and stood trial by jury. The trial lasted from October 18 to October 30, 1930. By consent of the court a mistrial was declared upon the withdrawal of a juror, at which time Anthony pleaded guilty.

The day of sentence was set for November 17, 1930. The Immigration Service of the U.S. Department of Labor was advised of Anthony's identification and conviction. A communication to the Court by the Immigration Service stated that "an officer will be on hand on November 17, 1930, to take this alien into custody in the event that he is discharged by the Court."

Apparently the Court thought it better for the State of New York to maintain Anthony in prison for some years rather than to deport him from the country. He was sentenced to Sing Sing Prison for a term of seven years.

Prison. Anthony remained at Sing Sing for more than a year and was transferred to Great Meadow Prison. Like his brother William, he gave no trouble as a prisoner. The prison psychiatrist reported that he was a "tense and restless individual with an I.Q. of 87½ and a mental age of 14. He very possibly will attempt another escape. He does not show any signs of maturity and prognosis is guarded."

Parole and Deportation. On May 18, 1936, at the end of five and one-half years, Anthony was paroled from Great Meadow Prison. He was then taken into custody by the Immigration Service. He nearly slipped out of hand again. According to a report of the immigration authorities, Anthony "was delivered to guard—at the Barge Office at 9:30 p.m. He was given supper and placed in room 314." The guard stated that "the two inspectors who turned this alien over to him informed him that the alien momentarily escaped at the 14th Street subway station. During the excitement of capture they lost both the alien's baggage and an inspector's brief case containing the alien's papers. The material was later recovered."

An application for a writ of habeas corpus was denied and Anthony, at 28 years of age, was placed by the immigration authorities aboard the SS Rex for deportation to Italy on June 27, 1936.

Illegal Return. On August 7, 1939, the American Consul at Naples notified the Department of State that "Anthony Esposito who was deported * * * to Italy is a stowaway on the SS Rex. Arriving at New York on August 10, 1939. The Italian Line was informed to advise the Captain of the ship." No stowaways were located aboard the Rex in New York harbor.

Expiration of Sentence. On November 18, 1939, Anthony, 34 years of age, was discharged from parole supervision by the State Board of Parole by reason of expiration of sentence. The New York Police Department had no contact with Anthony until his arrest at the scene of murder on January 14, 1941.

Summary. William and Anthony Esposito paid with their lives for taking the lives of others. Although they made excellent adjustments to prison life, they were menaces to society when out of prison. No one can say whether it would have been possible to alter their lives to the extent of re-directing the youths into a law-abiding existence through constructive efforts when they first entered upon criminal behavior. All we know is that they were moved from a destructive home setting to prison life and back again and that such moves produced no reformation.

With the advantage of hindsight, we can see that this pair of slippery criminals, once they had become recidivists, should have been continuously segregated from society by imprisonment. We cannot be certain, of course, that a Youth Correction Authority, if one had been in existence, could have seen behind their obedient prison behavior to gain insight into their true criminal natures. We are confident, however, that an Authority, in making an original diagnostic examination of their behavior and in re-examining them in the course of correctional treatment, would have made the effort to test them out not only under conditions of full restraint but also under conditions of partial freedom short of full parole.

The Youth Correction Authority bill provides that an offender who is within the jurisdiction of the Authority may be released to freedom following discernible evidences of rehabilitation; or he may be kept continuously under control, subject to approval of the Supreme Court, in case evidences of rehabilitation are lacking.

After a first imprisonment of such youths as Anthony and William, an Authority would attempt to set them on their feet to lead useful, law-abiding lives. It is to be expected that, following imprisonment in a maximum security prison, an Authority would interpose supervision in medium or minimum security settings as a means of preparing them for acceptance of responsibility under a plan of progressive release to freedom. If, after making every endeavor to fit them for return to the community, success could not be attained, the Authority would segregate them from society by imprisonment for as long as required. In either case—release upon rehabilitation or segregation when rehabilitation is unattainable—society would be protected. Protection of society would be the primary aim of the Authority. There would neither be a coddling of the unreformable nor useless imprisonment of the reclaimable youth offenders.

~ III ~

Probation Followed by Futile Workhouse Imprisonment

This is a thumbnail account of a sixteen year old Negro boy, Jacob W———, who was arrested at 3:00 a.m. on November 3, 1940, for breaking into a candy store.

Family Situation. Jacob was the youngest of five children. His father had deserted the family when he was three years of age. The mother had been dependent on the Department of Welfare for assistance. An older brother, convicted of larceny, had been committed to the Institution for Male Defectives at Napanoch.*

Arrest and Indictment. In company with another sixteen year old boy, Jacob had broken a padlock to gain admittance to a candy store. The boys' haul had consisted of two boxes of candy, two packages of gum, and two boxes of cough drops, all valued at ten dollars. Both boys were held at the Tombs for arraignment in Manhattan Felony Court. They pleaded guilty to the charge and were paroled from the bench pending indictment and trial. The indictment which followed was for burglary third degree, petit larceny and possession of a burglar's instrument.

Psychiatric Examination. The Probation Department of the Court of General Sessions requested that sentence be postponed for two weeks to permit the making of an examination by the Court's psychiatric clinic. The examination showed that Jacob was not psychotic and was of average intelligence, I. Q. 96, Bellevue Verbal Scale, and sixth grade educational level by Otis Educational Tests. "He is a very immature adolescent who

---

* Institution for the care, training and treatment of male mental defectives over 16 years of age convicted of criminal offenses. Commitment made by courts or by transfer from other correctional institutions.

was timid during the interview. He stated, as did his co-defendent, that he lost money in a crap game and was afraid to go home without money and therefore robbed the store. Under supervision he is apt to make a good adjustment—physical examination negative."

Probation. Jacob and his co-defendant appeared in the Court of General Sessions. On January 17, 1941, they pleaded guilty to petit larceny on the recommendation of the District Attorney. Sentences were suspended pending good behavior and probation supervision for a period of three years was ordered.

New Arrest and Sentence. On March 30th following, Jacob was arrested in Manhattan and charged with petit larceny. He was sentenced by the Court of Special Sessions to six months in the Workhouse.

Comment. Jacob failed on probation in that he committed a new offense in a little over two months. He had shown unmistakably that he needed some kind of guidance that was not to be found in his own home. No genuinely helpful new influence had been introduced in the boy's life during the period of probation. His lapse in behavior clearly signalized the need for more constructive measures of supervision and training. Instead he was merely punished by a short term of imprisonment for the petit larceny.

It can scarcely be supposed that a sixteen year old boy's admission to the regimented life of a jail, filled for the most part with drunkards, gamblers, petty thieves and vagrants, could yield much in the way of reformation. On the other hand, most persons would agree that the risks of contamination would be great. About the most that could be hoped for would be that the experience would be so unpleasant as to have a deterrent effect upon a young offender. Yet we know how illusory are the hopes of deterrence. The confusion in the minds of persons who rely on the deterrent effects of confinement to a prison cell, or even the threat of it under probation, arises from failure to understand that most young offenders are wanting in prudence and good judgment which would lead them to weigh thoughtfully the hazards of delinquent behavior. The trouble comes from expecting youths who are to some degree abnormal in their habits and attitudes, to follow a process of reasoning and to react with insight characteristic of normal persons. It takes more than fear of possible consequences to strengthen character and to induce a substitution of prudence for heedlessness.

~ IV ~'

Eventful Road to Sing Sing

In June, 1940, Bert L—— succeeded in getting his name in a newspaper under the heading "Young Thug Gets 15 Years." Some months earlier, at eighteen years of age, he had been shot by his intended victim in a hold-up. Seriously wounded in chest and abdomen, Bert had remained at a hospital for nearly six months. Upon leaving the hospital he was indicted and tried on a charge of robbery. A conviction followed and he was sentenced to Sing Sing Prison for not less than 15 and not more than 30 years.

Family Situation. Bert was the youngest in an Italian family of seven children. His father was a day-laborer but had long been unemployed and dependent upon the Department of Welfare for assistance. An older brother, with whom Bert had been associated in the above crime, had a record of arrests and prosecutions in the criminal courts. It appears that there was no stabilizing influence upon the youngster in his own home.

Earlier Experiences. At sixteen years of age Bert had been arrested in Queens on a charge of burglary. Upon trial he was convicted. The sentence was suspended and he was placed on probation under the supervision of the Queens County Court. No information could be obtained regarding the circumstances and conditions of his probation supervision.

Nearly a year later when seventeen, Bert was arrested late at night in Brooklyn for violation of Section 1141 of the Penal Code relating to the possession of obscene prints and articles. At the time of arrest he had been idling in a parked car with three companions, all of whom had police records. The four youths were arraigned in Magistrates' Court and discharged.

About four months later Bert, then eighteen, was arrested for possessing a revolver which was loaded with blank cartridges. The youth insisted that he was just having some fun over the Fourth of July, it then being the 10th.

Probation. Bert was arraigned in the Brooklyn Adolescents Court. The criminal charge of possessing a weapon was vacated and a wayward minor complaint was substituted. Pending final adjudication he was paroled to the custody of his parents. Upon arraignment for disposition it was disclosed by a probation officer, who had made a pre-sentence investigation, that Bert was at the time of probation under the supervision of the Queens County Court. The magistrate of the Adolescents' Court thereupon suspended sentence in order that the Queens Court of higher jurisdiction might continue to exercise probation supervision.

Robbery. Bert's culminating robbery offense, in which he was wounded, was perpetrated in company with his older brother and two other men aged 25 and 28 respectively. It is evident that probation supervision had not extricated the youth from personal associations of a destructive kind. Nor had fear of consequences operated as a deterrent.

Upon arraignment in the Court of General Sessions for sent-

ence, after a pleading of guilty to robbery second degree, the
Clerk of the Court put the question: Bert L—— "what have
you now to say why the sentence of the Court should not be
pronounced against you?" A colloquy ensued, in part as follows:

Defense Attorney: If Your Honor please, the probation
report is complete in this case, but there are some facts that
I think the court should know. This boy comes from a large
family. A brother of the co-defendant was dismissed.

Court: The defendant is a second offender.

Defense Attorney: Yes . . . and we took a plea to robbery
in the second degree. Mr. B. (associate defense attorney) had
the case, and we spoke to Your Honor about it several times
and we tried to get robbery in the third degree, and then it was
a question of whether or not his brother would go to trial with
him, or he would take this plea.

Court: Yes, and we adjourned this the last time for you to
see if you could get a lesser plea.

Defense Attorney: Yes, and we also adjourned it to find
out whether or not you could send him to Elmira.

Court: The sentence is mandatory.

Defense Attorney: Yes. He is about 18. He has three
bullet wounds in him. He has been in the hospital.
. . . we are faced with a situation where the boy at his age
will get 15 to 30 years.

Court: That is the law; I didn't make the law.

Defense Attorney: Well, could Your Honor do this: . . .
send him to Elmira, and if it is an improper sentence, he will
be returned.

Court: I cannot do it. The law does not permit it.

Defense Attorney: Will Your Honor then recommend a

minimum time commensurate with what Your Honor feels the punishment should be in this case, and I am sure that the Parole Board would honor Your Honor's feelings in the matter when he would come up for parole.

Court: —— (Bert——) you were indicted by the Grand Jury . . . for . . . robbery first degree together with —— ——. Pursuant to the recommendation of the District Attorney and with the consent of the Court, you were permitted to plead guilty to robbery second degree, and you now appear to be a second offender, and of course the laws of this state are mandatory on the Court.

This was a vicious crime. You, together with the co-defendants, entered a store and displayed loaded revolvers. The complainant, however, defended himself and fired 5 shots, 2 of which struck you. Your co-defendant was given not less than 15 to 30 years for robbery in Kings County on April 3, 1940.

The sentence of this Court is mandatory. I am obliged to send you to State Prison for not less than 15 years and not more than 30 years.

Defense Attorney: Will Your Honor make some recommendation?

Court: I will let the sentence stand.

Defense Attorney: Your Honor was inclined to give him robbery in the third degree, and I felt that there was a case in this court where there was a more vicious crime, and he got robbery in the third degree, and Your Honor posed that question to Mr. B., because shots were fired in both cases, and he was given robbery in the third degree and got 10 to 20 years, and he insisted on this boy taking a plea and getting 15 to 30.

Court: I will make a recommendation that after he has served not less than 10 years, that if he makes an application to the Governor, this Court recommend that he be released.

Comment. Two things stand out in Bert's correctional treatment experiences. In the first place, he enjoyed the freedom of probation without having to sacrifice the bad companions with whom he chose to associate. The habit of idling about with offenders leads almost inevitably to a fresh outbreak of crime. A person who drifts along with such companions simply is not taking his probation promises seriously. There can be no training in good habits under those circumstances, and good habits are essential to satisfactory adjustment on the part of a probationer.

In some instances, doubtless, judges reluctantly place youths on probation in the belief that the risk involved is outweighed by the risk of possible damage by imprisonment at an existing reformatory or prison. If facilities of correctional treatment, intermediate between probation and mass-imprisonment, were established under a Youth Correction Authority both risks could be avoided by commitment to the Authority.

The sentence, which resulted from the offense committed during the probation period, was mandatory and inflexible because of the nature and circumstances of the crime. After many years of imprisonment, the boy of eighteen grown into manhood, will be severely handicapped for a life of responsible living when at last he is released to freedom. Suppose it were possible to reclaim him after two years or three years of imprisonment. What good purpose is served by having him remain at prison for several years longer? That is what a mandatory sentence requires. A youth who is capable of readjusting himself at the end of the two or three years may not be equally well prepared for life in freedom at the end of fifteen years. In Bert's case the judge seemed disposed to give him an indeterminate sentence but his hands were tied by an inflexible provision of the law relating to the commission of a felony while armed.

Under a fifteen to thirty year sentence there is little encouragement to the prisoner or the prison officials to work for rehabilitation. In that way the initial long-term sentence undermines the opportunities for correctional treatment.

~ V ~

Leniency Yields Poor Fruits

Early in the evening of January 17, 1940, Ralph T——, aged seventeen, with three other youths escaped from jail by forcing open a barred window on the fourth tier of a cell block at the Queens City Prison. The youths lowered themselves on an improvised "rope" of sheets and blankets and swung themselves pendulum fashion to the top of the prison wall. Later that night the boys, joined by two others, robbed a druggist in Brooklyn.

Family Background. A significant account of Ralph's family background can be told in three lines: His father had been killed in a gambling row. His mother had a police record. She frequently deserted home and neglected her family. His brothers also had police records.

Early Delinquencies. At fourteen, Ralph had been before the Brooklyn Children's Court on a petition of delinquency. The case was dismissed. At sixteen, in company with a juvenile, he unlawfully entered a building through a skylight and stole a typewriter and an adding machine. Two days after the theft Ralph was arrested while attempting to sell the stolen articles. He was arraigned in the Brooklyn Adolescents' Court where the unlawful entry and larceny charges were set aside upon substitution of a wayward minor charge.

Commitment. Ralph was committed at sixteen to the Children's Village at Dobbs Ferry, a private non-sectarian training institution, of the cottage type, for white problem boys and girls aged nine to eighteen. He did not get along well with the other children and failed to benefit from the program of training which the Children's Village had to offer. He was returned in five months to the jurisdiction of the Adolescents' Court and was placed on probation. During the succeeding ten months of probation supervision very few contacts with Ralph were recorded, other than routine monthly reporting at the probation office. A recommendation of discharge from probation supervision was approved by the Court.

New Offense. Five days after his discharge from probation Ralph, seventeen, together with a companion, eighteen, entered a first floor apartment through the rear-court yard during the early evening and stole jewelry and miscellaneous articles valued at about $350. They were arrested by a patrolman as they were making their way out of the yard.

Indictments and Sentence. On December 17, 1939, the youths were arraigned in the Brooklyn Felony Court on a charge of burglary and held for the action of the Grand Jury. Pending indictment the youths, failing to produce bail in the amount of $2500, were held at the Queens City Prison under a new ruling to send youths to that prison rather than to the Raymond Street Jail in Brooklyn. One month later, Ralph and his co-defendant were indicted by the Kings County Grand Jury for burglary third degree and grand larceny first degree. Two days prior to the indictment the youths, with two others, made their escape from the Queens City Prison.

Three days after the escape, Ralph and one of his fugitive companions were arrested in their bunks at a cheap lodging house in Brooklyn. Ralph and his three companions were indicted by the Kings County Grand Jury for robbery first degree, grand larceny first degree, and assault second degree for robbery of the druggist in Brooklyn on the evening of their escape.

[25]

Later, the youths were indicted by the Queens County Grand Jury for escape from prison. In two weeks the youths withdrew their original pleas of not guilty and pleaded guilty to the charge of the indictment. Ralph and his three companions were sentenced by the Queens County Court to Sing Sing Prison for a term of 2 to 4 years.

Other Indictments. Following sentence by the Queens Court, the District Attorney of Kings County, taking into account the imposed term of imprisonment, stated that, as to the earlier burglary and robbery charges, the interests of justice would be satisfied by the Queens sentence. Concerning Ralph's robbery offense the District Attorney said: "In the instant case we understand that a screw driver and not a revolver was used in the holdup. We feel that the ends of justice are satisfied by the acceptance of a plea of attempted robbery in the third degree, which, when considered with the pleas of this defendant * * * for the Queens jail break would require sufficient punishment for this defendant, considering the fact that he is a seventeen year old youth."

Additional Sentence. Ralph T—— was sentenced to Sing Sing Prison for not less than 2½ years and not more than 5 years for robbery. This term of imprisonment was to run concurrently with the sentence of 2 to 4 years imposed by the Queens County Court for escape from jail.

Comment. Ralph perpetrated a series of criminal acts in short order after his release from probation. To what extent did the correctional treatment system contribute to making a full-fledged criminal of him? Considering the nature of his home background it may be supposed that the risks in placing him on probation were considerable. Yet he managed to get along for ten months without committing a new offense or, at least, he was not discovered to have committed one during that time. That would indicate a certain respect for a supervising authority. But it was a wholly negative factor in shaping his character and in fortifying him against exposure to persons and situations conducive to crime. A boy like Ralph may need to be supervised in a work camp or other training center where for a time he will come under the daily personal guidance of a leader who is experienced in re-directing the lives of youthful offenders.

When he was incarcerated in jail to await action of the Grand Jury on a bill of indictment, he was neither put on his honor nor guarded with a sufficient amount of care. The opportunity for escape presented itself and was siezed upon. Robbery was the next link in the chain of events. The youth having escaped from jail and lacking funds took desperate measures to acquire some money, avoiding exposure to friends or family while being sought by the police who knew his connections. Ordinary probation supervision was without avail in blocking the road to prison. Whatever his offenses and the tangle of circumstantial causation, Sing Sing was not the place for this seventeen year old boy.

~ VI ~

Mixture of Probation and Imprisonment

Stephen J—— was a youthful burglar who at the age of sixteen committed numerous thefts. He succeeded in stealing jewelry and in disposing of it by sale to a "fence." Early in January, 1937, he broke into a private house during the night, alone, and made his escape after taking jewelry, opera glasses, and other articles all valued at about $75. He was arrested in two days' time by a detective who knew and suspected him. Admitting the latest offense for which he was arrested, he also confessed that he had committed some fifteen other burglaries during the previous two months. The immediate outcome was a sentence to the New York City Reformatory at New Hampton.

Family Situation. Stephen's mother died when he was an infant and the responsibility for his upbringing was left to his older sisters and brothers. His father struggled with a small restaurant business and gave Stephen scant attention. One of his brothers was committed to the House of Refuge as a delinquent.

Early Delinquencies. When in the fifth grade at school and a little under 13 years of age, Stephen deserted his home. After an absence of four days he was found asleep in the Times Square subway station by a special policeman of the Interborough subway. In response to questions aimed to establish his identity and home address he stated that both his parents were dead and gave an incorrect home address. When the truth came out Stephen was taken to the Brooklyn Children's Court, adjudged delinquent, and remanded to the Shelter of the Society for the Prevention of Cruelty to Children.

Psychiatric Examination. Stephen was examined by the psychiatric clinic of the Children's Court. The report disclosed that he was "simple, undeveloped mentally, and behaves in the manner of a dull boy several years younger * * * is not greatly disturbed by his detention. In mood, he is fairly cheerful and pleasant. He cooperates with no spontaneity, but satisfactorily. * * * He grades as a borderline to a very dull normal type."

Probation. Upon the recommendation of an investigating probation officer, Judge I of the Brooklyn Children's Court placed Stephen on probation for a period of four months—from July to November. Stephen did not report to his probation officer during August. The officer therefore visited

Stephen's home and interviewed his father who stated that the boy was getting along very well. Stephen reported on probation once in September and the probation officer once visited his home. The father gave assurance that Stephen stayed home at night, did not play on the docks with undesirable companions, and was attentive to his religious duties.

In October Stephen failed to report to his probation officer. Inquiry was made of the father who was puzzled about his son's failure to report inasmuch as he seemed to be getting along very well at home and at school. It may be doubted that the father really knew much about the way the boy spent his time. A few days after the father's favorable report, an officer of the Bureau of Attendance, Board of Education, disclosed that Stephen had been a truant from school on four days in September and on ten out of the first eighteen days in October.

Special School. A day later Stephen was found asleep in the IRT subway. He was taken before the Children's Court on a truancy petition filed by the school attendance officer, and for failure to report on probation. Stephen was committed, on the truancy petition, to the New York Parental School in October. He did well enough at the disciplinary school, with a good conduct record, passing grades, and work in the carpentry and tailor shops.

Arrest. Nearly eight months elapsed before Stephen was again in trouble. At fourteen and a half years of age he unlawfully entered an apartment, alone, and stole a wrist watch. He was caught on the roof and identified by the tenant whose premises he had entered.

Probation Again. Stephen appeared in Children's Court with his father and older married brother. He was adjudged delinquent and remanded to a Shelter of the Society for the Prevention of Cruelty to Children for further investigation. It was learned that the boy and his father occupied a small, dark bedroom at the rear of a one-room restaurant in a condemned building. Stephen's married sister offered to take him into her home. Judge II of the Manhattan Children's Court placed Stephen on probation with the understanding that he would live with his sister in the Bronx and that supervision of probation be transferred to the Bronx Children's Court.

Probation Failure. Stephen failed to report to his probation officer. He continued to live with his sister but did not attend school. The sister had suggested to the probation officer that Stephen be sent to live with his brother. Because of continued failure to report on probation, Judge III of the Children's Court issued a bench warrant for the boy's return to court. Three weeks were required to catch up with him.

Restored to Probation. He was brought before the court accompanied by the older brother, previously mentioned. He explained that he had been with friends on a two-weeks' camping trip in the Catskills, having left his sister's home because, as he said, she was unable to support him. Accepting his promise to do better, Judge IV of the Children's Court restored Stephen to probation and instructed him to live with his brother. There followed a period of six weeks during which Stephen satisfactorily met the conditions of his probation. Apparently, however, he was very much on his own whether living with his brother or his father, to whom he returned without the knowledge or consent of his probation officer.

Asleep In Subway. In mid-July an IRT special policeman found Stephen asleep in a subway station. He was permitted to depart on the promise that he would go to his home. Later in the day a police officer found him asleep in the same station and took him to a Shelter of the Society for the Prevention of Cruelty to Children.

Remand. Stephen was again before the Children's Court for violation of probation. On July 22, 1935, Judge IV remanded him to the New York Catholic Protectory until September 3rd. The boy's father and brother were notified to be in court at the expiration of the remand period. Stephen earned a favorable report at the Protectory. No member of his family had visited him during the entire time of his stay at the institution. He was returned from the institution to the home of his father. Judge V of the Children's Court dealt with Stephen's case at this juncture and directed that he be restored to probation. His probation officer stated in a report that, "I urged the boy to do well and he promised to do so."

Aimless Month. For the next month Stephen disregarded home, school, and probation officer. When it became known that he had run away from his father's home, a bench warrant was issued for his return to court. He was not found for service of the warrant. His public school reported that he had been absent for thirteen days out of sixteen school days in September. Stephen had gone for many months without committing an offense so far as known. His derelictions consisted of sleeping in a subway train or in a subway station and failure to report on probation. It would appear from the record that his family had only a casual interest in him. He was on the loose in the community. No constructive plan had been thought out for him. Something more than an occasional appearance before a probation officer was needed for the guidance of a boy in a situation corresponding to that of Stephen's.

Burglary. In October, 1935, Stephen, at fifteen years of age, was caught, while alone, in the act of breaking into an apartment. He appeared in court on the same day with his older brother. Judge V of the Children's Court adjudged him to be delinquent and directed that he be remanded to Bellevue Hospital for examination. Stephen's father told the court that he thought the boy should be sent to an institution. The older brother and his wife indicated that they did not care to assume further responsibility for his supervision at that time.

Psychiatric Report. The following is a summary of the psychiatric examination made of Stephen by Bellevue Hospital: "Without psychosis; inferior intelligence; deep-seated neurotic tendencies of a rather complicated type; neurotic type of personality deviate; growth factors which indicate indefinite endocrine tendency; neurological findings which may indicate an organic basis for the beginnings of his personality change. The findings indicate this is *not* a proper case for a state hospital nor for a state school. * * * It is suggested that this boy be placed for an extended period of time in a custodial or correctional institution where he can receive continued psychiatric analysis and treatment. While the prognosis is not held especially hopeful * * * we believe that this boy may still be rehabilitated to a certain extent if he can be removed from his environment to an institution."

Commitment. Stephen, with his father and married sisters, appeared before the Brooklyn Children's Court at the end of October. Probation was terminated and Stephen was committed by Judge VI of the Children's Court to the Children's Village at Dobbs Ferry until May 29, 1936, a period of seven months. Near the end of the period, Children's Village reported that Stephen was "trustworthy, a good worker and dependable. * * * We are recommending that he be discharged from the institution to his home, but the probation officer will probably need to make a careful investigation of the home situation and supervise Stephen, if your Honor decides to place him on probation."

On the day of his return from the institution Stephen appeared with his father in Children's Court. The probation officer who had previously supervised him recommended that he be again placed on probation, noting that the home situation had been improved since the father had moved around the corner from the condemned building to one which was cleaner and lighter. That would seem to be an extremely narrow basis for evaluating the adequency of a home setting for a boy of Stephen's background of experience and circumstances. He was placed on probation by Judge VII of the Children's Court with instruction to report to his probation officer on June 9th. He failed to report.

Arrest. A week later the probation officer learned from a detective that Stephen had been arrested for unlawfully entering a house, alone. Stephen stated falsely that he was sixteen years of age and was therefore arraigned in the Brooklyn Adolescents' Court rather than in the Children's Court. His true age, fifteen, was reported by the probation officer and he was taken next day before Judge VIII of the Brooklyn Children's Court. The judge took testimony but did not adjudicate the case. Stephen was remanded for five days to the Society for the Prevention of Cruelty to Children to permit the making of a further investigation. Stephen had vigorously denied his guilt, insisting that he was in the private home looking for a friend whom he had known at Children's Village. He was permitted to return to his father's home. A day or so later the Children's Village informed the court that the friend lived in Queens and not at the Brooklyn residence which Stephen had entered.

Neither Stephen nor his father appeared in court on July 7, 1936, the day appointed. Bench parole to the custody of the father was continued until July 10th. The court later learned that Stephen had run away from his father's home on July 7th. A warrant was issued for his arrest but the warrant officer was unable to find him. There was no further contact with Stephen until February, 1937.

Burglary. During the first week of February, 1937, Stephen, then sixteen years and four months old, burglarized a residence He was arrested and arraigned in the Brooklyn Adolescents Court where he pleaded not guilty. He was held for the action of the Grand Jury.

Imprisonment. Stephen was indicted for burglary and was arraigned in the Kings County Court. With the consent of the court and the District Attorney, he withdrew his plea of not guilty of burglary and pleaded guilty to the misdemeanor offense of petit larceny. He was returned to the Raymond Street Jail to await the pronouncement of sentence. A month later he was sentenced to the New York City Reformatory at New Hampton. All told he had been in the Raymond Street Jail for 62 days from day of arrest to day of sentence.

There is not a more disheartening thing about the criminal justice system than the apparent indifference to a youth's languishing in jail awaiting disposition of his case. Although rehabilitative training is in the offing, the system tolerates the seriously deteriorative effects of a long stay in a jail cell before the somewhat more constructive correctional regime gets under way.

New Offense. In about nine months Stephen was paroled from the Reformatory. He had been out of the Reformatory on parole for eleven days when he committed a new offense. Accompanied by an unknown associate who escaped, he broke into a factory building at night and stole two electric drills valued at about $50. He was intercepted by an alert patrolman who shot him upon his failure to stop when ordered to do so. The wound was not serious but required attention at a hospital for about two weeks.

Re-commitment. Stephen was indicted for burglary third degree and petit larceny. Upon arraignment in the Kings County Court toward the end of March, he pleaded not guilty. The court did not try the case but ordered Stephen's return to the Reformatory for violation of parole.

Penitentiary. About eight months later, on November 16, 1938, Stephen was transferred from the New Hampton Reformatory to the City Penitentiary at Rikers Island. The following notation was made in the record relating to the transfer: "Stephen is mature, prison-wise and troublesome." The little fellow, who five years earlier had wandered until he was exhausted and fell asleep in the subway, had traveled a long way on a dangerous, dead-end road.

Probation. As Stephen's maximum term of imprisonment at New Hampton-Rikers Island was about to expire (April 12, 1940) he was taken from Rikers Island to the Kings County Court where he was arraigned to answer the charge of burglarizing the factory two years earlier, the offense which led to his return to New Hampton Reformatory as a parole violator. With the consent of the court and the District Attorney, he withdrew his plea of not guilty of burglary third degree and petit larceny and pleaded guilty. He was thereupon sentenced to Sing Sing Prison, 3 to 10 years, but "execution of sentence suspended during good behavior—probation."

Failure. Stephen adopted an assumed name of Polish origin for his new start in life and began working for a moving and trucking company. He had several jobs as a laborer and managed to save a little money but it was not a clear saving for he owed $25 in back rent for a room from which he had moved. He admitted the debt in discussing his affairs with the probation supervisor and reluctantly agreed to pay it back gradually. Stephen failed to report on probation in June, 1941, and his whereabouts were unknown. A warrant was filed at the Kings County Court for his arrest as an absconder. He was nearing his twenty-first birthday.

Comment. Stephen J—— grew from childhood through adolescence into manhood under the almost continuous supervision of an agent or agency designated by a court. It was an abnormal atmosphere, too long endured, for a youth's proper growth and development.

The boy was not wholly cast off by his family. Yet, in being shifted about from father to brother to sister, it appeared that there was no home where he was unmistakably wanted or where he could enjoy the feeling of security and satisfaction so necessary to the adolescent. When he was sent to the Reformatory after a long stay in jail he became "mature, prisonwise, and troublesome." In Stephen's case there seems to have been, over a period of years, too much and too little supervision—too little supervision on probation and too much mass-imprisonment. The reason for it, no doubt, was the lack of suitable intermediate facilities for the training and treatment of youths in similar circumstances.

~ VII ~

Long History of Failure

Arthur B——'s "adult" criminal history began when he was a little under seventeen years of age. Upon conviction for the offense of snatching a woman's pocketbook, he was sentenced to the New York City Reformatory at New Hampton.

Early History. Arthur's parents died when he was an infant. He was raised by an aunt who had the reputation in her neighborhood of being a reliable, hard-working person. No difficulties were encountered in bringing up the boy until he was nearly thirteen when he began to desert his home and classes at school. His aunt, recognizing that she was unable to manage the boy, presented a delinquency petition to the

Children's Court. The court hearing resulted in Arthur's being placed on probation. He continued to live at the home of his aunt.

Probation Failure. During the first month of probation Arthur stole some hats from a shop. A new investigation was made by the probation department of the Children's Court. Although the supervising probation officer was dissatisfied with Arthur's progress and reported his opinion to the court, probation was continued. In a short while Arthur was apprehended, with other boys, for stealing cases of beer. For that offense he was committed, in April 1933, to the House of Refuge at Randall's Island. A month later, upon the opening of the New York State Training School for Boys at Warwick, Arthur was transferred there to become a ward of the State Department of Social Welfare.

Parole. After a stay of ten months at Warwick, Arthur was paroled, not for the reason that he had made a satisfactory adjustment at the school but because the training school authorities believed their institutional program was not helping him. He then came under the supervision of one of the institution's social workers. Later, the theft of newspapers and small change from a newsstand was recorded against Arthur but no change was made in his parole status on that account.

In a few months, however, it was learned that Arthur had burglarized a grocery store and had also been caught sneaking through a subway turnstile without payment of the fare. In May, 1935, when fifteen years of age, Arthur was returned to Warwick for violation of his parole.

Psychiatric Examination. Just prior to his return to Warwick the psychiatric clinic of the Children's Court reported that Arthur "shows deeply ingrained delinquency pattern * * * little desire to reform * * * Aggressive type who will readily involve other boys * * * Fairly capable, but cannot confine

[37]

attention to wholesome types of activity * * * Should be watched closely."

Disappearance. After a further stay of eleven months at Warwick, Arthur was granted leave for a brief stay at his aunt's home. He failed to return at the end of the appointed time and disappeared from home. Eluding detection for approximately three months, Arthur was at last caught by his Warwick parole officer. As he was being put on a bus for return to the institution, he broke away and made good his escape.

Warwick Gives Up. Following the escape, the Warwick institution evaluated its training program in relation to Arthur and decided that a longer stay at the institution would be of no benefit to the boy. Accordingly his discharge from Warwick was recommended. The investigation leading to that decision disclosed that Arthur's behavior had become increasingly antisocial. Although he was only sixteen he was absorbed in gambling and was known to have been living with, and supported by, a prostitute.

Case Closed Without Solution. When a parolee from Warwick fails under supervision and is deemed unsuitable for further treatment at the institution it appears to be customary practice for the institution to wash its hands of the delinquent. Theoretically, the Children's Court, which originally ordered the commitment to Warwick, has power to exercise control over such delinquent until he reaches twenty-one years of age. But apparently the institution "closes" its cases of failure without returning the failing delinquents to the court of origin. Thus, the youth who is most in need of close supervision is given none. There is a hiatus, often brief, between discharge from the control of the institution and the commission of a crime which, upon discovery and arrest, sets in motion a new order of correctional treatment by the criminal court.

Doubtless the reason for failure to re-establish the control of the Children's Court in such cases is that there is no suitable place to which the delinquent may be sent by the court after his final discharge from Warwick. The New York State Vocational Institution at Coxsackie is available but the transfer from the jurisdiction of the State Department of Social Welfare to the Department of Correction appears to be a too drastic·move in the absence of a proved new offense. If a Youth Correction Authority were in existence, the transfer of a youth to its control would be appropriate and readily effected.

Larceny and Arrest. On January 12, 1937, Arthur snatched a pocketbook containing about $60. The machinery of criminal justice administration worked efficiently and without undue delay up to the time when the court began to consider what kind of correctional treatment should take place. He was arrested on his seventeenth birthday, January 21, 1937, and was arraigned in Felony Court on the following day, at which time he pleaded not guilty. He was held at the Tombs. On January 28th an indictment for grand larceny in the first degree was handed down by the Grand Jury and on February 3rd Arthur pleaded not guilty. He was returned to the Tombs, his case having been set for a jury trial in the Court of General Sessions.

At that point Arthur was sent by the Court to Bellevue Hospital for a mental test and for treatment of gonorrhea. The hospital reported that he was of average intelligence. One month and a week later Arthur was brought before General Sessions. Upon the consent of the district attorney and the Court, the charge was reduced to petit larceny to which Arthur pleaded guilty.

Commitment and Parole. In March, 1937, the Court of General Sessions sentenced Arthur to the New York City Reformatory. He was paroled from the institution a year later. In the sixth month of the parole period, Arthur and two other boys beat a man who refused to give them cash which they demanded. The boys had used a piece of lead pipe, a broken bottle, and a knife in the assault. They escaped but a detailed description by the victim lead to the later arrest of Arthur. He was then returned to the Reformatory as a parole violator.

Assault. Three months after his return to the Reformatory, Arthur assaulted three of the institution's officers, severely injuring one of them. He was tried for that offense in the Orange County Court and sentenced to the County Jail for eleven months and twenty-nine days. He served six months of the time in jail and was returned to the Reformatory. Shortly afterwards he was transferred from the City Reformatory to the City Penitentiary at Rikers Island because he presented problems of discipline too difficult to be dealt with at the Reformatory.

Jail. In mid-March, 1940, at the expiration of his maximum Reformatory sentence of three years, Arthur was discharged from the Penitentiary and was confronted by the service of a warrant for his return to the Orange County Jail to complete the sentence imposed for assaulting the Reformatory officers.

Release. In mid-June, 1940, Arthur was released from the Orange County Jail. The County Sheriff in response to an inquiry about the status of Arthur's imprisonment wrote, "When he was serving time here we used him as a trusty and he did his work well. We never had any trouble with him."

Vagrancy. Arthur was arrested in New York City about three months later on a charge of vagrancy. At that time he was nearly twenty-one years of age. He was sentenced as a vagrant to six months in the Workhouse.

Comment. Arthur was a failure but so also was the administration of correctional treatment in his case. The series of imprisonments were negative in their rehabilitative effects. The last incarceration of six months at the Workhouse could have little effect one way or the other. Imprisonment was an old story to Arthur. It could scarcely have any particular value as a deterrent. The short term at the Workhouse was more in the nature of an inconvenience to the prisoner; it held no worth-while possibilities in the way of training and reformation. He marked off the days on his calendar as they passed and left the institution no better and perhaps worse off than when he entered. There was no consistent design or plan in the correctional treatment which was given him by numerous agencies of criminal justice.

~ VIII ~

One Psychiatric Examination After Another

Max B——, at sixteen years of age, was arrested for a childish attempt at extortion by demanding money in letters to a large New York department store. He was convicted of attempted extortion and sentenced to the New York City Reformatory at New Hampton.

Family Background. When Max was six years old his father deserted the family. No more is heard of the father who left his wife with four children to care for. Five children were born of a subsequent marriage. Max was the third oldest of the nine children. Social investigations revealed that the stepfather was uninterested in the home and was a harmful influence on the children. He was an alcoholic and deserted the home frequently. The family was for years in an extremely impoverished condition. At various times the children were before the Children's Court on petitions of neglect. They were aided by the Children's Division of the Department of Welfare, and were cared for by institutions or distributed among relatives.

First Offense. At fourteen years of age, Max entered a building in Manhattan during the daytime and stole a typewriter. He told the arresting officer that he was seventeen and so was dealt with as an adult.

The Tombs. Max was unable to furnish $1500 bail and was held at the Tombs to await court action. Arraigned in Manhattan Felony Court on October 4, 1937, he pleaded guilty to burglary and was returned to the Tombs. He was indicted for burglary third degree and petit larceny. Upon arraignment in the Court of General Sessions on October 14th, he pleaded guilty to petit larceny. The date of sentence was set for October 28th and the boy was returned to the Tombs. When he again appeared in court a question was raised as to his age. Sentence was postponed until November 10th and Max remained at the Tombs.

Psychiatric Examination. The psychiatric clinic of the General Sessions Court examined Max but owing to his refusal to cooperate with the examining psychiatrist it was impossible to establish his I.Q. The report stated that "we have come to the conclusion he is not psychotic * * * He has become embittered into a self-conscious, self-willed role of intense egocentricity and anti-sociality * * * It is still possible that he might learn to work for society instead of against it. It is obvious that he will require the most careful sort of retraining * * * We think his commitment should be for a long-term period. May we therefore suggest * * * New York State Vocational Institution at West Coxsackie."

Probation. After a further postponement of five days Max again appeared in General Sessions Court. It was determined that he was under sixteen years of age and he was therefore placed in the custody of the Society for the Prevention of Cruelty to Children, pending further disposition in the Manhattan Children's Court.

Max was adjudged delinquent by the Children's Court. He had admitted the commission of numerous burglaries, all of which were later verified. An investigation revealed that prior to his court appearances Max had been absent from his home, whereabouts unknown. Upon recommendation of the probation department of the Children's Court he was placed on probation. Two weeks later he failed to report to his probation officer. The school attendance officer reported that Max had not been attending school.

Probation Failure. A bench warrant was issued on December 23, 1937, to bring Max before the Children's Court for violation of probation. At this time the principal of a public school accused him of stealing approximately $1000 worth of school property over a period of several weeks.

While the Children's Court was waiting for the appearance of the mother or stepfather, Max was released on bench parole. During that time he committed several burglaries. On January 4, 1938, he was again brought before the Children's Court and was committed to the New York Catholic Protectory, an institution for delinquent Catholic boys. When escorted from the courtroom he remarked to an attendant, "They finally caught up with me."

Trouble-maker. Max and his mother were again in Children's Court following a petition to the court by the Protectory requesting the boy's removal. The institution reported that Max had "a typical psychopathic outlook on life and was considered to be a dangerous individual. He took part in the difficulties on June 26, 1938, by breaking windows, pulling down pipes, and contributing to the general excitement." The "diffi-

[43]

culties" related to a serious disturbance during which Max, a ring-leader, attempted to escape disguised as a member of the Catholic Brotherhood.

Probation. The commitment to the Protectory was vacated by the Presiding Justice of the Children's Court on August 19, 1938, and Max was placed on probation. His mother and maternal grandmother had pleaded with the court to permit the boy to live with his grandmother at her home in Rockland County, New York.

An earlier report in the court records relating to a brother of Max described the grandparent's home as a "dilapidated old shack located in an uninviting and deserted section near the water front * * * The quarters are congested and entirely inadequate for the purpose of all the members now residing at the house * * * The shabby and poorly constructed shacks in the neighborhood are mostly settled by a lawless element of white and black people."

Max made what appeared to be a very sincere plea to the judge for another chance and promised that he would desist from stealing. The judge was doubtful of the boy's sincerity but the probation officer reinforced the plea for leniency. Max was instructed to go with his grandmother for an indefinite stay. His case was referred to the Rockland County probation service for supervision. Max remained upstate for about two weeks. It was supposed that he had returned to the home of his mother in New York City. A notice was mailed to Max and his mother for their appearance at the Children's Court on October 7th. They did not appear.

Arrest. On November 21st, Max was arrested in Rockland County and was held at the Bronx County Jail on a charge of burglary committed on November 17th. It was learned on investigation that he had burglarized the same house a week earlier. He was arraigned in the Bronx Felony Court.

It was revealed that Max was only fifteen years of age, hence he was transferred to the jurisdiction of the Children's Court. He was again adjudged delinquent and was remanded on December 9, 1938, to the Psychiatric Division of Bellevue Hospital for examination.

Psychiatric Examination. Bellevue Hospital reported that Max was "an individual of abnormal make-up who might be technically classified as a psychopathic personality * * * His first preoccupations appear to deal with his desire to become a gangster * * * Unless he is able to form an emotional transfer to somebody whom he can respect and in whom he can have confidence, he will become a definite leader in crime."

Commitment. Early in January, 1939, Max was committed to the New York State Training School for Boys at Warwick. Although he was regarded as a "model boy" at Warwick with respect to behavior at the institution, he did not hesitate to discuss with staff members his plans to do bigger jobs and escape detection. After a stay of eight months at Warwick, Max was permitted to visit his home. He did not return to the institution and the authorities were unable to catch up with him until his arrest on December 27, 1939.

Extortion. Max had turned sixteen while he was absent without leave from Warwick. He now aspired to large returns from crime which he thought could be safely obtained. A series of extortion letters were sent to a large department store. He mailed to the store a key to a subway locker where he demanded that the sum of $4000 be deposited. He threatened to bomb the store unless payment was made.

Max was arrested and held at the Tombs to await the action of the Grand Jury. On January 2, 1940, he was indicted for blackmail, attempted extortion, and sending a threatening letter.

Psychiatric Examinations. Upon appearance in the Court of General Sessions, Max was committed to the psychiatric ward of Bellevue Hospital for observation and examination. After ten days he was taken to court where he pleaded guilty to attempted extortion. He was returned to Bellevue for further observation and treatment.

After a stay of about two months at Bellevue a report was made to General Sessions stating that nothing was found "which would indicate psychotic process and he was found not mentally defective. After prolonged observation * * * it is our opinion that he has apparently suffered from a transitory mental upset, which has been diagnosed as a hypomanic attack but which has subsided at the present time * * * Basically he is an abnormal type of individual, as indicated in his immaturity and in his anti-social conduct, but this abnormality in make-up does not imply that he is suffering from a psychosis." The hospital made no specific recommendation to the Court for further treatment.

Just prior to sentence, the psychiatric clinic of the General Sessions Court reported on April 8, 1940, that "This boy * * * passed through a transient mental illness, which terminated in March of this year * * * We find now that he is advanced along the line of maturity, and this time there is every prospect that he will not return to this earlier boyish method of behavior."

Sentence. Max was before the court for sentence on April 10, 1940. He was committed to the New York City Reformatory at New Hampton.

Parole Requirements. The New York City Parole Commission determines, in advance, the approximate date on which youths committed to New Hampton shall be released. In this case a high number of conduct marks was allotted in a communication to the Superintendent of the institution: "At a meeting of the Parole Commission on June 13, 1940, Max B—— was allotted 7,386 marks to earn before he will be considered for parole. Kindly notify the inmate, and when he has earned the marks allotted, kindly forward to the Commission a report of his institution record, prospective home and employment, and the recommendation of the prison officials. The committing court will then be notified, pursuant to Section 3 of the Parole Commission law, and his eligibility for parole determined." The Commission also directed that a mental report on Max be submitted prior to his release.

Psychiatric Report. A psychiatric report submitted on June 30, 1941, by the Division of Classification and Education at New Hampton stated that it was "impossible to gain information regarding his home relationships, but his running away a number of times indicates they were unsatisfactory * * * institutional adjustment superficial although no infraction reports * * * excitable, quarrelsome and resentful in butcher shop, although a good worker * * * impresses as being a psychopathic personality who will have considerable difficulty in effecting an adequate post-institutional adjustment. His present tendencies also indicate an anti-social trend." Max was released on parole from the New York City Reformatory eight days later, on July 8, 1941.

Parole Failure. Max reported regularly to the City parole authorities until mid-October. Toward the end of November his mother notified the Parole Commission that she had not seen Max during the preceding six weeks. A warrant was issued by the Commission for his arrest as an absconder. Max remained at large.

Comment. Psychiatric examinations swelled the treatment record accumulated by Max. Several wholly independent psychiatric units of court and institutions made diagnoses. The examining psychiatrist would have his say and the youth would be passed on to another jurisdiction where the process was repeated. Small returns may be expected from that kind of unintegrated procedure. Under such circumstances the psychiatric examination amounts to little more than providing a generally descriptive label couched in scientific terms. The psychiatric service should be intimately related to the entire correctional treatment plan. All of it, examination and treatment, should be unified within the hands of a single agency for treatment. The Youth Correction Authority would provide such unification for youths over sixteen, building its treatment plan and making necessary modifications of it on the basis of continuous responsibility for what, after all, should be a continuous task of re-establishing a youth offender.

~ IX ~

Bad Companions Graduate to Elmira

Edmond T—— began stealing in his childhood and continued at it. His experiences in social welfare and correctional institutions failed to divert him to desirable companionships but instead cemented his friendship for a thieving associate.

Family Background. Born in 1920, Edmond was next to the youngest of four children. His father and mother had excellent references from prominent persons who had employed them as domestic servants. But unemployment took its toll of the family in the early nineteen thirties. The family received assistance from both public and private agencies. The record of a private family service agency indicated that the father was probably an alcoholic. He was burned to death in an accident when Edmond was fourteen years of age.

Delinquencies. In January, 1934, Edmond then fourteen, was arrested for stealing coal from the platform of a Manhattan Elevated Station. He sold the coal for fifty cents and was taken into custody upon his return to the "L" station. The Children's Court adjudged him delinquent for this offense and placed him on probation. Two months later Edmond was again in Children's Court for stealing two sweaters from a store. A store clerk stated that it was not his first offense. He was remanded to the Catholic Protectory for a period of five months.

Probation Failure. Edmond was under probation supervision following his return from the Protectory. He continued to truant from school and his conduct at home was unsatisfactory. At length he ran away from home. When found he was returned to court for violation of probation. Under threat of commitment to an institution, he pleaded for another chance with abundant promises of good behavior. His behavior, however, did not improve on probation.

Burglary. On the day before Christmas in 1934, Edmond, nearly fifteen, was involved with three adults in the burglary of a candy store. The stolen articles were worth about $200.

Commitment. Edmond was committed by the Manhattan Children's Court to the New York State Training School for Boys at Warwick. He was examined by a psychiatrist at Warwick who reported that, "Mentally he is slow and lacking in concentration and initiative, but there is probably no serious defect in mental capacity * * * This boy gives a very good impression but his innocent mood is so striking that one wonders if he is not acting especially for the occasion * * * No sense of responsibility." I.Q. 79—dull normal or borderline.

After a six-month stay at the institution, Edmond was granted a three day leave to visit his home in New York City. He failed on two appointed occasions to meet the bus leaving for Warwick. Later he was apprehended and once more established in his program of institutional training.

He seemed to adjust very well at the institution but one worker was positive that his adjustment was only outward and superficial. He learned to handle tools fairly well, to drive a truck, and make minor repairs on machinery. Members of the Warwick staff expressed some concern about his friendship for another Warwick boy, James N——, who was not doing well at the institution.

Parole. On April 21, 1936, Edmond was paroled from Warwick. He failed to improve, however, under the supervision of the Warwick social worker. Most of the summer was spent swimming in the East River, shooting craps, and drinking beer with questionable companions. He continued to associate with James, the companion whom he had known at Warwick.

Burglary. While on parole from Warwick, Edmond, at sixteen years of age, in company with James and another accomplice broke the locks of a building in Long Island City and stole some $200 worth of copper cable. The youths were bound over to the Queens County Grand Jury. A few days later the Warwick parole supervisor visited Edmond's home and learned of his arrest. At that point Warwick withdrew from the case.

Sentence. Edmond and his two companions were indicted for burglary third degree and grand larceny. The youths pleaded not guilty. The case went to trial on October 28, 1936, at the conclusion of which the three youths withdrew their original plea and pleaded guilty to burglary third degree and petit larceny. All three were sentenced in the Queens County Court to the State Reformatory at Elmira.

At sixteen years of age Edmond was received at Elmira where he was put to work in the blacksmith and electrical shops. The institution's classification clinic recorded that he was of dull normal intelligence, I.Q. 88, according to the Army

Alpha tests, and gave evidence of emotional instability. His attitude and cooperation were found to be poor. The prognosis was regarded as "doubtful in view of poor home environment and instability."

Parole. Nearly two years later, Edmond, eighteen, was paroled from Elmira to live with his mother. He obtained a job at $10 per week and worked for seven months. For a year he reported faithfully on parole. An officer of the State Board of Parole made numerous visits to his home and to his place of business.

New Offense. Shortly before the end of his first year on parole, Edmond was arrested at 5 o'clock one morning while attempting to break into the premises of a Manhattan bar and grill. James N——, his companion at Warwick, in the burglary of 1936, and at Elmira, participated in the instant offense. The youths told the arresting officer that they had been drinking beer all night and wanted to obtain some more.

Sentence. The original burglary charge was changed to the misdemeanor charge of unlawful entry and the case was heard in the Court of Special Sessions. In September, 1939, Edmond was sentenced, under the alias Patrick O'Keefe, to the Penitentiary for an indeterminate term not to exceed three years.

Psychiatric Examination. A psychiatric examination made at the Penitentiary indicated that Edmond was "a rather weak-willed and suggestible individual who might easily be used as a tool * * * seems to be ambitionless and without interest of any kind and seems to be quite resentful of authority * * * refused to take mechanical test because he 'had taken so many tests already.'" The Penitentiary recommended maximum custody and general labor.

Parole Revocations. Edmond's true name and his criminal record having been disclosed, the State Board of Parole lodged a warrant at the Penitentiary for his eventual return to the

Parole Board's jurisdiction. He still owed six years and eleven months of his maximum sentence of November, 1936. The New York City Parole Commission decided to release Edmond on February 25, 1941. On that date he was paroled from the Penitentiary and was taken immediately to the Tombs to await return to Elmira Reformatory as a parole violator. He was readmitted to Elmira.

Comment. One bad companion on parole can outweigh the possible benefits of vocational and correctional training at an institution. In this case Warwick held on too long and at last Edmond drifted into criminal activity of a serious nature. The later shifts from the State's control at Elmira to the City's control at the Penitentiary and back again to Elmira, shows that there is no consistent policy as to what governmental authority should be responsible for the correctional training and treatment of the State's youth offenders. One may well ask, as to correctional treatment—whose business is it?

~ X ~

Temporizing With a Criminal Career

The concluding case relates to a youth who, for too long a time, was mistakenly trusted to straighten himself out. As a result, crime was compounded upon crime and he will grow to middle age at Sing Sing or some other prison, a burden to the State.

Family Background. Juan S—— was the only son in a family who moved from Central America to New York a few years ago. Although the cultural background of the father and mother was above average, they were unable to get along in New York without some assistance from public and private agencies. The parents were graduates of a foreign university. The mother earned a few dollars in giving piano lessons; the father was a cardiac, semi-invalid. They were respected and admired in the shabby neighborhood where they lived. Juan was an altar boy at his church. He was described as a "good boy but easily led."

First Offense. Juan, a high school student seventeen years of age, was arrested on November 13, 1939, while acting as a lookout for another youth who was stealing gasoline from a parked car. His companion escaped. The police discovered that Juan was the owner, at least the reputed owner, of an automobile parked around the corner. A search revealed that the car contained stolen goods. The license plates were removed by the police.

Arraignment. Juan was arraigned in a Magistrates' Court on a charge of disorderly conduct. The youth was referred on bench parole to a worker in the Court's Social Service Bureau. An attempt was made to have Juan take part in the activities of a well-known Social Settlement House.

New Offense. On the following day, November 14, 1939, Juan was again arrested and taken before the Magistrate for removing a radio and heater from a parked car. The Court's Social Service Bureau worker talked with the car owner who recommended leniency in dealing with Juan, although he was of the opinion that Juan had been associated with a gang of thieves. The Magistrate adjourned the case until December 12, pending a further social investigation by the Social Service Bureau.

Investigation. Juan had made a favorable impression and it was thought he could be straightened out if he could be persuaded to make better use of his leisure time at the Settlement House. But, as it turned out, Juan did not like the boys at the Settlement. Juan's mother was said to have lost all confidence in the boy, indicating the kind of rejection at home that constitutes a most serious obstacle to rehabilitation under probation supervision within the home setting.

Probation. Upon obtaining the consent of the car owner, the disorderly conduct charge of November 14th was set aside and Juan was adjudged to be a wayward minor. He was placed on probation for one year by the Magistrate, who suggested that a psychiatric examination be made and requested the social service worker to keep in close touch with the Court's probation officer. The probation officer, it should be noted, never established contact with Juan.

New Offense. About mid-June 1940, Juan and an unknown companion, in the night-time, stripped the wheels and tires from a parked car belonging to an out-of-town owner. Later that same night the car owner caught Juan with the stolen wheels and tires in a tow-truck and he was arrested.

Juan was arraigned and charged with petit larceny. He adopted an alias, Joseph A——, in dealing with the arresting officer and the magistrate. The case was adjourned for five days. Bail was set at $100 and, failing to produce it, Juan was held at the Tombs. The social worker, referred to above, learned that Juan was being held under an assumed name at the Tombs and visited him there. His explanation was that he had been drunk and did not know what he had been doing. Some days later a parish priest notified the court of Juan's true identity. The youth was released on bail, his mother having borrowed money to provide it.

Special Sessions. On June 21, 1940, Juan was arraigned in the Manhattan Court of Special Sessions charged with petit larceny. He was released on his own recognizance until June 27th. He failed to appear in court on the appointed date and a warrant was issued for his arrest. Juan eluded the warrant officer for two and one-half months. He was becoming accustomed to wriggling out of his difficulties with the courts.

Serious Crime. Before the arrest warrant could be executed, Juan, with a companion on the evening of September 15, 1940, held up at the point of a revolver a bartender who handed over $24. When Juan demanded "give me it all," the bartender threw a handful of quarters in his face, seized his revolver, and knocked him to the floor where he was held until a police officer arrived. His companion escaped during the fracas.

Hospital. Juan was arraigned in court on a charge of robbery. He requested an adjournment of the examination which was granted for four days. He was returned to the Tombs. On the following day he was transferred from the Tombs to Bellevue Hospital on the advice of the Tombs' physicians. There was some indication that Juan may have sustained injuries when he had been beaten by a gang prior to the barroom robbery. The examination at Bellevue revealed a possible fracture of the jaw and other contusions. In addition to the jaw injury there was found a gun-shot wound on the right foot, apparently sustained about two weeks previously. It was noted that Juan was undernourished.

Explanations. Juan revealed to the Bellevue physician that he had been in bad company. He stated that he had borrowed a friend's car and that the carblock had frozen, costing the owner sixty dollars for repairs. It must have been as far back as the cold weather of the previous winter. The owner kept demanding money from Juan, who could not pay. At last the aggrieved youth, who sought payment for the repairs, with some others assaulted Juan and threatening him with a gun compelled him to hold-up the bartender. The youth whose car Juan had borrowed accompanied him but escaped during the scuffle in the bar and grill.

Indictment. On September 26, 1940, Juan was indicted by the New York County Grand Jury for robbery first degree, assault first degree, and possessing a pistol. On first appearance in the Court of General Sessions, Juan pleaded not guilty. Ten days later, October 10th, he withdrew his original plea and pleaded guilty to robbery third degree.

Psychiatric Examination. The psychiatric clinic of General Sessions reported, upon examination, that Juan was neither psychotic nor mentally defective. "He is a rather ineffectual, suggestible sort of individual, who is obviously dominated by more aggressive types. He does not seem to have any chronic tendency toward viciousness; he appears to be the type who rarely takes the initiative. There are no definite neurotic traits in evidence."

Probation. On October 28, 1940, Juan was arraigned for sentence in the Court of General Sessions.

Clerk: What have you now to say why the sentence of the court should not be pronounced upon you?

Counsel (for defendant): . . . Several boys, whose company was anything but desirable as it later turned out, took advantage of his (Juan's) mechanical skill to help them fix their cars . . . and eventually he became indebted to one of those boys, and as a result they kept hounding him for repayment of this money to such an extent that on September 15, 1940, several of these boys took him down to the dock and assailed him, beat him up, and forced him into the commission of this stick-up. The fact that he was under duress is corroborated by the fact that the hospital record shows he was detained at Bellevue for several days, and the record shows he was severely injured. The bartender here in court testified that at the time he was approached in this so-called stick-up that the defendant had marks on his forehead of bruises, that his clothes were all bloody.

Now Juan has tried to be cooperative with the authorities, and he has helped them in every way in giving them whatever information he could with respect to those boys with whom he has been associated and who are downright scoundrels, one by the name of ———. He was in on this stick-up with him, and the one who forced him to go through with it. The defendant has been cooperating all along, and I am sure that he would still be willing to cooperate in the event that any of these boys are picked up.

Court: Well, suppose they pick him up and get him to do another stick-up?

Counsel: Well, I think if once he is kept away from this neighborhood and from these boys that he will probably straighten out.

Court: How is that going to be effected—that he is going to be kept away from this neighborhood and these boys?

Counsel: I don't know. I leave that to the discretion of the court with his greater knowledge of these things and the behavior of these boys under similar circumstances.

Court: There is some evidence that this young man may have been forced into this affair, but how am I going to know that if I let him out he is not going to be forced into another affair or cajoled into it and the next time shoot somebody?

Counsel: I think he has certainly learned a lesson. I think he has been sufficiently scared and sufficiently impressed with the majesty of the law that he is going to behave himself, and I think that he is at a critical period in his life now, and the treatment that he gets now as an ailing member of society, so to speak, which calls for treatment at this moment in his career and calls for leniency at this time.

Court: How old is he?

Counsel: 18 . . . I think he has enough good in him to be

worth salvaging both to **himself and society**, and I think if we could get him straightened out, he would make a good mechanic, and Uncle Sam is going to need lots of men soon

Court: I hope I don't hear that very often about what Uncle Sam is going to need. I am tired of having men charged with crime saying they are going to join the army. The Army don't want crooks. There are plenty of decent men ready to fight for this country. That cry is going to be the standard cry of every man charged with crime from now on—that he is going to defend Uncle Sam. He can't live a decent life, it seems, but he can save his country in time of war. There used to be a time when pirates were enrolled to save the country, but I don't think we need them now, so I hope I won't hear very much more of that sort of twaddle.

Now I don't know whether the court is foolish in taking a gamble on this boy or not. He is only 18 . . . but has a good background, and there is some evidence that he was forced into this crime by older and more experienced thieves. It may be that he will go straight from now on, and if he does, I will be very happy because I am going to let him go despite the fact that he is guilty of robbery.

I am going to place you on probation for a period of ten years. Do you understand that?

Juan: Yes, Your Honor.

Court: If you come back here for any reason, if my probation department reports to me that you are keeping bad company, that you refuse to cooperate with them and don't get a job, or that in any way you give evidence that you are going to lapse into your former habits of life and you are brought back here, I am going to put you in State Prison for a term that will be a severe deterrent to you for at least 15 years. Do you understand that?

Juan: Yes, Your Honor.

Counsel: Your Honor, may I submit this letter from one of his teachers?

Court: Yes. We will let the defendant stand aside, and I will put the sentence over until tomorrow.

Juan was arraigned on the following day for sentence in General Sessions. Suspended sentence. Probation 10 years.

Ten years is a long period for probation and seems fantastic on the face of it. What new element of a constructive nature was introduced into the boy's life at the time the judge announced his decision? Would the counsel of a probation officer be sufficient? Would not the probation officer be handicapped in any endeavor to work constructively with his probationer because the boy would view the officer as a personification of the overhanging threat of 15 years imprisonment?

Old Charge. One month later Juan was in the Court of Special Sessions to answer the charge of petit larceny for theft of tires and wheels on June 13th. He pleaded not guilty and was paroled to the custody of his counsel pending trial at a later date. The Special Sessions procedures appear from time to time in this story as meaningless interludes in the major prosecution for robbery.

Robbery. A little over a month later, on January 4, 1941, Juan and a companion, both nineteen years of age, held up with a loaded revolver and robbed a couple in Queens County, taking $165 in currency and a bottle of liquor. The youths were not arrested at the time for this offense. Juan's companion, it was learned later, had previously been sentenced by the Court of Special Sessions for possession of burglars' tools and had also been convicted earlier on felony charges, once in Kings County and once in Queens County.

Robbery. Ten days later, Juan, with a companion aged twenty-five, and a second companion unknown, while armed with a loaded revolver held up a clerk in a Manhattan wine store. They were not apprehended until later. The twenty-five year old accomplice had a record of several arrests and convictions. Notice should be taken of the kind of companions Juan had during the initial months of his ten-year probation period.

Robbery. Robbery seemed to be working out very well in Juan's criminal designs, for six days later he again teamed up with his nineteen year old friend and an unknown companion to rob the clerk of another wine shop, taking $25 in currency. Again the trio escaped.

Interlude. On the following day, an application to withdraw the charge, made by the complainant whose wheels and tires Juan had stolen, was denied by the Court of Special Sessions.

Taxicab Theft. At the end of an eventful month of several crimes and no arrests, Juan, with three unknown companions, stole a taxicab in Queens County. He was arrested when he failed to give a satisfactory explanation of his possession of the cab. On the last day of January, 1941, Juan was arraigned before a magistrate in Queens and was ordered to be held in the Long Island City jail for a later hearing. On the same day he was officially discharged from probation by the Manhattan Magistrates' Court. The record indicated that he had never seen the Court's probation officer.

General Sessions In Action. On February 4, 1941, the Court of General Sessions, apprised of Juan's arrest in Queens County and acting on the violation of probation, lodged a warrant at the Long Island City jail for his transfer to the Tombs for disposition by that court. The transfer was made.

Special Sessions In Action. On February 10th, the Court of Special Sessions revoked its bench parole of Juan to the custody of his counsel pending trial on the wheels and tires misdemeanor charge, and lodged a warrant with the warden of the Tombs. On February 11th, Juan was before Special Sessions and was remanded to the Tombs to await sentence on February 17. On three successive dates, February 17th, 19th and 28th, Juan was before Special Sessions and remanded to the Tombs, sentence finally being put over to March 14th pending disposition by General Sessions.

Arraignment. Juan appeared in the Court of General Sessions for sentence on March 13, 1941, but the day of pronouncement was adjourned until March 24th and he was returned to the Tombs. The compiler of this history was in court and observed Juan as he was brought up for sentence. He was a tall, good-looking, well-built youth, neatly dressed. There was evidently no attorney, friend, or member of his family present. His face was absolutely expressionless, nor could one notice any gestures or mannerisms which might have given some indication of his feelings and attitudes at the moment.

Queens Indictment. Juan and companion were indicted for the hold-up committed in Queens on January 4, 1941—robbery first degree, grand larceny, and assault. A bench warrant was issued for Juan's arrest and disposition in Queens County.

New York Indictments. Juan and his twenty-five year old accomplice were indicted by the New York County Grand Jury on March 28, 1941, for robbery first degree, assault second degree, and for criminally possessing a pistol, in connection with the hold-up committed in Manhattan on January 14th. On April 16th, Juan pleaded not guilty to the indictment.

On April 22nd, Juan and his first companion in robbery were indicted by the New York County Grand Jury for attempted robbery first degree, and assault first degree, for the Manhattan hold-up committed on January 20th. Juan pleaded not guilty to this indictment.

Plea of Guilt. After several appearances and adjournments in the Court of General Sessions, Juan was again in court on

May 21st, at which time he withdrew his original plea of not guilty and pleaded guilty to attempted robbery first degree and at this time he also pleaded guilty to robbery first degree for the hold-up of January 14th.

Sentence by Special Sessions. On June 20, 1941, Juan was before the Court of Special Sessions for sentence in connection with the larceny of the wheels and tires. He was first arraigned in Special Sessions for that offense one year earlier, lacking a day, June 21, 1940. He was sentenced to the City Penitentiary at Rikers Island for an indeterminate term not to exceed three years. However, the execution of sentence was suspended because of the certainty of his commitment to State Prison by the Court of General Sessions.

Sentences by General Sessions. On June 24, 1941, Juan was in the Court of General Sessions for sentence relating to the following:

Offense	*Sentence*
Violation of General Sessions probation on January 30, 1941, by reason of arrest in Queens County.	Suspended sentence, and probation of October 29, 1940, was set aside and vacated. Sentenced to State Prison for term of not less than 5 nor more than 10 years, said term to run concurrently with sentence imposed for robbery of January 20, 1941.
Robbery first degree committed on January 14, 1941.	Suspended sentence for term of 60 years, as Juan was sentenced to State Prison on two other indictments.
Attempted robbery first degree committed on January 20, 1941.	Sentenced to State Prison at Sing Sing for not less than 15 years nor more than 30 years.

Comment. Automobiles caused trouble for Juan in the first instance. Over and over his liking of cars led him to pilfering and major theft. As a high school student and son of parents who required outside financial assistance he was in no position to support a car, so to speak. It takes money to operate a car whether it is borrowed, owned on a shoestring purchase or owned free of debt. A youth who is without resources is under strong pressure to get money to satisfy a recreational hobby. If he is a youth of strong character and is living among desirable associates he will work hard and learn to spend his money in the light of the effort required to get it. If he is a weak person and falls in with bad companions, theft all too often provides the key to immediate satisfaction and ultimate sorrow.

Juan early supplied clear warning signals of danger. His return to stealing and adoption of an alias showed that he was not ready to be trusted in the comparative freedom of probation. Left to manage his own affairs, he quickly became involved with a criminal group. The easy money obtained in one criminal episode led him to another and another.

The long process of trial and error in the handling of Juan, throughout the steady succession of his offenses, served neither to provide intelligent treatment for the boy nor to protect society. In the conspicuous absence of constructive measures, the burden of reform was placed entirely upon him. But he was not the self-reclaiming type. The day came when he had to be dealt with as a criminal of a dangerous sort. At last the community was afforded the only kind of protection then possible, a long prison sentence. Now the State and its taxpayers must carry year upon year the heavy expense of an unconstructive regimen of segregation at a maximum security prison.

Conclusion

The brief histories given in the foregoing accounts show that youthful offenders circulate in various situations according to the decisions of numerous authorities in the criminal justice system. The cases indicate repeated failure of probation, parole, and mass-imprisonment as rehabilitative measures. There are, of course, numerous other cases showing the success of probation and parole supervision. What appears to be most lacking in the cases under review in this study is continuity of supervision and intensive personal guidance in the correctional training and treatment of individual offenders.

It is impossible to tell from the bare records why New Hampton Reformatory is chosen in preference to the State Reformatory at Elmira. The City institution receives youths convicted of misdemeanor offenses and the State institution receives those convicted of felonies. In the case of many commitments to New Hampton, however, the actual offenses were felonies, the charges having been reduced to lesser offenses upon acceptance of pleas of guilty.

Two factors are known to be at work in the reduction of pleas. Prosecutors and judges wish to spare certain guilty youths the record of a felony conviction. In other instances, the element of bargaining with the defendant appears. A prospective lighter sentence on a misdemeanor charge is held out as an inducement for an indicted youth to plead guilty. Neither of those reasons is relevant to the issue of whether the State or City should assume responsibility for correctional treatment of an offender who has been found guilty.

The New York City Reformatory was established in 1905 because at that time there was no state reformatory to which misdemeanants could be sent. A few years ago the state established the Vocational Institution at Coxsackie. Boys aged 16 to 19 may be committed there upon conviction for a misdemeanor or felony offense. Thus the state has accepted a responsibility for the correctional treatment of youthful misdemeanants but the City of New York carries on as before in treating with misdemeanants and with young felony offenders whose pleas of guilt are reduced to the misdemeanor level.

An overlapping of city and state responsibility extends beyond the maintenance and operation of correctional institutions. Parole supervision is likewise duplicated, the city exercising control over youths released on parole from New Hampton and the state parole service caring for those released from the Coxsackie Institution and from Elmira Reformatory. We believe that such division of responsibility between city and state should be ended. The State of New York alone should be equipped to deal with all youths who are committed to correctional institutions.

The hope of substantial progress in the field of youth-crime control lies in the development of a unified service for the rehabilitation of youth offenders. It should be the responsibility of the State of New York to provide a unified and integrated correctional service. At present the state expends immense sums for its prisons and reformatories. It can afford to spend more than is now being allotted for genuinely constructive undertakings to reclaim its youthful offenders. There is a clear need for consolidation of existing services and facilities and for the creation of new facilities unlike the present institutions for mass-imprisonment and mass-vocational training. A state-wide Youth Correction Authority suitably provided with personnel and facilities for the training and treatment of youth offenders would supply the unmet need. An Authority would bring about a consistent policy, a plan of correctional treatment, and a unified, responsible administration of policy and plan that are now wanting.

The Proposed Youth Correction Authority
Its Powers and Responsibilities

It is necessary, of course, to examine in detail the proposed legislation providing for the creation of a Youth Correction Authority, in order fully to understand its duties and responsibilities. A useful description may, however, be given briefly in a few paragraphs.

The bill provides for setting up a state-wide Authority of three members to have charge of youths, aged 16 to 21, committed by the courts for correctional treatment. The Authority is given power to organize regional offices, to appoint the necessary professional and administrative staffs under civil service regulations, to establish new types of correctional facilities including small institutions, training camps, hostels, and boarding homes for the rehabilitation of youth offenders under its control, and to use any suitable existing public institutions and facilities.

Youths in the 16 to 21 age group arrested for criminal offenses would be arraigned in courts of appropriate jurisdiction and tried, as at present. The purely judicial function of determining the guilt or innocence of accused youths would be exercised exclusively by the courts, as heretofore. At the conclusion of the trial of fact, the courts would render judgments of acquittal, pronounce sentences upon offenders punishable by death or life imprisonment, impose fines for lesser offenses, and place certain convicted offenders on probation under the court's supervision. As to all other convicted offenders in the 16 to 21 age group not disposed of as above, the courts would merely pronounce sentences of commitment to the Youth Correction Authority without recommendations or conditions affecting their further disposition. The Authority would then assume full control over the youths committed to it.

The Authority would be required to conduct a physical and mental examination of a youth as soon as he is committed and to investigate his personal capacities and behavior record, his family, school, and community background. On the basis of such composite diagnostic examination and social investigation, the Authority would determine, initially, the type of medical, psychiatric, and custodial care and treatment required in the case of each youth.

A basically important feature of the Authority plan is the recognition of the need for flexibility in kind of treatment and control of committed youths. No human agency can foretell the changes that will take place in human beings, particularly adolescents, when they are tried out in new surroundings and under new influences. The only way to know when a youthful offender is ready for a change in form of supervisory control, or for release to limited or full freedom in the community, is to work with him toward that end, from day to day. The Authority would be unhampered in making prompt modification of any course of correctional treatment whenever a youth shows the need for it.

As to custody, the Authority may place a youth under supervision corresponding to probation, in his own home setting or in a controlled residence away from home. Or it may assign him to a place of semi-confinement or full confinement for disciplinary training and treatment, or segregate him by confinement in an appropriate penal institution maintained by the state. For the purpose of carrying out prescribed training and treatment, a youth may be placed in a maximum or medium security institution, in a training school, a hostel, or foster home. The Authority is empowered to make use of any suitable private agencies and facilities which may be available for the training and treatment of youths in the age group with which the Authority would deal, having regard for the religious affiliations of the youths and the agencies.

The bill contains a provision that the Authority shall re-examine all persons under its control at least once a year. But more frequent administrative reports would be prepared to show the progress being made by a youth under supervision of one kind or another. Examinations, measures of treatment, follow-up of results, and re-examinations would be fully integrated under the direction of a single administration, responsible alike for initial decisions, modifications based on experience with the youths' responses, and final decisions regarding correctional treatment.

If necessary, several placements of a youth may be made and one kind of disposition may be followed by any other, in the discretion of the Authority. A youth would be moved in the direction of greater freedom or to closer confinement according to the nature of his reactions to measures undertaken for his rehabilitation. Thus, there would be flexibility of method of treatment as well as variety of form which is not at present attainable.

The Authority would have the power to parole offenders as soon as they are believed to be ready for release. Depending upon their age at the time of apprehension and the seriousness of the offense, offenders must be released, in ordinary cases, by the time they reach 21 years of age, or within three years after their commitment, and in more serious cases by the time they reach 25. In order to protect the public, in extraordinary cases, against offenders who are believed to be dangerous by reason of some mental or behavior abnormality, the Authority may apply to the Supreme Court of the State for extension of control over such offenders for two or five year periods. The offenders' legal rights are fully protected.

A provision of the act empowers the Authority to restore an offender "to liberty on parole under such supervision and upon such conditions as it believes conducive to law-abiding conduct." In exercising supervision and prescribing the conditions, it is anticipated that the Authority will establish agencies and services to aid persons paroled or discharged to find employment and establish themselves safely in the community.

When discharged by the Authority as rehabilitated, a youth's civil rights would be fully restored, according to the terms of the bill, and disqualifications now attaching to a conviction for a criminal offense would not apply to him. A youth would be helped to restore himself in every reasonable way, but he himself would have to show his worthiness by favorable response to the help given him. The basic aim of the plan is to protect society; it would accomplish that aim in so far as it might attain success in the reclamation of youths who had started on the wrong road.

The Authority is proposed as a means of introducing administrative efficiency in the difficult task of correctional training and treatment of youth offenders. It would utilize all existing treatment facilities and any others that may prove themselves effective in the future; it would encompass all measures into an integrated system so that the courts of the state may have available the widest variety of resources to meet the needs of the different personalities that come before them.

The Authority would rely primarily on personal guidance by leaders qualified to deal effectively with older adolescents and young men. Such guidance and training would be carried out for the most part with relatively small groups of youths distributed among places suited to the characteristics, aptitudes and particular needs of the individual offenders.

While the assignment of youths to appropriate settings would be an important part of the Authority's diagnostic and classification service, the major emphasis would not be upon institutions and institutional management but upon the element of human contacts in undertaking to redirect the lives of plastic youths. It will not be an easy task to recruit leaders gifted in influencing difficult young persons. So much the more important, then, that a single responsible agency be charged with concentrating its attention on the prime requirements of personal service in its task of reclaiming youth offenders.

These objectives are sometimes described by the skeptical as being idealistic and, because of that, not readily attainable. Advocates of the Authority plan make no apology for their idealistic aims since they know that the aims must inevitably be pursued along strictly practical lines. The task of the Authority would consist of everyday administration of workable measures for the rehabilitation of youths. The Authority alone would be responsible for the measure of success it achieves. It would, therefore, be intent on practical operations for, if not practical, there would be no success. The stimulus to endeavor will be an idealistic one but the endeavor itself will be eminently practical.

This book set up and printed by
THE LIVINGSTON PRESS
operated by patients at
THE POTTS MEMORIAL INSTITUTE
(for the rehabilitation of the tuberculous)
Livingston, Columbia County, New York

CHILDREN AND YOUTH
Social Problems and Social Policy

An Arno Press Collection

Abt, Henry Edward. **The Care, Cure and Education of the Crippled Child.** 1924

Addams, Jane. **My Friend, Julia Lathrop.** 1935

American Academy of Pediatrics. **Child Health Services and Pediatric Education:** Report of the Committee for the Study of Child Health Services. 1949

American Association for the Study and Prevention of Infant Mortality. **Transactions of the First Annual Meeting of the American Association for the Study and Prevention of Infant Mortality.** 1910

Baker, S. Josephine. **Fighting For Life.** 1939

Bell, Howard M. **Youth Tell Their Story:** A Study of the Conditions and Attitudes of Young People in Maryland Between the Ages of 16 and 24. 1938

Bossard, James H. S. and Eleanor S. Boll, editors. **Adolescents in Wartime.** 1944

Bossard, James H. S., editor. **Children in a Depression Decade.** 1940

Brunner, Edmund DeS. **Working With Rural Youth.** 1942

Care of Dependent Children in the Late Nineteenth and Early Twentieth Centuries. Introduction by Robert H. Bremner. 1974

Care of Handicapped Children. Introduction by Robert H. Bremner. 1974

[Chenery, William L. and Ella A. Merritt, editors]. **Standards of Child Welfare:** A Report of the Children's Bureau Conferences, May and June, 1919. 1919

The Child Labor Bulletin, 1912, 1913. 1974

Children In Confinement. Introduction by Robert M. Mennel. 1974

Children's Bureau Studies. Introduction by William M. Schmidt. 1974

Clopper, Edward N. **Child Labor in City Streets.** 1912

David, Paul T. **Barriers To Youth Employment.** 1942

Deutsch, Albert. **Our Rejected Children.** 1950

Drucker, Saul and Maurice Beck Hexter. **Children Astray.** 1923

Duffus, R[obert] L[uther] and L. Emmett Holt, Jr. **L. Emmett Holt:** Pioneer of a Children's Century. 1940

Fuller, Raymond G. **Child Labor and the Constitution.** 1923

Holland, Kenneth and Frank Ernest Hill. **Youth in the CCC.** 1942

Jacoby, George Paul. **Catholic Child Care in Nineteenth Century New York:** With a Correlated Summary of Public and Protestant Child Welfare. 1941

Johnson, Palmer O. and Oswald L. Harvey. **The National Youth Administration.** 1938

The Juvenile Court. Introduction by Robert M. Mennel. 1974

Klein, Earl E. **Work Accidents to Minors in Illinois.** 1938

Lane, Francis E. **American Charities and the Child of the Immigrant:** A Study of Typical Child Caring Institutions in New York and Massachusetts Between the Years 1845 and 1880. 1932

The Legal Rights of Children. Introduction by Sanford N. Katz. 1974

Letchworth, William P[ryor]. **Homes of Homeless Children:** A Report on Orphan Asylums and Other Institutions for the Care of Children. [1903]

Lorwin, Lewis. **Youth Work Programs:** Problems and Policies. 1941

Lundberg, Emma O[ctavia] and Katharine F. Lenroot. **Illegitimacy As A Child-Welfare Problem, Parts 1 and 2.** 1920/1921

New York State Commission on Relief for Widowed Mothers. **Report of the New York State Commission on Relief for Widowed Mothers.** 1914

Otey, Elizabeth Lewis. **The Beginnings of Child Labor Legislation in Certain States;** A Comparative Study. 1910

Phillips, Wilbur C. **Adventuring For Democracy.** 1940

Polier, Justine Wise. **Everyone's Children, Nobody's Child:** A Judge Looks At Underprivileged Children in the United States. 1941

Proceedings of the Annual Meeting of the National Child Labor Committee, 1905, 1906. 1974

Rainey, Homer P. **How Fare American Youth?** 1940

Reeder, Rudolph R. **How Two Hundred Children Live and Learn.** 1910

Security and Services For Children. 1974

Sinai, Nathan and Odin W. Anderson. **EMIC (Emergency Maternity and Infant Care):** A Study of Administrative Experience. 1948

Slingerland, W. H. **Child-Placing in Families:** A Manual For Students and Social Workers. 1919

[Solenberger], Edith Reeves. **Care and Education of Crippled Children in the United States.** 1914

Spencer, Anna Garlin and Charles Wesley Birtwell, editors. **The Care of Dependent, Neglected and Wayward Children:** Being a Report of the Second Section of the International Congress of Charities, Correction and Philanthropy, Chicago, June, 1893. 1894

Theis, Sophie Van Senden. **How Foster Children Turn Out.** 1924

Thurston, Henry W. **The Dependent Child:** A Story of Changing Aims and Methods in the Care of Dependent Children. 1930

U.S. Advisory Committee on Education. **Report of the Committee, February, 1938.** 1938

The United States Children's Bureau, 1912-1972. 1974

White House Conference on Child Health and Protection. **Dependent and Neglected Children:** Report of the Committee on Socially Handicapped — Dependency and Neglect. 1933

White House Conference on Child Health and Protection. **Organization for the Care of Handicapped Children, National, State, Local.** 1932

White House Conference on Children in a Democracy. **Final Report of the White House Conference on Children in A Democracy.** [1942]

Wilson, Otto. **Fifty Years' Work With Girls, 1883-1933:** A Story of the Florence Crittenton Homes. 1933

Wrenn, C. Gilbert and D. L. Harley. **Time On Their Hands:** A Report on Leisure, Recreation, and Young People. 1941